Professional Practice in Governance and Public Organizations

"Professional Practice in Governance and Public Organizations" offers cutting-edge insights and practical guidance for professionals in the areas of economics, politics, public policy and public administration, and those working at international organizations. The series features concise and accessible books on the latest developments in governance, organizational and political strategies, institutional policies, policy instruments, public management, and finance. Leadership and digitalization issues are a core topic throughout the series. All volumes are written by practitioners, experts and leading authorities from think tanks, non-governmental organizations, and public and international organizations. While the books are explicitly intended for professionals in the above-mentioned fields, students of economics, political science, public policy and public administration will also benefit from these practical guides for their future careers.

Tankiso Moloi
Editor

Digital Transformation in South Africa

Perspectives from an Emerging Economy

 Springer

Editor
Tankiso Moloi
Johannesburg Business School
University of Johannesburg
Johannesburg, South Africa

ISSN 2731-9776 ISSN 2731-9784 (electronic)
Professional Practice in Governance and Public Organizations
ISBN 978-3-031-52405-9 ISBN 978-3-031-52403-5 (eBook)
https://doi.org/10.1007/978-3-031-52403-5

This Springer imprint is published by the registered company Springer Nature Switzerland AG
The registered company address is: Gewerbestrasse 11, 6330 Cham, Switzerland

Paper in this product is recyclable.

Preface

This book examines digital transformation from the lenses of researchers in the emerging world. A broader introduction to digital transformation and an overview of the book are provided in first chapter, whereas in second chapter, the book details digital transformation in the enterprise risk management environment. The third chapter details digital transformation in the banking and financial sector. This chapter recognises that like every other financial institution, banks seek to maximise their profits by reducing operational expenses or reaching out to more customers. Hence, the need to embrace the disruptive tendencies of digital transformation that are changing the organisational landscape and how businesses and individuals conduct their daily activities. The fourth chapter investigates the current state of digital transformation, the challenges that are faced, the existing digital gaps and digital literacy, and the potential benefits associated with the use of digital technologies in rural areas and areas under the tribal authorities. The fifth chapter acknowledges that the finance function is one of the most affected fields of work by digitalisation, which is a common feature in all companies, sectors, or various country applications. As such, the chapter discusses digital transformation and the process improvements in the general finance environment.

The sixth chapter discusses the development of corporate reputation into e-reputation against the background of a global digital transformation as part of the Fourth Industrial Revolution. It is underpinned by the theories of legitimacy and signaling. The seventh chapter acknowledges that digital technologies are shaping the Industrial Revolution, extending beyond industry and influencing markets and customer experiences. It argues that their transformative power is noticeable, particularly in the field of marketing. In this chapter, the concept of digital transformation in the marketing environment is dealt with. The eighth chapter discusses digital transformation in finance and banking with a specific focus on servicing customers' changing behaviors, the use of big data and analytics to make informed decisions as well and operational efficiencies required when customer-centric models are adopted, while ninth chapter sought to examine the adoption of digital technologies in the auditing environment through the lenses of Technology Task Fit (TTF) Theory.

The tenth chapter explores the role of technologies in digitalising corporate reporting through a consistent and efficient configuring and restructuring of the most informative quantitative and qualitative data from the source to the end users of corporate reports. The eleventh chapter recognises that tax revenue constitutes a large share of the total national revenue of most developing and emerging economies. Digital transformation by its nature speaks to technologically transforming processes and operations. Accordingly, for tax administration, it signals the need to embrace digital tools in delivering tax administration functions of assessing tax liability, communicating with taxpayers and other revenue authorities as well as facilitating tax compliance. Finally, twelfth chapter investigates the impact of digital transformation on small businesses and offers insights into best practices for its implementation.

This book is an exciting resource for graduate students, researchers, strategists, business executives, digital transformation practitioners, boards of directors, and relevant board committees.

Johannesburg, South Africa   Tankiso Moloi
November 2023

Acknowledgements

I thank all the authors and peer reviewers for contributing to the success of this project. I also thank my family for allowing me time to work on this project until its delivery.

Contents

A High Level Introduction

Tankiso Moloi ⓘ

Abstract In this chapter, we discuss the overarching concept of digital transformation. We make an argument that literature on digital transformation is dominated by
scholars in the developed world. Literature is scarce on the views and case studies
in the developing world. This book is an attempt to look at digital transformation
from the lenses of scholars in the developing world.

The book consists of twelve chapters covering digital transformation in enterprise risk management (ERM), the role of digital transformation in driving financial
inclusion and accessibility and the challenges limiting the adoption of digital transformation by banks and other financial institutions, the current state of digital transformation, the challenges that are faced, the existing digital gaps and digital literacy,
and the potential benefits associated with the use of digital technology in rural areas,
and digital transformation and process improvement in the general finance
environment.

It further covers the effects of digital transformation on reputation management,
the concept of digital transformation in the marketing environment, the adoption of
digital technologies in the auditing environment through the lenses of Technology
Task Fit Theory, the role of technologies in digitalizing corporate reporting through
a consistent and efficient configuring and restructuring of the most informative
quantitative and qualitative data from the source to the end users of corporate
reports, digital transformation by tax authorities and the impact of digital transformation on small businesses and offers insights into best practices for its
implementation.

T. Moloi (✉)
Johannesburg Business School, University of Johannesburg, Johannesburg, South Africa
e-mail: tankiso.moloi@jbs.ac.za

© The Author(s), under exclusive license to Springer Nature
Switzerland AG 2024
T. Moloi (ed.), *Digital Transformation in South Africa*, Professional Practice in
Governance and Public Organizations,
https://doi.org/10.1007/978-3-031-52403-5_1

1

1   Introduction

Various definitions of digital transformation have emerged in the past couple of years. Vial (2019) defines digital transformation as a process that aims to improve an entity by triggering significant changes to its properties through combinations of information, computing, communication, and connectivity technologies. Heavin and Power (2018) argue that the primary aim of digital transformation can simply be stated as solving challenges concerning efficiency and effectiveness in organisational processes.

When referring to digital transformation, Mckinsey and Company (2023) think of it as a process of rewiring an organisation by consistently using technology to create and capture value along the value chain. An important distinction is made between digital transformation and business transformation. From the perspective of business transformation, McKinsey and Company (2023) emphasise that the project will come to an end once a certain behavior has been achieved.

On the other side, digital transformation is a lifelong commitment by those charged with running the affairs to rewire an organisation by consistently using technology to create and capture value along the value chain. This view is consistent with Warner and Wäger (2019) definition of digital transformation where the process is viewed as an ongoing process of strategic renewal that uses advances in digital technologies to build capabilities that refresh or replace an organization's business model, collaborative approach, and culture.

According to Lamarre et al. (2023), the value of digital transformation lies in the creation of value that cannot be copied. In this regard, digital leaders would create this value that cannot be copied, thus delivering better performance to their shareholders compared to the laggards.

2   The Case for Digital Transformation in the Developing World

Kraus et al. (2022) point to the fact that the concept of digital transformation has been heavily promoted by large consulting companies such as McKinsey and Boston Consulting, which are companies that are incorporated in developing nations. Even from the research perspective, few studies in existence look into the concept of digital transformation from the lenses of the developing world.

According to Matthess and Kunkel (2020), developing countries have high hopes for digital technologies to drive the transformation of the economy towards prosperity. Digital transformation drives the transformation of the economy by increasing productivity and this in turn increases economic development (Aly, 2020). Given these benefits, digital transformation has to be studied from the perspectives of developing nations.

3 Demarcation of Chapters

Chapter "Digital Transformation in Enterprise Risk Management" discusses digital transformation in enterprise risk management (ERM). ERM is a strategic business discipline that helps organisations achieve their goals by addressing all of their risks and managing the combined impact of those risks in an integrated manner.

Chapter "Digital Transformation in Finance and Banking Sectors" discusses the role of digital transformation in driving financial inclusion and accessibility. It further discusses the challenges limiting the adoption of digital transformation by banks and other financial institutions and the future trends and prospects for banks and financial institutions as they embrace digital transformation.

Chapter "Digital Transformation in Areas Administered by Traditional Authorities" acknowledges that traditional authorities in South Africa are only beginning to embrace digital transformation; there are numerous obstacles to be addressed. As such, the chapter investigates the current state of digital transformation, the challenges that are faced, the existing digital gaps and digital literacy, and the potential benefits associated with the use of digital technology in rural areas.

Chapter "Digital Transformation and the Process Improvements in General Finance Environment: The Good Governance Perspective" points to the fact that digital transformation should start with a well-defined digital strategy and be implemented within the framework of a digital business model. Although this practice is for organizations at the micro level, it is also a relevant approach that should be followed at the macro level based on sectors and countries. This chapter outlines digital transformation and process improvement in the general finance environment.

Chapter "Digital Transformation in Corporate Reputation" describes the development of corporate reputation into e-reputation against the background of a global digital transformation as part of the Fourth Industrial Revolution, based on the theories of legitimacy and signaling. The importance of corporate reputation in the long-term sustainability and success of organisations was illustrated, and the effects of digital transformation on reputation management were highlighted.

Chapter "Lessons on Digital Transformation in the Marketing Environment" acknowledges that digital technologies are shaping the Industrial Revolution, extending beyond industry and influencing markets and customer experiences. It argues that their transformative power is noticeable, particularly in the field of marketing. In this chapter, we discuss the concept of digital transformation in the marketing environment.

Chapter "Digital Transformation in the Finance and Banking Sector" is premised on the argument that the implementation of digital transformation initiatives and strategies could unlock costs and process efficiencies and ensure sustainable growth, and improved service delivery which ensures improved customer experiences. This chapter discusses digital transformation in finance and banking with a specific focus on servicing customers' changing behaviors, the use of big data and analytics to make informed decisions as well as operational efficiencies required when customer-centric models are adopted.

Chapter "Digital Transformation in the Auditing Environment" sought to examine the adoption of digital technologies in the auditing environment through the lenses of Technology Task Fit Theory (TTF). It describes the factors that affect the adoption of digital transformation in auditing engagements. It further examines the adoption of digital technologies in the auditing space as well as how auditing has been transformed by digital technologies including implications of DT on International Standards on Auditing (ISA).

Chapter "Digital Transformation of Corporate Reporting" explores the role of technologies in digitalizing corporate reporting through a consistent and efficient configuring and restructuring of the most informative quantitative and qualitative data from the source to the end users of corporate reports.

Chapter "Digital Transformation by Tax Authorities" argues that revenue authorities around the world are digitally transforming their engagements and interactions with taxpayers and other stakeholders. These tax authorities are now remodeling their tax administration functions, technologically enabling the filing of tax returns and reporting requirements, as well as digitalising their auditing functions and procedures.

Chapter "Digital Transformation in the Small Businesses Sector" investigates the impact of digital transformation on small businesses and offers insights into best practices for its implementation.

References

Aly, H. (2020). Digital transformation, development and productivity in developing countries: is artificial intelligence a curse or a blessing? *Review of Economics and Political Science.*. Retrieved November 21, 2023, from https://www.emerald.com/insight/content/doi/10.1108/REPS-11-2019-0145/full/html

Heavin, C., & Power, D. J. (2018). Challenges for digital transformation–towards a conceptual decision support guide for managers. *Journal of Decision Systems, 27*, 38–45.

Kraus, S., Durst, S., Ferreira, J. J., Veiga, P., Kaila, N., & Weinnmann, A. (2022). Digital transformation in business and management research: An overview of the current status quo. *International Journal of Information Management, 63*, 102466.

Lamarre, E., Chheda, S., Riba, M., Genest, V., & Nizam, A. (2023). The Value of Digital Transformation. *Harvard Business Review*. Retrieved November 21, 2023, from https://www.mckinsey.com/featured-insights/mckinsey-explainers/what-is-digital-transformation

Matthess, M., & Kunkel, S. (2020). Structural change and digitalization in developing countries: Conceptually linking the two transformations. *Technology in Society, 63*, 101428.

Mckinsey and Company. (2023). What is digital transformation? Retrieved November 21, 2023, from https://www.mckinsey.com/featured-insights/mckinsey-explainers/what-is-digital-transformation

Vial, G. (2019). Understanding digital transformation: A review and a research agenda. *Journal of Strategic Information Systems, 28*(2), 118–144.

Warner, S. R., & Wäger, M. (2019). Building dynamic capabilities for digital transformation: An ongoing process of strategic renewal. *Long Term Planning, 52*(3), 326–349.

Digital Transformation in Enterprise Risk Management

Sylvester Senyo Horvey (iD) **and Tankiso Moloi** (iD)

Abstract This chapter discusses digital transformation in enterprise risk management (ERM). ERM is a strategic business discipline that helps organisations achieve their goals by addressing all of their risks and managing the combined impact of those risks in an integrated manner. This approach offers several benefits to an organisation, compared to the traditional risk management system, as it offers a holistic approach to managing risk. Despite the importance of ERM, organisations are seeking innovative ways to improve their efficiency and effectiveness. The shift to Industry 4.0 suggests the need to integrate digital technologies into the ERM system. Digital transformation also offers risk managers a window into the array of risks facing organisations.

As a result, this chapter conceptualises the need to digitalise ERM. We further outline the role of digital transformation in the ERM process. The study points out that digitalisation provides a more holistic perspective of the risks identified, their characteristics, causes and interdependencies. It enables companies to overcome risk oversight issues, make judgments and efficiently handle challenging risk situations. Hence, risk managers should leverage these digital tools, such as machine learning, big data, ERM software and AI-powered models, to identify and understand risks previously thought to be unknown. It is crucial for organisations that desire effective ERM programs to make sure that the risk management function and IT function collaborate to improve or develop ERM support systems. Therefore, ERM program executives should keep working with important stakeholders and other important functional areas to find ongoing investments, support, and resources to promote the use of digital tools for ERM throughout an organisation.

S. S. Horvey (✉)
Wits Business School, University of the Witwatersrand, Johannesburg, South Africa
e-mail: sylvester.horvey@wits.ac.za

T. Moloi
Johannesburg Business School, University of Johannesburg, Johannesburg, South Africa
e-mail: tankiso.moloi@jbs.ac.za

© The Author(s), under exclusive license to Springer Nature
Switzerland AG 2024
T. Moloi (ed.), *Digital Transformation in South Africa*, Professional Practice in
Governance and Public Organizations,
https://doi.org/10.1007/978-3-031-52403-5_2

1 Introduction

The fourth industrial revolution has brought about a digital shift in how individuals, businesses, and governments operate. This has led to modern technological advancements changing the business world. Coupled with the COVID-19 pandemic, this has brought attention to the necessity for businesses to accelerate their digitalisation initiatives. It has sped up the adoption of digital technologies and compelled businesses to swiftly implement remote work and digital procedures. The fast change in the corporate environment brought about by digital transformation across industries presents exponentially more opportunities for new projects and capabilities (George & Paul, 2020). Hence, the rapid shift in digitalisation is compelling companies to re-examine how they do business. With increased mobile networks, internet connectivity, and the evolution of artificial intelligence (AI), businesses are now changing their operation patterns. The drive to adopt the new technology and operating paradigms required to reap these advantages keeps growing (Van Veldhoven & Vanthienen, 2022). As a result, organisations are becoming more digitally savvy to maintain their competitiveness, adjust to shifting market conditions, seize new growth opportunities and improve their business operations.

To speed up the digital transformation journey in business organisations, business executives must view technology as the most effective differentiator to support their new business models. They must extend their digital capabilities beyond limited perspectives to the entire organisation. If this is on the cards, then enterprise risk management (ERM) also needs to be digitalised. The Committee of Sponsoring Organisation of the Treadway Commission (COSO) (2004, p. 2) defines ERM as: "A process, effected by an entity's board of directors, management and other personnel, applied in a strategy setting and across the enterprise, designed to identify potential events that may affect the entity, and manage risk to be within its risk appetite, to provide reasonable assurance regarding the achievement of entity objectives." This approach provides a top-down holistic view of risk and is believed to provide a robust approach to managing the risk of an organisation in an integrated manner, which enhances business performance and shareholder value (Horvey & Odei-Mensah, 2023).

Further, DeLoach (2000, p. 5) defines ERM as: "A structured and disciplined approach: it aligns strategy, processes, people, technology, and knowledge with the purpose of evaluating and managing the uncertainties the enterprises face as it creates value." This suggests the critical role of digital transformation in the ERM process. This is because ERM's effectiveness depends on its available resources, including technology (Patterson, 2015). Hence, it is important to digitalise the ERM system. Digitalising ERM involves utilising digital tools and data-driven strategies to improve the efficiency and effectiveness of ERM procedures within a business (Saeidi et al., 2019). This improves our understanding of risk interconnections. Therefore, to get the most out of their digital activities, companies must manage both the risks that are brought into the environment and their effects on the current ecosystem in addition to undergoing digital transformation.

ERM has previously been based on manual, compartmentalised processes, but a shift toward digitisation is required to keep up with the complexity and unpredictability of the modern corporate environment. Also, a digitalised risk function offers improved monitoring, control, and more efficient regulatory compliance. These include ensuring the control environment remains effective and assisting the risk function in using technology to satisfy regulatory expectations more effectively in crucial areas, such as risk measurement, aggregation, and reporting. Thus, significant improvement in ERM practices can be achieved through digital transformation. Therefore, organisations must manage risk stemming from the internal and external environment and its impact on their current ecosystem to drive value from their digital initiatives (Bautista & Krutzen, 2018). Hence, despite all the challenges and risks that the changing environment presents, organisations cannot overlook the potential that digital transformation brings forth, in addition to the profound impact that it shall have on them. This helps to detect, assess, monitor, and manage risks across diverse business activities.

Digitalising ERM is important because risk managers have been under intense pressure to fulfil changing regulatory standards and the ongoing global digital transformation. Also, the growing dynamics in the business environment have led to very volatile, uncertain, complex and ambiguous (VUCA) risks, which are difficult to manage. This requires high-level digital capabilities to manage these risks effectively. Given this, digitalising ERM provides an avenue to address the complex risks that keep unfolding. Also, digitalisation comes with so many risks which organisations cannot ignore. More so, risk managers may not have all the technical know-how to identify and manage some of the modern forms of risks, such as cyber risk. Organisations can proactively identify and mitigate risks related to digital transformation activities by implementing a thorough framework for digital risk management (Quinn et al., 2022). Therefore, technology is essential for businesses striving to control risk, but at the same time, as technology is used more frequently, risk is created that cannot be ignored, which makes the digitalisation of the ERM system crucial.

Digitalising the ERM system is an urgent need which transcends beyond geographical boundaries, affecting not only developed but also emerging economies, where the concept of digitalisation and ERM is gaining much prominence. Emerging economies face several constraints, including infrastructure and resource constraints regarding ERM. Also, Silva et al. (2019) point out that emerging economies face several challenges, such as political and institutional risk and the volatility of interest rate and exchange rate risk, compared to the developed economy, making the digitalisation of ERM imperative. This can boost emerging economies by offering affordable and efficient risk management solutions, fostering economic growth, and reducing vulnerabilities.

As a result, the risk management system of business organisations needs to be digitalised it allows them to transform operations fundamentally, improve customer experiences, spur innovation, and enhance ERM effectiveness. Therefore, the premise of this chapter lies in how ERM implementation can be improved through digital transformation. It explains the concept of ERM and its importance over the traditional risk management system. Further, it highlights how digitalisation improves the ERM process, thereby offering insight to academics and practitioners on the importance of digitalisation and how to incorporate this in the ERM process.

2 Enterprise Risk Management Versus Traditional Risk Management

2.1 Traditional Risk Management (TRM) System

In the traditional risk management system, risks were managed in silos; thus, firm managers placed responsibilities on business units or departmental heads to manage risks within their areas of responsibility (Beasley, 2016). This is because different departments and/or functions manage risks within their discipline. Each function adopted and developed tools that were independent of each other. Hence, the TRM system is viewed as a disintegrated approach to managing risks. Different kinds of risks are managed separately in different departments within the firm. For instance, liquidity, market, credit and operational risks, were separately managed in different silos (Hoyt & Liebenberg, 2011).

Figure 1 presents an overview of the TRM approach. Regarding this system, each silo leader is responsible for managing or elevating risks within their silo.

Fig. 1 Traditional Risk Management Approach; *Source*: Beasley (2016)

Therefore, in the silo system, the human resource head is only concerned about risks that affect the business unit, while the IT department head also concentrates on risk within this business unit, and the same applies to the other business units. However, this method of risk management does not help. Beasley (2016) revealed some limitations of the traditional/silo risk management system. Some of these limitations are that some risks can "fall between the silos" that none of the silo leaders can see, leading to risk oversight issues. Also, there may be risks that can have multiple effects on silos in different ways. In light of this complexity, individual silo leaders who put up measures to manage such risks do not know how those measures are likely to impact other silo managers, and mostly, silo leaders are tempted to focus only on internal aspects of risk management while ignoring external factors (Pagach & Warr, 2011). Moreover, managing the same risk in different silos can lead to duplication and waste of resources and is more defensive than offensive since most business units do not have risk expertise and are not proactive in managing risk (Hoyt & Liebenberg, 2011). More so, TRM creates a lot of inefficiencies and inconsistencies because there is a lack of coordination. According to the Organisation of Economic Cooperation and Development (OECD), this approach to risk management contributed greatly to the 2007/08 global financial crises (Moloi, 2018). As a result, organisations and risk managers have begun to embrace ERM, which offers a broader perspective on risk management and overcomes the shortcomings of the TRM system (Beasley et al., 2005).

2.2 Enterprise Risk Management (ERM) System

Enterprise risk management is a response to the inadequacies of the TRM system. The ERM approach to managing risk helps manage each risk as a feature of the firm's overall risk portfolio managed in an integrated manner (Horvey & Ankamah, 2020). The primary characteristic that sets ERM apart from the traditional risk management system is the more holistic or integrated approach employed. ERM is seen as a concept that unifies the management of all risks in various ways rather than as a novel or innovative strategy. As a result, when a company considers every risk it faces and how those risks can affect its strategy, initiatives, and operations, it is starting to use an enterprise risk management approach (Hopkin, 2018). Enterprise risk management is also known as Enterprise-Wide Risk Management, Strategic Risk Management, Holistic Risk Management, Corporate Risk Management, Integrated Risk Management, Portfolio Risk Management, Business Risk Management and Scientific risk management because it involves a body of knowledge and processes.

ERM has been explained from diverse perspectives by individuals and organisations. ERM is believed to reduce firm risks and, in turn, increase performance and shareholder value (Bromiley et al., 2015). The importance of ERM implementation and its impact on performance is revealed in the following definitions. Sobel and Reding (2004) highlight that ERM is a well-disciplined and structured approach that helps management know and manage uncertainties encompassing all business risks using a holistic approach. Meulbroek (2002) also defines ERM as a process requiring managers to collectively identify and assess organisational risks that affect performance and adopt a strategic risk management approach to manage those risks to achieve an effective risk management strategy. From these definitions, it can be deduced that ERM has two main characteristics. First, it must be comprehensive (thus, a detailed inclusion of all kinds and different ranges of risks). Second, it must be integrated; it should cut across all business lines, functions and departments (Horvey & Odei-Mensah, 2023).

International organisations such as the Casualty Actuarial Society (CAS) (2003) define ERM as integrated management of operational, hazard, strategic and financial risks. In addition, the International Organisation for Standardisations (ISO) explains ERM as a set of activities brought together to direct and control an organisation's risk affairs. The Risk and Insurance Management Society (RIMS) in 2011 also revealed ERM as a strategic approach supporting an organisation to achieve its goals by identifying and managing all risks to reduce their impact. COSO (2017) further explains ERM as an art and science because it involves a body of knowledge and expertise to manage an organisation. These definitions highlight the significance of ERM as a strategic function in achieving organisational goals by identifying and managing all risks, linking the concept to the idea that ERM makes companies resilient and responds to change. This is due to their proactive nature in identifying possible risks and deviations and how to respond to these deviations. ERM reveals the strengths and weakness of a firm's strategy while evaluating alternative methods within a changing environment and how strategy can help with the attainment of a firm's mission and vision (Horvey & Odei-Mensah, 2023). A good risk management system instils trust and confidence in stakeholders.

Based on the above-noted definitions, it can be viewed that these studies provide a gist of the value of ERM implementation. While some authors view ERM as a system that helps to achieve organisational goals and objectives, others see it as a way of mitigating the large problems facing an organisation, whereas other scholars view it as a way of creating value for an organisation. Generally, these definitions reveal that ERM is a system that combines all risk activities of a firm, manages them in an integrated manner, and facilitates the identification of such interdependencies to achieve the firm's strategic objectives. These definitions further explain that ERM, as a new paradigm, offers better opportunities and a competitive edge than the traditional risk management system. Table 1 provides a summary of the difference between ERM and TRM.

3   The Enterprise Risk Management Process

Several ERM frameworks have been developed to explain the risk management process. These include the ISO 31000 ERM framework, RIMS risk maturity model ERM framework, and the Australian/New Zealand risk standard, among others. However, this study shall explore the COSO ERM framework, which is one of the

Table 1 Difference between TRM and ERM

TRM	ERM	Source
Manage risk separately (Fragmented)	Manage risk Holistically (Integrated)	Liebenberg and Hoyt (2003); Pagach and Warr (2011)
They identify and respond to internal risks	They identify and respond to internal and external risks	Beasley (2016)
Risk is considered an individual hazard	Risk is part of firm strategy	Beasley et al. (2008)
Takes a bottom-up approach	Takes a top-down approach	Gatzert and Martin (2015); Beasley et al. (2008)
More defensive	Very offensive	Gatzert and Martin (2015)
Does not consider all risks (Narrowly focused)	Encompasses all risks (Broadly focused)	Beasley (2016); COSO (2004); Horvey and Ankamah (2020)
Focus on People	Focus on people and process	McShane et al. (2011); DeLoach (2000)
Does not consider its effect on other business units	Considers its effects on all business units	Beasley (2016); Lundqvist (2014)
Very reactive and Cost-Based	Proactive and Value-Based	Deloach (2000)
There is an information asymmetry	Information asymmetry is reduced, thereby improving communication	Hoyt and Liebenberg (2011); Beasley et al. (2008)
Leads to the duplication of resources	Avoids duplication of resources	Beasley (2016); Hoyt and Liebenberg (2011)
Managed by functional/ departmental managers	Managed by risk experts such as CRO or risk manager	Gatzert and Martin (2015)
There is no centralised risk committee/board	A centralised risk committee/ board is dedicated to managing risk	Horvey and Odei-Mensah (2023)
No formal report to the board	Submits a formal report to the board at least annually	Sekerci and Pagach (2019)
Does not consider shareholder value and responsibilities to investors	Considers shareholder value and responsibilities to investors	Manab et al. (2010)
It does not involve all employees at all levels of the organisation	Involves all employees at all levels of the organisation	Horvey and Odei-Mensah (2023)
Negative and Ad-hoc	Positive and Process-driven	Deloach (2000)

Source: Authors Compilations

most widely used frameworks. Even though most countries and organisations have developed their frameworks, the basic steps are similar and are mostly consistent with the COSO internal control process (Hopkin, 2018), which is the motivation for choosing this framework.

The COSO ERM framework provides a comprehensive understanding of an ERM approach. It captures risk management and internal controls within its scope. It is viewed as a multidirectional and iterative process in which practically every component is related to the other. The main emphasis of the COSO framework is to provide a flexible evaluation standard against which to evaluate the current ERM process instead of focusing on the specific activities of the risk management process itself. The COSO ERM framework can be seen in Fig. 2 below:

The COSO framework is a three-dimensional matrix with a cube-like shape. It creates a connection between the objectives that must be attained and the ERM process, which details the steps necessary to accomplish the objectives. The third dimension, which stands for the organisational units, illustrates the model's capacity to concentrate on the organisational units and the overall.

3.1 COSO ERM Objectives

The main objectives of the COSO framework can be seen on top of the cube. These are strategic, operations, reporting and compliance. These are further explained below:

- *Strategic:* These are the high-level goals of an organisation which must be aligned with and support the organisation's mission statement.
- *Operations:* This has to do with the daily activities of an organisation and the ongoing management process.
- *Reporting:* This objective deals with the protection of an organisation's assets and quality of financial reporting
- *Compliance:* The last objective explains the ability of the organisation to adhere to rules and regulatory policies.

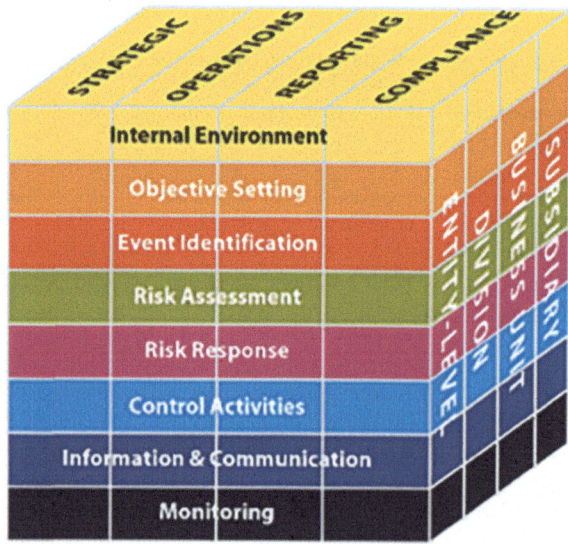

Fig. 2 COSO ERM framework; *Source*: COSO

3.2   COSO ERM Dimensions

The right-hand side of the COSO ERM framework reveals the different levels that must be considered to achieve the overall objectives of an ERM system. These include;

- Subsidiary level
- Business unit level
- Division level and
- Entity level

3.3   COSO ERM Components

The front side of the COSO ERM cube specifies the individual components that must be considered for enterprise risk management implementation. The COSO ERM cube, which consists of eight connected sections, is a very effective risk management system. These are produced by how management manages a company and are weaved into the management process.

(a) *Internal Environment:* One of the major arguments of the ERM process is where it starts. COSO believes that the ERM process begins with the internal environment, which is mostly defined by the board of directors. As a result, the internal environment, which is initiated by the board, sets the organisational tone, which also affects risk appetites and elements such as board oversight, attitudes toward risk management, and ethical principles (Moeller, 2011). A board that lacks diversity, solid and independent voices, proper technical understanding, and balance is unlikely to set the correct tone (Scott, 2004). The work that directors conduct on board committees can also significantly affect the tone, with the audit and risk committees' operations being of special significance.

(b) *Objective setting:* Once the internal environment has been defined, the board should establish goals that advance the organisation's mission and align with its risk appetite (Hopkin, 2018). Objective setting refers to providing a foundation for operations, reporting, and compliance goals and establishing strategic goal-setting objectives. Before management may identify possible events affecting the attainment of the objectives, these objectives must first be set. The board should also think about its risk tolerance and decide how much risk it is willing to absorb on a broad scale.

(c) *Event Identification:* This is where the organisation identifies events likely to affect the organisation's goals. The organisation must determine the internal and external factors affecting the realisation of its goals. The COSO guidance distinguishes between situations with a negative impact, representing threats and situations with a positive impact, representing opportunities that should inform strategy setting. Organisations should analyse prospective events to find them, but it is also critical to spot and address any early warning indications of risks (Hopkin, 2018). Also crucial in this context is the distinction between operational and strategic risks. Organisations must be aware of potential operational disruptions and threats to accomplishing strategic goals.

(d) *Risk Assessment:* Risks are evaluated in order to decide how to manage them by analysing their impact and likelihood (Scott, 2004). Likelihood represents the probability of occurrence, and impact represents the severity of the most probable risk events (Patterson, 2015). The risks can be categorised into financial, market, operational, regulatory, cyber risk, etc. Managers need to map the interrelationships between specific risks in addition to the likelihood and impact of each risk. A combination of qualitative and quantitative risk assessment approaches should be used, according to COSO's recommendations. Organisations can employ tools such as the risk matrix, risk map, forced ranking, and bow-tie technique, among others, for risk assessment. The organisation should evaluate residual risks that remain after risk management steps have been taken, in addition to the inherent risk levels (Hopkin, 2018).

(e) *Risk Response:* After assessing the nature of risks, management must select the best course of action to balance risks with their appetite and tolerance levels (Hopkin, 2018). The four main responses at this stage are treat (high likelihood, low impact), transfer (low likelihood, high impact), tolerate (low likelihood, low impact) and terminate (high likelihood, high impact). Risks, however, might wind up being handled separately from the organisation's overall situation. The risk response chosen must be realistic, considering the costs of responding and the impact on risk. It is important to highlight that an organisation's environment affects its risk responses. Highly regulated organisations, for example, have more complex risk responses and controls than less regulated organisations.

(f) *Control Activities:* This refers to the rules and guidelines that support implementing management's risk response strategies. According to COSO, a combination of controls, including manual and automated controls and prevention and detection, will be effective. Once created, the controls must function properly (Scott, 2004).

(g) *Information and Communication:* This refers to the right information being identified, recorded, and transmitted to the right people in the right format and amount of time. The management team must receive pertinent and high-quality information. Additionally, it must address each of the goals listed on the cube's top. Communication with personnel is necessary. By instilling risk awareness in staff members' minds, sharing risk areas that are pertinent to their work is a key strategy for improving the internal environment (Hopkin, 2018).

(h) *Monitoring:* This simply means overseeing, consistently checking and carefully observing. It also means to identify the present status and to judge whether expected performance levels are essentially being achieved or not (Gjerdrum & Peter, 2011). This process consists of the approval that the various risk management components and activities are working effectively in conjunction with the organisation's expectations. It helps to identify any gaps, such as emerging risks and changes in prevailing risks due to variations in objectives and environmental conditions (Hopkin, 2018). Monitoring involves consistent scanning of the environment by risk managers, control assertion, bringing together new material available, and drawing conclusions about the various risks and their controls from the analysis of success and failure.

4   Conceptualising the Digitalisation of Enterprise Risk Management

Digitalising ERM is the process of employing digital technologies and data-driven techniques to manage an organisation's risks in a holistic and far-sighted manner. Thus, digital transformation involves using artificial intelligence, automation and other technological tools to assist in the ERM process (Deloitte, 2018; Platsis, 2022). The ultimate purpose of digital transformation of the ERM system is to ensure the efficiency, proactiveness and adaptability of the risk management process in the rapidly evolving environment. This enhances the organisation's resilience and capacity to accomplish its strategic goals in a world that is becoming more complicated and data-driven. Digital transformation also offers risk managers a window into the array of risks facing the organisation. It helps to revise risk management decisions, assess emerging risks and make strategic changes accordingly.

   Despite the advantages ERM has over the silo approach, most organisations still rely on the manual approach to its implementation. This approach tends to be time-consuming and highly prone to human error. Another major issue regarding the manual approach to ERM has been the lack of reliable data and information on which to make decisions (Moloi & Iredele, 2020). Again, risk data is mostly dispersed throughout the organisation and is not shared across silos of business units, which poses a difficulty for risk managers. This is because most risk management departments lack the resources to capture and use risk data more effectively (Patterson, 2015). In essence, this asserts that missed opportunities for the company are a possibility and might be anticipated. Hence, it calls for the digitalisation of the risk management process.

   By digitalising the ERM process, companies can eliminate these challenges and ensure the efficiency and effectiveness of the ERM system. For instance, digitalising ERM reduces the required response time by clearly revealing existing threats and opportunities. Ernst and Young (2014) claim that by using technology, we could start to witness a decline in missed opportunities and realised risks. This is because technology allows risk management activities to be carried out with improved insight, efficiency, and effectiveness, freeing up time for risk management resources to spend on risk identification, assessment, and control of future risks. In light of these arguments, more effort is required to elevate ERM to fully take advantage of the developments in a digital world and advanced analytics to embed deeper and more insightful risk information in strategy-setting, performance management, and decision-making processes. According to Patterson (2015), the use of digital tools in the ERM process helps to:

- Capture and assess the potential impacts of identified risks
- define, convey, monitor, and track the organisation's levels of risk appetite and risk tolerance
- appoint a responsible party to carry out ongoing risk monitoring and internal control actions
- report on the success of continuing risk management for an organisation.

In today's complicated and dynamic environment, digitalising the ERM process is not just a choice. It is a need. Digitalising the ERM system provides precision, real-time capabilities, better decision-making, efficiency, and adaptability. By so doing, organisations would be able to deal with the dynamic realities of the twenty-first century (Mckinsey, 2017; Bayuk, 2018). Through digitalisation, companies are able to have a more holistic perspective of the risks identified, their characteristics, causes and interdependencies. It enables companies to make judgments and efficiently handle challenging risk settings. This ensures that companies adapt and respond to the VUCA portfolio of risks. This argument is affirmed by Patterson (2015), who states that the ERM process is effective if integrated with the digital technology employed by the organisation. This involves developing a risk-based architecture which is aligned with the organisation's digital needs and operating environment. Knopjes (2017) supports this viewpoint by highlighting that businesses can use emerging technology to integrate various systems to gather and analyse enormous amounts of data from infinite sources across numerous places. Organisations benefit from improved operational processes, quicker reporting, and data-driven preventative actions through this method, putting them miles ahead of possible risks.

According to Davis et al. (2002), digital transformation shortens the time processes in risk management. For instance, modern technologies make it easier to store important data, which allows for transferring previous project expertise to new projects and improves scheduling, budgeting, communications, and time spent on requirements that are not repetitive (Cho & Kim, 2008). It also supports the integration, flexibility, and compatibility of the ERM process at all levels. Another essential role of digitalising the ERM process is that it streamlines the integration of the risk management process and makes it cost-effective (Anand, 2010). PwC (2017) support this statement, concurring that information technology governance, risk and compliance ensure that the activities and functions of the organisation support the objectives, achieve the benefits it has to offer against the strategy and manage critical information technology resources effectively.

5 The Role of Digital Transformation in the Enterprise Risk Management Process

In our opening discussion, we indicated the importance and the need for digital transformation in ERM. In this section, we shall discuss the role of digital transformation in the ERM process.

(a) *Risk Identification:* Good data is the foundation of an efficient risk management strategy because it gives the organisation reliable statistics for decision-making. As a result, organisations must create reliable front-end systems, data architecture with minimal human intervention, databases, and business intelligence technology to capture excellent data (Schutte & Marx, 2018). Digital transformation provides this capability. It offers technological software and tools for risk identification (Deloitte, 2018). For instance, the automation of digital technologies such as "Big data", cloud computing and ERM software in the risk identification process enables businesses to proactively recognise and address risks, enhancing risk management and boosting organisational resilience. Also, the digitalisation of the risk identification process helps organisations find hidden risks that conventional methods might not be able to reveal. This involves gathering data from many internal and external sources. These include financial data, market trends, social media, and historical records (Patterson, 2015). This vast data repository makes it easier to spot potential risks and provide detailed reports. Again, digitalisation helps risk managers connect to different databases for risk information, which may not be manually possible.

(b) *Risk Assessment:* It can be difficult to analyse data from a wide range of risk types, business lines, and geographical locations using conventional methods. It is onerous to assess the direction and velocity of risk, appreciate the elements that drive risk, take into account risk in the context of company strategy, and enable a strong risk appetite debate because traditional risk reporting lacks insight into the underlying realities. As a result, it frequently requires too much human work to compile information from various sources, update metrics, and create PowerPoint presentations that meet the demands of decision-makers. Digitalisation helps to overcome these challenges and makes the risk assessment process more effective and efficient (Wilkinson, 2011). For instance, with the integration of digital technologies, risk managers can capture, extract, transform, and use legacy databases to perform risk assessments, stress tests, and risk scenario analyses. By so doing, risk managers gain an in-depth understanding of the magnitude and velocity of the risk. Through digitalisation, companies can have a more holistic perspective of the risks identified, their characteristics, causes and interdependencies. Statistical modelling tools can help support an ERM system's risk analysis as they allow for risk scenarios that are even more diverse to be evaluated, which results in better decision-making (Patterson, 2015). Although not easy or cheap to implement and manage, these digital evolutions will become less costly over time and greatly impact how organisations track and manage risks (Patterson, 2015).

(c) *Risk Response:* Traditional risk response strategies of the ERM system are frequently slow and reactive, which makes it challenging to manage risks that are fast emerging. A strategic objective that improves agility, reactivity, and resource efficiency in managing the complexity of contemporary risk landscapes is the digitisation of the risk response process. The automation of regular risk response duties is made possible by digitalisation, which enables firms to spend resources more wisely. Digital solutions can also give firms complete visibility into risk data, allowing them to make data-driven decisions and allocate resources more effectively for risk response activities.

(d) *Control Activities:* Given the significance of the human factor, it follows that many control failures are caused by issues with how managers and staff use controls. These include mistakes, staff cooperation, failure to operate controls because they are not taken seriously, and management ordering staff to override controls. With digital transformation, firms are able to efficiently deploy resources to improve the effectiveness of risk control procedures through the automation of risk control tasks.

(e) *Information and Communication:* A key component of an effective ERM programme is having timely information. For instance, when an organisation is immediately aware that a key supplier has experienced significant disruptions in its raw materials supply chain, timely information can help compensate for this risk (Patterson, 2015). Since timely information is such a critical component, many organisations can employ digital tools to monitor the operational activities of businesses to collect and process information promptly (Patterson, 2015). Also, the risk committee and employees need a more thorough, understandable, and actionable snapshot of their organisations' risk profile to make prudent decisions. This helps risk officers, board members, and shareholders feel more confident that they understand their critical risks and can act quickly when risk levels rise or fall. Technology, therefore, becomes a crucial tool for efficiently managing and communicating risks across all levels of an organisation. It allows firms to use data to identify risks, improves communication and reporting procedures, and makes remote collaboration easier, all of which help create more effective risk management strategies. Digital tools such as mobile technology and cloud computing make it possible for teams to communicate and work together on risk management initiatives wherever they are. This facilitates information dissemination compared to the manual approach.

(f) *Monitoring and Review:* Digitalisation has sped up organisational change, which motivates risk managers to monitor how ERM is impacted. Real-time monitoring of risk indicators is made possible by digital tools. For example, by using "big data" as a risk management tool, managers could anticipate risks and monitor the emergence of risk events as they affect the firm. When odd patterns or threats appear, automated warnings can be set up to notify the appropriate stakeholders promptly. Routine monitoring operations can be automated to reduce human error and to derive valuable insights from data at a size and speed that would be unattainable with conventional processes. These advantages result in stronger risk mitigation techniques and a more durable organisation (Schutte & Marx, 2018).

6   Key Points

- ERM is a system that combines all risk activities of a firm, manages them in an integrated manner, and facilitates the identification of such interdependencies to achieve the firm's strategic objectives.
- In the wake of digital evolution, the effectiveness and efficiency of the ERM process can be improved by employing digital tools for the risk management process. This drives the ERM capabilities, thereby ensuring the organisation's performance.
- Through digitalisation, companies can have a more holistic perspective of the risks identified, their characteristics, causes and interdependencies. It enables companies to overcome risk oversight issues, make judgments and efficiently handle challenging risk situations.
- The data-driven fourth industrial revolution is a period of intense automation and digitisation. With the advent of machine learning, data formerly regarded as unusable can now be found to be useful. Hence, the board and risk managers can leverage these data through AI-powered models to identify and understand risks previously thought to be unknown.
- It is crucial for organisations that desire effective ERM programs to make sure that the risk management function and digital function collaborate to improve or develop ERM support systems.
- Therefore, ERM program executives should keep working with relevant stake-holders and other principal functional areas to find ongoing investments, support, and resources to promote the use of digital tools for ERM throughout an organisation.
- Additionally, organisations should consider including digital experts in the risk committee and ensure that the ERM program is part of the organisation's entire digital process. This will help risk managers embrace future evolutions in risk management technologies and help obtain the necessary digitalisation level. Also, the risk managers need to be retrained to evolve and respond to the growing demand for digitalising ERM.

References

Anand, S. (2010). Technology and the integration of governance, risk management and compliance. *The Financial Executive, 26*(10), 57–58.

Bautista, M. C., & Krutzen B. (2018). Digitisation of risk management: Equipping the business to make informed risk decisions. Retrieved April 12, 2023, from https://www.compact.nl/en/articles/digitization-of-risk-management/

Bayuk, J. (2018). Technology's role in enterprise risk management, 2. Retrieved October 06, 2023, from https://www.isaca.org/resources/isaca-journal/issues/2018/volume-2/technologys-role-in-enterprise-risk-management

Beasley, M. S. (2016). *Enterprise risk management*. ERM Initiative, North Carolina State University. https://erm.ncsu.edu/az/erm/i/chan/library/What_is_Enterprise_Risk_Management.pdf

Beasley, M. S., Clune, R., & Hermanson, D. R. (2005). Enterprise risk management: An empirical analysis of factors associated with the extent of implementation. *Journal of Accounting and Public Policy, 24*, 521–531.

Beasley, M., Pagach, D., & Warr, R. (2008). Information conveyed in hiring announcements of senior executives overseeing enterprise-wide risk management processes. *Journal of Accounting, Auditing & Finance, 23*(3), 311–332.

Bromiley, P., McShane, M., Nair, A., & Rustambekov, E. (2015). Enterprise risk management: Review, critique, and research directions. *Long Range Planning, 48*(4), 265–276.

Cho, T., & Kim, T. S. (2008). Probabilistic risk assessment for the construction phases of a bridge construction based on finite element analysis. *Finite Elements in Analysis and Design, 44*(6-7), 383–400.

Committee of Sponsoring Organisations of the Treadway Commission. (2017). *COSO enterprise risk management: Integrating with strategy and performance*. AICPA.

Committee of Sponsoring Organizations of the Treadway Commission (Coso). (2004). *Enterprise risk management-integrated framework* (p. 2). Committee of Sponsoring Organizations of the Treadway Commission.

Davis, P. S., Dibrell, C. C., & Janz, B. D. (2002). The impact of time on the strategy–performance relationship: Implications for managers. *Industrial Marketing Management, 31*(4), 339–347.

DeLoach, J. W. (2000). Enterprise-wide risk management: strategies for linking risk and opportunity. *(No Title)*.

Deloitte. (2018). Managing risk in digital transformation. Retrieved May 21, 2023, from https://www2.deloitte.com/content/dam/Deloitte/in/Documents/risk/in-ra-managing-risk-in-digital-transformation-1-noexp.pdf

Ernst & Young. (2014). Retrieved October 04, from https://www.ey.com/Publication/vwLUAssets/EY-leveragingtechnology-and-data-for-cost-effective-riskmanagement/$File/EYLeveraging-technology-and-data-for-cost-effectiverisk-management.pdf

Gatzert, N., & Martin, M. (2015). Determinants and value of enterprise risk management: Empirical evidence from the literature. *Risk Management and Insurance Review, 18*(1), 29–53.

George, B., & Paul, J. (2020). *Digital transformation in business and society*. Springer International Publishing.

Gjerdrum, D., & Peter, M. (2011). The new international standard on the practice of risk management–A comparison of ISO 31000: 2009 and the COSO ERM framework. *Risk Management, 31*(21), 8–12.

Hopkin, P. (2018). *Fundamentals of risk management: understanding, evaluating and implementing effective risk management*. Kogan Page Publishers.

Horvey, S. S., & Ankamah, J. (2020). Enterprise risk management and firm performance: Empirical evidence from Ghana equity market. *Cogent Economics & Finance, 8*(1), 1840102.

Horvey, S. S., & Odei-Mensah, J. (2023). The measurements and performance of enterprise risk management: A comprehensive literature review. *Journal of Risk Research, 26*(7), 778–800.

Hoyt, R. E., & Liebenberg, A. P. (2011). The value of enterprise risk management. *Journal of risk and insurance, 78*(4), 795–822.

Knopjes, B. (2017). Why IoT is the future of integrated risk management. Retrieved October 12, 2018, from https://www.isometrix.com/iot-in-risk-management/

Liebenberg, A. P., & Hoyt, R. E. (2003). The determinants of enterprise risk management: Evidence from the appointment of chief risk officers. *Risk Management and Insurance Review, 6*(1), 37–52.

Lundqvist, S. A. (2014). An exploratory study of enterprise risk management pillars of ERM. *Journal of Accounting, Auditing & Finance, 29*(3), 393–429.

Manab, N. A., Kassim, I., & Hussin, M. R. (2010). Enterprise-wide risk management (EWRM) practices: Between corporate governance compliance and value. *International Review of Business Research Papers, 6*(2), 239–252.

McKinsey. (2017). Digital risk: Transforming risk management for the 2020s. Retrieved Juene 25, 2023, from https://www.mckinsey.com/capabilities/risk-and-resilience/our-insights/digital-risk-transforming-risk-management-for-the-2020s

McShane, M. K., Nair, A., & Rustambekov, E. (2011). Does enterprise risk management increase firm value? *Journal of Accounting, Auditing & Finance, 26*(4), 641–658.

Meulbroek, L. K. (2002). Integrated risk management for the firm: a senior manager's guide. *Available at SSRN 301331*.

Moeller, R. R. (2011). *COSO enterprise risk management: Establishing effective governance, risk, and compliance processes* (Vol. 560). John Wiley & Sons.

Moloi, T. (2018). Analysing the human capital capabilities in the enterprise risk management function of South Africa's public institutions. *Business and Economic Horizons, 14*(2), 375–388.

Moloi, T., & Iredele, O. O. (2020). *Risk management in the digital era: the case of Nigerian banks* (pp. 229–246). Digital Transformation in Business and Society.

Pagach, D., & Warr, R. (2011). The characteristics of firms that hire chief risk officers. *Journal of risk and insurance, 78*(1), 185–211.

Patterson, T. (2015). *The use of information technology in risk management*. IBM.

Platsis, G. (2022). Digital transformation and risk management must go together. Retrieved October 09, 2023, from https://securityintelligence.com/articles/digital-transformation-risk-management-different-together/

PricewaterhouseCoopers (PWC). (2017). IT governance, risk and compliance. Retrieved July 13, 2017, from http://www.pwc.com/la/en/risk-assurance/itgrc.html

Quinn, S., Ivy, N., Chua, J., Scarfone, K., Barrett, M., Feldman, L., & Gardner, R. (2022). *Information and Communications Technology (ICT) Risk Outcomes: Integrating ICT Risk Management Programs with the Enterprise Risk Portfolio (No. NIST Special Publication (SP) 800-221A (Draft))*. National Institute of Standards and Technology.

Saeidi, P., Saeidi, S. P., Sofian, S., Saeidi, S. P., Nilashi, M., & Mardani, A. (2019). The impact of enterprise risk management on competitive advantage by moderating role of information technology. *Computer Standards & Interfaces, 63*, 67–82.

Schutte, B., & Marx, B. (2018). The role of information technology in the risk management of businesses in South Africa. *Journal for New Generation Sciences, 16*(2), 92–111.

Scott, A. (2004). COSO ERM framework released. *Internal Auditor, 61*(5), 17–19.

Sekerci, N., & Pagach, D. P. (2019). Firm ownership and enterprise risk management: Evidence from Continental Europe. *Available at SSRN 3366489*.

Silva, J. R., Silva, A. F. D., & Chan, B. L. (2019). Enterprise risk management and firm value: Evidence from Brazil. *Emerging Markets Finance and Trade, 55*(3), 687–703.

Sobel, P. J., & Reding, K. F. (2004). Aligning corporate governance with enterprise risk management. *Management Accounting Quarterly, 5*(2), 29.

To, C. A. S. (2003). The Casualty Actuarial Society Forum Summer 2003 Edition Including the 2003 Enterprise Risk Management & Dynamic Financial Analysis Modeling Call Papers.

Van Veldhoven, Z., & Vanthienen, J. (2022). Digital transformation as an interaction-driven perspective between business, society, and technology. *Electronic Markets, 32*(2), 629–644.

Wilkinson, M. (2011). *The role of information technology in risk management*. Retrieved July 13, 2023, from https://www.towerswatson.com/en-GB/Insights/IC-Types/Ad-hoc-Point-ofView/2011/Insights-The-role-of-technology-in-riskmanagement

Digital Transformation in Finance and Banking Sectors

Toluwa Celestine Oladele ⓘD

Abstract This chapter discussed the effect of digital transformation in the banking and financial sector. This chapter examined the overview of banks and the financial sector and the role of COVID-19 in increasing the pace and adoption of digital transformation by banks and other financial institutions. Also, the chapter examined the important role digital transformation plays in the banking and financial sector and how digital transformation is reshaping the banks and financial sector. Emphasis was given to the key technologies driving digital transformation in the banking and financial sector and the key dimensions of banks' digital transformation. The chapter also discussed the role of digital transformation in driving financial inclusion and accessibility. The chapter equally discussed the challenges limiting the adoption of digital transformation by banks and other financial institutions and the future trends and prospects for banks and financial institutions as they embrace digital transformation. The final lap of the chapter is the summary of the key findings from the chapter.

Like every other financial institution, banks seek to maximise their profits by reducing operational expenses or reaching out to more customers. Hence, the need to embrace the disruptive tendencies of digital transformation that are changing the organisational landscape and how businesses and individuals conduct their daily activities. The Covid-19 outbreak caused a significant shift in how banks and other financial institutions operate. More internet-based services than ever are available in the banking sector. Digital services are now more crucial than ever, even though traditional banking services still entail going to a banking hall or the offices of any financial organisation. Transactions made during and after Covid-19 surpassed those made before the outbreak. The banking and finance industry is undergoing a complicated and continuing digital transformation process. The diverse effects of digital technology on the sector have been examined in this chapter, from improving customer experiences and operational efficiencies to addressing legal issues and

T. C. Oladele (✉)
Department of Banking and Finance, University of Ibadan, Ibadan, Nigeria
e-mail: ct.oladele@mail1.ui.edu.ng

© The Author(s), under exclusive license to Springer Nature
Switzerland AG 2024
T. Moloi (ed.), *Digital Transformation in South Africa*, Professional Practice in
Governance and Public Organizations,
https://doi.org/10.1007/978-3-031-52403-5_3

cybersecurity risks. Financial institutions must innovate and adapt as technology develops in order to be competitive in this quickly changing environment. Those who embrace this shift will be best positioned for success in the future. There is little doubt that the future of banking and finance lies in digital technology.

1 Introduction

The banking and financial sector has changed over the years due to digital technology advancements. This section explored how digital transformation has impacted aspects of the industry, including customer experiences, operational efficiencies, regulatory challenges, and cybersecurity. This chapter delved into trends, emerging technologies and strategies institutions employ to stay competitive in the digital era. The COVID-19 pandemic has further accelerated technology adoption across industries, including banking and finance (Versal et al., 2022). Embracing digitalisation is crucial for the banking sector as it enables the development of capabilities and effective collaboration across industries. Digital transformation involves integrating technologies throughout all areas of a business or industry, fundamentally reshaping operations and providing customer value.

In the context of banking and finance, digital transformation entails adopting and utilising technologies such as intelligence (AI), machine learning (ML), blockchain technology and robotic process automation (RPA) (Jayalath & Premaratne, 2021). These technologies enable institutions to streamline operations, enhance customer experience, automate processes and strengthen security measures against fraud. The transformation process involves an overhaul of conventional systems and procedures, embracing digital channels and platforms to meet the changing requirements of the digital era. Banks and financial institutions can foster innovation, improve effectiveness and maintain competitiveness in a growing landscape by harnessing the power of digital technologies (Taka & Bayarçelík, 2023).

2 Overview of the Banking and Financial Sector

In contemporary economies, the banking and financial sector is crucial because it drives economic development, risk management, and capital allocation. Its organisational structure consists of several institutions and services that cater to the different financial demands of people, organisations, and governments (Versal et al., 2022). The industry is undergoing revolutionary developments, including technological breakthroughs and a push toward ethical and sustainable investment, even with regulatory changes and cybersecurity dangers. A fluid environment that adapts to social, technical, and economic advancements will determine how the banking and financial industry develops in the future.

The financial industry has been greatly affected by the introduction of new technology. Banks that offer financial services have experienced significant changes due to these advancements. In the past, banks controlled the financial markets in many countries, particularly in payments, deposits, and credit. However, with increasing competition, financial technology—fintech—companies have started to dominate these industries more and more. This shift has been highlighted by Singh et al. (2022) in their study.

The digitalisation of the economy, especially in the financial markets, has led to changes in consumer behaviour and the marketing activities of commercial banks. With cutting-edge technologies, such as AI and mobile applications, banks can simplify processes like onboarding by allowing customers to submit required documents through their smartphones (Singh et al., 2022). This saves time and effort for both customers and workers and enables swift analysis of financial history and customer data to assess loan applications.

The focus on quality characteristics of banking services becomes vital in this changing landscape. By leveraging technology, banks can simplify processes like onboarding and improve operational efficiency. Mobile applications enable customers to submit required documents, saving time and effort. Additionally, AI technology allows for quick financial history and customer data analysis, facilitating faster loan application assessments. The focus on quality characteristics of banking services becomes crucial in this digital age.

3   COVID-19 and Digital Transformation Demand in the Banking and Financial Sector

During the Covid-19 pandemic, the banking and financial industries experienced a major increase in digital change. Due to the pandemic's constraints, individuals and companies were compelled to rely on internet channels for service delivery. Due to company closures and customers being forced to trade and access money from home, it became increasingly crucial to make digital interactions as customised and seamless as possible (Indrawati et al., 2022; Khandelwal & Dave, 2022). Because of this behaviour change, many banks and financial institutions took advantage of the new chances to connect with their consumers through mobile applications, chatbot interactions, or by using big data and working with big tech to understand customer expectations better.

A dramatic change in how the Covid-19 pandemic brought about banks and other financial organisations work. The banking sector offers more internet-based services than ever (Ionaşcu & Barbu, 2023). Although traditional banking services still include visiting a banking hall or the offices of any financial organisation, digital services are now more important than ever (Keshari, 2022). Transactions carried out before the pandemic were dwarfed by those carried out during and after Covid-19. As a result, the pandemic has led to significant advances in the financial sector, particularly with the growth of Fintech firms and the rising need for digital transformation in the industry. (Mishra & Sant, 2021; Priyadarshini et al., 2022).

4   Importance of Digital Transformation in the Banking and Financial Sector

Digital transformation is of utmost importance in the banking and financial sector due to its profound impact on various aspects of the industry. Banks all around the world understand how investments in digital technology may enhance their strategies for acquiring new clients, as well as how they can raise customer satisfaction while lowering total expenses for both the banks and the clients (Annenkova, 2023; Bubnova, 2021).

Some of the benefits of digital transformation to the banking sector include an improvement in the customer experiences. Banks and financial institutions may now offer smooth, customised customer experiences thanks to digital transformation. Customers may access services through digital channels at any time and from any location, and they get a smooth and simple banking experience. Customer loyalty and satisfaction increase as a result. Another importance of digital transformation in the banking and financial sector is the Operational efficiency. Automating and simplifying numerous banking operations using digital technologies increases operational efficiency. Automation may be used to reduce manual mistakes and boost productivity in processes, including account opening, loan processing, and transaction processing. This enables banks to more efficiently manage resources, speed up procedures, and optimise costs.

The COVID-19 pandemic also accelerated adoption of digital transformation in the banking and financial sector. With physical branches temporarily closed or operating with limited capacity, customers have turned to digital channels for their banking needs. Banks have rapidly scaled up their digital capabilities to meet the increased demand for online banking services. In the area of regulatory difficulties, digital transformation can aid in addressing the many regulatory problems the banking industry confronts. Banks can more easily and successfully comply with rules thanks to digital platforms. Utilising digital solutions lowers the risk of non-compliance and related fines by assisting with data management, risk assessment, and compliance reporting.

In terms of Cybersecurity especially now that we have become more dependent on digital platforms, banks now have a serious issue regarding cybersecurity. Thanks to digital transformation, strong security measures may be implemented to safeguard consumer data and financial activities. To improve security and defend against cyber attacks, cutting-edge technology such as biometrics, multi-factor authentication, and encryption are deployed.

Another area of importance of digital transformation to the banking and financial sector is in the area of Cost Savings. Digital transformation allows banks to reduce costs significantly. By automating manual processes, banks can optimise their workforce, reduce operational expenses, and streamline their infrastructure. Additionally, digital channels reduce the need for physical branches, saving real estate and maintenance costs.

Similarly, digital transformation gives room for all-day banking. Thanks to digitalisation, customers may access their accounts all day, eliminating waiting in line for even the smallest transactions. The convenience of being able to bank whenever and wherever, thanks to mobile apps, considerably improves the customer experience. With the development of real-time customer support channels like live chat and co-browsing, which are very successful for inquiry resolution, the rise of digital banking has also boosted customer service in the banking industry. Also, the advent of digital transformation has made access to banking activities easier. Banks can simplify the process for customers and employees through a thorough digital onboarding process made possible by cutting-edge technologies. For instance, when setting up a new account, a client must provide many papers, such as proof of identification, employment, and residency. It is possible to allow customers to submit these documents utilising mobile phones thanks to modern technologies. Everyone will save time and frustration if the data is processed and updated immediately in the bank's systems. With AI, it is also possible to quickly analyse customer data and mortgage applicants' financial histories to determine the likelihood of default and reach a conclusion on the application's result immediately.

Blockchain, robotic process automation (RPA), artificial intelligence (AI), machine learning (ML), and other technologies are being used by banks to hasten the digital transformation process. Banks may improve decision-making, uncover fraud, analyse vast data, and expedite operations while providing individualised services through these technologies. Digital transformation is crucial for the banking and financial sector to remain competitive, meet customer expectations, improve operational efficiency, address regulatory issues, ensure cybersecurity, and provide cost savings. The COVID-19 pandemic has pushed the adoption of digital transformation in the industry and emphasised its significance.

5   How Digital Transformation is Reshaping the Bank and Financial Sector

The financial sector is currently undergoing a significant transformation due to digital innovation. Digital transformation has disrupted traditional banking, insurance, and investment practices in recent years, completely changing how financial institutions operate, interact with customers, and handle data (Elsheikh, 2022). One of the ways in which digital transformation is reshaping the financial landscape is in the area of digital banking. The advent of digital transformation has dramatically altered the way we bank. Traditional physical branches are being supplemented or even replaced by digital banking platforms that allow customers to conveniently bank using their smartphones, tablets, or computers. Online banking, mobile apps, and digital payment services have become the norm, providing round-the-clock access to account information, fund transfers, and bill payments. This shift has reduced costs for banks and increased convenience for consumers. Another area in which digital transformation is reshaping the financial sector is in the area of Fintech Disruption. The rise of financial technology (fintech) businesses has hastened the financial sector's digital transformation. Fintech companies are upsetting existing financial institutions by providing cutting-edge solutions like peer-to-peer lending, robo-advisors, and blockchain-based services. These businesses frequently work with agility, utilising digital technology to provide services more quickly, effectively, and affordably, leading traditional banks to rethink their plans.

Another area in which digital transformation is transforming the financial sector is the advent of Blockchain and cryptocurrencies. Financial institutions can fundamentally alter how they manage transactions, settlements, and security thanks to the blockchain technology that underpins cryptocurrencies like Bitcoin. Blockchain promises lower transaction costs, transparency, and immutability. Several institutions are investigating or implementing blockchain solutions for cross-border payments, trade financing, and identity verification. Additionally, cryptocurrencies are transforming the world of international commerce and are a key component of investment portfolios. Data analytics and Artificial intelligence (AI) is another area in which digital transformation is reshaping the financial sector. Financial institutions are utilising these technologies to their full potential to gather insightful knowledge about client behaviour, preferences, and risk management. Banks and insurance firms can customise their services, spot fraud, and make better loan choices by analysing vast amounts of data. AI-powered virtual assistants and chatbots also improve customer service by offering immediate assistance and solutions to frequent questions.

Regulatory Compliance has also benefited from the advent of digital transformation. The financial sector's regulatory compliance has also been influenced by digital transformation. Regulators are creating new laws and standards for digital financial services in an effort to keep up with the rapid speed of technological development. Institutions are managing compliance more effectively thanks to regtech (regulatory technology) solutions, which lowers the danger of breaking the law and incurring penalties. In the area of Cybersecurity and risk management, digital transformation has made financial services to become digitalised even though new cybersecurity problems have emerged. The security measures used by financial institutions must be updated regularly to secure consumer data and counter online threats. Tools for risk management driven by AI and machine learning are helping banks discover and respond to possible threats in real-time, increasing the overall security of the financial system. In the area of Financial Inclusion, more people especially in the rural areas now have access to financial services. Due to digital transformation, underserved and unbanked groups have better access to financial services, especially in emerging market like South Africa. Digital wallets and mobile banking have opened new avenues for financial inclusion, allowing people in rural or economically underprivileged areas to engage in the formal economy. In order to use digital technology for financial inclusion and social development, governments and financial institutions are working together.

The digital revolution of the financial sector is already underway and changing the sector. Financial institutions are becoming more customer-centric, effective, and adaptive due to the development of digital banking, fintech innovation, data analytics, and blockchain technology. The benefits in terms of accessibility, cost-effectiveness, and innovation are pushing the sector towards a more dynamic and inclusive future, even if there are still obstacles to be addressed, notably in terms of cybersecurity and regulatory compliance. As technology develops, more new financial industry breakthroughs that benefit customers, companies, and the global economy might be anticipated.

6 Key Technologies Driving Digital Transformation in Banking and Financial Sector

Digital transformation in the banking and finance sector is being fueled by several significant technologies that are revolutionising how financial organisations function, interact with customers, and manage data. These technologies are revolutionising the industry by enhancing efficiency, security, and customer happiness (Guitart, 2021; Lai & Luo, 2022; Taka & Bayarçelík, 2023).

Blockchain and Distributed Ledger Technology (DLT) is one of the technologies driving digital transformation in the banking and financial secrtor especially in South Africa. By delivering a visible and impenetrable record, blockchain technology has the ability to improve security, speed up transactions, and eliminate fraud. It is utilised for several applications, including smart contracts, cross-border payments, and digital identity verification. Similarly, big data analytics enables banks to gain valuable insights from large datasets. It helps identify patterns, trends, and customer preferences, which can be used to tailor financial products and services. In addition, Machine learning (ML) and artificial intelligence (AI) are technologies utilised in data analysis, credit scoring, fraud detection, and customer service. Artificial intelligence-powered chatbots and virtual assistants offer round-the-clock client service. Additionally, risk management and investment decision-making are aided by AI and ML.

Cybersecurity Solutions is another technology that drives digital transformation. Cybersecurity is paramount as the financial industry moves toward more digitalisation. Technologies, including sophisticated encryption, multi-factor authentication, and behavioural analytics, are utilised for safeguarding sensitive data and systems. Cloud computing is another driver of digital transformation. The scalability, cost-effectiveness, and flexibility of cloud technology are advantages. In order to manage their data and applications more effectively while upholding high standards of security and compliance, financial institutions are moving to the cloud. Robotic Process Automation (RPA) also contributes significantly to the advancement of digital transformation. RPA automates repetitive, rule-based tasks, reducing operational costs and increasing efficiency. It applies to compliance reporting, account reconciliation, and customer onboarding.

Mobile banking and payment solutions have become increasingly popular due to the spread of smartphones and the development of digital wallets. These technologies allow customers to manage their accounts and make payments simply and securely. Regulatory Technology, or RegTech, leverages technology to help financial institutions comply more efficiently and cost-effectively with regulations. It involves solutions like automated reporting, identity verification, and risk management tools. Internet of Things (IoT). IoT devices are used for asset tracking, insurance telematics, and improving the efficiency of banking operations. For example, smart ATMs and sensors in bank branches can help monitor and optimise services.

Quantum Computing is also a major driver of digital transformation in the banking and financial sector. Even though it is still in its infancy, quantum computing holds the potential to tackle challenging financial and risk modelling issues far more quickly than conventional computers. Risk evaluation and portfolio optimisation might both be revolutionised by it.

The use open banking APIs also encourage innovation and competition by enabling outside developers to develop financial services and apps. Customers may give these applications access to their bank data so they can get a more complete picture of their finances. The use of biometrics for authentication is another driver of digital transformation in the banking and financial sector. For ease and security in banking, biometric authentication techniques like fingerprint and face recognition are becoming increasingly crucial. These techniques enable clients to access their accounts and conduct transactions safely. These technologies are related, and many financial institutions have used them differently. Banks and financial institutions must invest in and adapt to these technologies to satisfy the changing needs of clients and regulators while upholding the strictest security and compliance requirements if they want to stay competitive.

7   Key Dimensions of Bank Digital Transformation

To remain competitive, banks are under pressure to change from a product-centric to a more customer-centric strategy in their business models. The bank perceives digital transformation as the answer to the problems it must overcome. In truth, technology is just one aspect of a bank's digital transformation. Sadigh et al. (2021) highlighted five factors that comprise the digital transformation elements. These are as follows:

People who collaboratively work for the bank. The second is the Processes call for a thorough lifecycle analysis of the value provided to the customer and how each customer interacts over the customer experience lifecycle to improve bank efficiency and build new digital business models. The third dimension is that technology may interact to enable growth-oriented information management through integrated information infrastructure. The information structure is essential for data and content management to discover the links between information categories.

The fourth dimension is that the content entails managing customer-focused content and internal company information to evaluate all digital assets and give product information that reflects consumer preferences. Finally, because it includes a lot of valuable and sensitive personal data, the state must pay more attention to the banking industry's digital transition. It requires improved processes and information security to stop the bank from suffering unreported losses.

Winasis (2020) offered another viewpoint on the components of digital transformation, stating that top level factors include strategy and management, technology and regulation, customer and employee involvement, market knowledge and goods, and public benefit. For banks' digital transformation, each element is broken down into several smaller components, each discussed in great depth. Feher and Varga (2019) emphasise that leadership, digital trends, digital transformation skills, digital strategies, application of digital technologies, and customer-centric approach are the fundamental digital transformation practices impacting the bank's digital maturity levels. These practices also affect the bank's degree of adoption of new technologies. Shanti et al. (2022) emphasised that the Code Halo group contended that aspects of digital banking also include data and data analysis methods, business process strategies, and strategies for mobile devices and social networks.

Digital banking is a phrase that is often used in the context of bank digital transformation. However, it should be distinguished from electronic banking, which is well-established in virtually all banks. The following are the differences between them that Rogers (2016) highlighted and which may be viewed as a dimension of bank digital transformation.

While in electronic banking, customers may contact the bank via electronic channels that offer services in a one-way manner, customers can access bank services through virtual channels akin to social media in digital banking. Similarly, electronic banking offers a variety of accounts in its products and services, whereas digital banking often uses mobile-based applications for its products and services. In addition, In digital banking, products and services are flexible and dependent on the consumer's needs at the time of engagement with the bank. On the other hand, the services and products offered by electronic banking are not created with the demands of the clients in mind. Another difference between digital transformation and digital banking is the guiding concepts of digital banking which is the integration of infrastructures and technologies. This is in contrast to electronic banking, which employs a variety of both old and modern technology. Finally, establishing new legislation results in opportunities that can be utilised in digital banking, but they typically become a limiting factor in the design of electronic services.

8   Financial Inclusion and Accessibility Driven by Digital Transformation

Financial inclusion refers to the availability and accessibility of financial services to all people, especially those who live and work in underprivileged and marginalised communities. It significantly affects social and economic improvement (Mishra & Sant, 2021). Over the past few years, banks' digital revolution has advanced financial inclusion in emerging markets like South Africa. This transition has been fueled by technological improvements, which have substantially increased access to financial services and benefited both banks and customers. One of the ways that digital transformation is fostering financial inclusion is in the area of inclusion of the unbanked and underbanked. Due mostly to financial and geographic constraints, a sizeable segment of the world's population remains unbanked or underbanked. This divide has been closed by the advent of creative digital transformation solutions. For instance, mobile money services have grown in popularity and now allow users to save, send, and receive money using their mobile devices even if they do not have a regular bank account.

Similarly, Banks are utilising various technologies to speed up their digital transformation, including blockchain, robotic process automation (RPA), artificial intelligence (AI), and machine learning. With these technologies, banks may streamline operations, analyse massive volumes of data, detect fraud, enhance decision-making, and offer specialised services. The banking and financial sector must transform digitally to meet consumer expectations, solve regulatory concerns, assure cybersecurity, and reduce costs while remaining competitive. The COVID-19 epidemic has accelerated industry adoption of digital transformation and raised awareness of its worth.

The expenses related to banking transactions are greatly lowered by using digital banking. High fees are sometimes charged by traditional banking for simple services and transactions. Digital banking enables decreased transaction costs, making access to and usage of financial services more accessible and cheap for people with limited means. The digital transformation has enabled banks to develop secure and reliable remote identification and verification processes, eliminating the need for physical presence when opening accounts. This is crucial for people with difficulty moving about or limited access to identifying papers. Banks can now collect a ton of data on consumer behaviour thanks to digital transformation, which they can then use to create financial products and services that are tailored to individual customers' requirements. For instance, using modern data analytics, banks might provide microloans or savings products customised to each customer's income and spending habits. This level of personalisation improves financial inclusion by accommodating a wide range of requirements and tastes.

9 Challenges to the Adoption of Digital Transformation by Banks and other Financial Institutions

In recent years, the world of banking and finance has seen a significant transition, with the advent of digital transformation at its forefront. Integrating digital technology into every part of an organisation, radically altering how it functions and provides value to consumers, is known as "digital transformation." Despite the evident advantages of digital transformation, banks and other financial organisations confront several obstacles that prevent them from successfully using new technologies (Ayhan & Darici, 2022). The studies of Vavousis and Βαβούσης (2021) and Diener and Spacek (2020) highlighted some of the obstacles that the banking and financial industry faces in implementing digital transformation to include the legacy systems and infrastructure The burden of legacy systems and infrastructure is one of the biggest problems that banks and financial institutions face. Many of these institutions have depended on antiquated equipment and procedures for decades. These systems can be expensive, complicated, and time-consuming to replace or modernise. Additionally, the possibility of system failures during the transition is a major worry because even a short period of downtime may result in losses in revenue and reputational harm. There is also an issues with regulation and compliance. The banking sector is highly regulated to protect consumer assets, data security, and privacy. Numerous national and international laws and regulations must be followed while using digital transformation technology. The effort of navigating this regulatory environment is difficult. Heavy fines, legal ramifications, and reputational harm may occur from failing to comply with these rules. As a result, financial institutions need to spend money on complex compliance systems and keep up with changing laws.

Cyber security threat is another major concern militating against ther full implementation of digital transformation. Digital transformation exposes banks and other financial organisations to higher cybersecurity dangers. Cybercriminals have a greater opportunity to take advantage of weaknesses as data becomes more digitalised and disseminated. Financial institutions must invest extensively in cybersecurity measures, such as data encryption, intrusion detection systems, and personnel training because attackers' level of complexity is only increasing. This is a big financial burden that requires continual attention. The issue of Data Privacy is another major concern. Customer data privacy has become increasingly important due to recent high-profile data breaches. Banks and other financial companies handle large volumes of private consumer data. The difficulty is in providing seamless digital services while preserving this data. It might not be easy to balance client convenience and data security. To earn customers' trust, establishments must invest significantly in effective data security procedures and convey their dedication to privacy. Another area of concern to the full implementation of digital transformation is people's resistance to change. Organisational culture must frequently change significantly due to digital transformation. Staff members could resist new technology and procedures used to conventional banking procedures. Strong leadership, extensive training programs, and a distinct future vision are required to overcome this reluctance. Internal disagreements and project delays might result from a digital transformation's failure to handle the human dimension. The area of manpower is another area of concern especially in an emerging market like South Africa. The demand for tech-savvy professionals in the banking sector has skyrocketed. Many banks and financial institutions struggle to find and retain the necessary talent to implement digital transformation initiatives successfully. Attracting the right talent can be challenging, as competition is fierce across industries, and salaries for technology professionals are often higher elsewhere. Cost control is another major challenge. Making the switch to a digital economy is costly. From the purchase of new equipment to the hiring of trained individuals, the expenditures might quickly mount. Banks and other financial institutions must manage their budgets carefully to avoid using all available resources. They need a strategic plan to prioritise tasks and distribute resources effectively.

Banks and other financial institutions must undergo digital transformation to live and remain competitive in the current world. There are several barriers in the road, including legacy systems, legal limitations, cybersecurity dangers, privacy concerns over customer data, resistance to change, a lack of expertise, and cost management. Strategic preparation, a commitment to security and compliance, and an ability to respond swiftly to changing circumstances are required to overcome these obstacles.

Financial institutions will be better able to fulfil their clients' changing requirements and expectations, cut operating costs, and put themselves in a position for long-term success in the digital age if they can effectively traverse these hurdles and embrace digital transformation. Although the path to change may be difficult, the payoff promises to be one of creativity, effectiveness, and expansion.

10 Future Trends and Prospects for Banks and Financial Institutions as they Embrace Digital Transformation

The financial services industry is profoundly transforming, driven by technological advancements and changing consumer expectations. Traditional banks and financial institutions are evolving rapidly to keep pace with the digital revolution (Lottu et al., 2023). Here, we explore some prospects and future trends for financial institutions as they embrace digitalisation.

Enhanced Customer Experience. The pursuit of an improved customer experience is one of the main forces behind digital transformation in the banking sector. Online banking, smartphone applications, and chatbots are progressively taking the role of traditional banking procedures (Yakovleva, 2022). Thanks to this technology, customers may easily and quickly access their accounts, complete transactions, and get help. We may anticipate even more advanced improvements to customer experience in the future thanks to the application of artificial intelligence (AI) and machine learning to tailor financial services, provide in-the-moment help, and anticipate client demands. The Integration of FinTech is another area that digital transformation would disrupt in the future. Banks and financial institutions are progressively incorporating FinTech solutions into their business operations due to the financial technology (FinTech) businesses' years-long disruption of the sector. These alliances and joint ventures enable established financial institutions to benefit from the cutting-edge technology created by FinTech startups (Shrivastava & Shah, 2021). The future looks bright for banks since this integration may result in lower costs, quicker service delivery, and more access to new sources of income.

Blockchain and cryptocurrencies has come to stay. The financial sector has grown substantially because blockchain technology is renowned for its secure and open ledger. Banks are investigating blockchain technology for use in smart contracts, trade finance, and international payments. A larger audience is also accepting cryptocurrencies, led by Bitcoin and Ethereum. As a result of rising client demand and regulatory certainty, more banks will likely provide cryptocurrency services in the future, including trading, custody, and investment choices. Data analytics and artificial intelligence ia an area that can longer be taken for granted by financial institutions. Since data is the lifeblood of the contemporary financial sector, banks are utilising these technologies to understand client behaviour better, manage risk, and make data-driven choices. As new technologies enable more precise credit scoring, fraud detection, and investment strategies, the future for banks looks bright. In order to improve business outcomes, machine learning models may be used to assist in identifying industry trends and optimise the customer experience.

Another emerging trend for banks and financial organisations is open banking, which is motivated by regulatory adjustments and consumer desire for greater financial transparency. Open banking lets Customers securely exchange their financial information with outside suppliers. Better financial product comparisons, cutting-edge services, and more individualised financial guidance are made possible. Increased market penetration and the potential to become financial service aggregators are two advantages that banks that adopt open banking can enjoy. It is becoming more and more crucial to maintain cybersecurity and abide by rules as the digital transformation process continues. Banks and other financial institutions must make large investments to protect consumer data and adhere to constantly evolving regulations. The ability of banks to develop robust compliance frameworks and cybersecurity measures that boost trust and lower the risks associated with digital transactions will determine how successful they are in the future.

The concepts of environmental, social, and governance (ESG) and sustainability investing. These concepts are increasingly incorporated into the financial industry. Financial institutions such as banks increasingly provide sustainable investing choices and consider ESG considerations when making lending and investment decisions. As they position themselves to serve a rising market of socially and ecologically sensitive investors while encouraging sustainable business practices, banks have good prospects going forward.

11 Key Points

- Banks must embrace change, make technological investments, and modify their business models to match the rising needs of the tech-savvy customer if they are to prosper in this quickly changing environment.
- Digital transformation in the banking and financial sector has come to stay. Any bank or financial institution that wants to remain in business for a long time must innovate. This innovation includes investing in digital technology and staff training, among others.
- In the age of digital transformation, possibilities abound for banks and other financial organisations. Exciting opportunities for these institutions include improved customer experiences, FinTech integration, blockchain and cryptocurrencies, data analytics and AI, cybersecurity and compliance, open banking, and sustainability.
- The banks and other financial sector can longer ignore digital currencies like cryptocurrencies. While there is a need to exercise some caution in the acceptability, conventional banks can no longer ignore its presence.
- Banks and banking services are no longer restricted to a physical building operated by a bank. Banking services have gone beyond the physical building with conventional operating hours. Bank services are now available anytime of the day as against the operating hours usually employed by the traditional bank.
- Banks embracing digital transformation are more likely to perform better than their counterparts, focusing more on traditional banking.
- The cybersecurity threat is real. Hence, banks and other financial institutions must invest heavily in technology that can protect resources and customer data.
- The disruption caused by the FinTechs will force banks and other financial institutions to integrate FinTech solutions into their businesses. With the aid of these partnerships and joint ventures, established financial institutions can use the cutting-edge technology FinTech startups developed.

References

Annenkova, E. (2023). The mechanism of digital transformation of Russian banks in modern conditions. *Intellect Innovations Investments, 3*, 42–51.

Ayhan, F., & Darici, B. (2022). Digital transformation and new approaches in trade, economics, finance and banking.

Bubnova, Y. B. (2021). The role of the state in ensuring digital transformation of banking sector. In *SHS Web of Conferences*.

Diener, F., & Spacek, M. (2020). Implementation barriers in digital transformation: A qualitative perspective on German banking. In *The 14th international days of statistics and economics, Prague, September 10–12, 2020*.

Elsheikh, A. S. (2022). Blockchain analytics reference architecture for FinTech - A positioning paper: Advancing FinTech with blockchain, data analytics, and enterprise architecture. In *Proceedings of the Federated Africa and Middle East Conference on Software Engineering*.

Feher, P., & Varga, K. (2019). Digital transformation in the Hungarian banking industry. *Experience with Design Thinking, Society and Economy, 541*, 239–310.

Guitart, C. V. (2021). Spanish financial institutions facing the challenge of digitalisation: The case of payment systems. *Finance, Markets and Valuation, 7*(2), 73–99.

Indrawati, A., Putri, F. H., & Wahyudi, R. (2022). Analisis Kinerja Bank Syariah Negara OKI pada Era Digital: Studi Masa Pandemi Covid-19. *Journal Of Institution And Sharia Finance, 5*(2), 51–65.

Ionaşcu, A., & Barbu, C. A. (2023). Digital transformation in the banking sector: A pre-and post-Covid-19 analysis.

Jayalath, J., & Premaratne, S. (2021). Analysis of Digital Transformation challenges to overcome by Banks and Financial Institutions in Sri Lanka. *International Journal of Research Publications, 84*, 1.

Keshari, S. (2022). Impact of mobile banking and Internet banking during covid-19 pandemic. *International Journal of Scientific Research in Engineering and Management, 10*(1), 749–757.

Khandelwal, P., & Dave, D. M. (2022). COVID-19 pandemic- the emerging trend of banking digitalisation in India.

Lai, Z., & Luo, H. (2022). How does intelligent technology investment affect employment compensation and firm value in Chinese financial institutions? *International Journal of Emerging Markets, 17*(4), 945–966.

Lottu, O. A., Abiola, A., Daraojimba, D. O., Alabi, A. M., John-Ladega, A. A., & Daraojimba, C. (2023). Digital transformation in banking: a review of Nigeria's journey to economic prosperity. *International Journal of Advanced Economics, 5*(8), 215–238.

Mishra, P., & Sant, T. G. (2021). Role of artificial intelligence and internet of things in promoting banking and financial services during COVID-19: Pre and post effect. In *2021 5th International Conference on Information Systems and Computer Networks (ISCON)*.

Priyadarshini, K., Nath, A., Saha, U., Saha, S., Chakravarty, G., & Mukherjee, D. (2022). Pre and post changes of AI, IoT, and cloud computing in financial services and banking sector during pandemic COVID-19. *International Journal of Health Sciences, 6*(S1), 11559–11574.

Rogers, D. L. (2016). *The five domains of digital transformation: Customers, competition, data, innovation, value. Digital transformation playbook*. Columbia University Press. https://doi.org/10.7312/roge17544-001

Sadigh, A. N., Asgari, T., & Rabiel, M. (2021). Digital transformation in the value chain disruption of banking services. *Journal of the Knowledge Economy, 13*(2), 446–461.

Shanti, R., Avianto, W., & Wibowo, W. A. (2022). A systemic review on banking digital transformation. *Jurnal Administrare: Jurnal Permikiran Ilmiah Dan Pendidikan Administrasi Perkantoran, 9*(2), 543–552.

Shrivastava, U., & Shah, M. (2021). Determinants of cross selling through mobile apps in Indian Banks – A factor analysis approach. *Journal of University of Shanghai for Science and Technology, 23*, 161.

Singh, S., Sharma, M., Kaur, S., & Prasad, E. S. (2022). The future of money: How the digital revolution is transforming currencies and finance. *Journal of Evolutionary Economics, 32*, 1391–1394.

Taka, M. E., & Bayarçelík, E. B. (2023). Sustainable digital transformation of financial institutions. *Business & Management Studies: An International Journal, 11*, 253.

Vavousis, K., & Βαβούσης, Κ. (2021). User and infrastructure security and privacy with regard to compliance.

Versal, N., Erastov, V., Balytska, M., & Honchar, I. (2022). Digitalisation Index: case of banking system. *Statistika Statistics and Economy Journal, 102*(4), 426–442.

Winasis, S. (2020). Impact of digital transformation on Employee engagement Influenced by work stress on Indonesia's private banking sector. In *Proceeding of the international conference on industrial engineering and operations management.*

Yakovleva, A. K. (2022). Theory and practice of implementation of strategies of digital transformation of financial and credit organisations into technological companies. *Russian Journal of Industrial Economics, 15,* 1066.

Digital Transformation in Areas Administered by Traditional Authorities

Sylvia Siphugu and Tankiso Moloi (iD)

Abstract The concept of digital transformation has garnered considerable attention across many industries, including traditional authorities in South Africa. The objective of this chapter is to improve an understanding of digital transformation within domains governed by traditional authorities in South Africa through a review of relevant literature. Through literature review, this chapter investigates the current state of digital transformation, the challenges that are faced, the existing digital gaps and digital literacy, and the potential benefits associated with the use of digital technology in rural areas. Traditional authorities in South Africa are only beginning to embrace digital transformation; there are numerous obstacles to be addressed. However, by addressing issues such as limited digital infrastructure, lack of digital skills, and resistance to change, traditional authorities can unlock the potential benefits of digital transformation. Improved service delivery, increased efficiency, enhanced transparency, and better decision-making are some of the advantages that can be derived from embracing digital technologies. Further research and collaboration between traditional authorities, government agencies, and other stakeholders is needed to drive digital transformation in this sector and ensure its successful implementation.

1 Introduction to Traditional Authorities and Digital Transformation

Rural communities have encountered challenges in maintaining pace with advancements in digital connectivity (Salemink et al., 2017). Despite the extensive integration of information and communication technology (ICT) within South Africa, there persists a notable gap in Internet access among rural households, with a very small

S. Siphugu · T. Moloi (✉)
Johannesburg Business School, University of Johannesburg, Johannesburg, South Africa
e-mail: sylvia@intalpower.co.za; tankiso.moloi@jbs.ac.za

© The Author(s), under exclusive license to Springer Nature
Switzerland AG 2024
T. Moloi (ed.), *Digital Transformation in South Africa*, Professional Practice in
Governance and Public Organizations,
https://doi.org/10.1007/978-3-031-52403-5_4

percentage having connectivity (Aruleba & Jere, 2022). Specifically, as of 2018, only 1.7% of rural households across the country, 0.6% in Limpopo, and 0.8% in North West had the means to connect to the Internet (Aruleba & Jere, 2022; Pretorius et al., 2022). In contrast, a significantly higher percentage of households in urban areas and cities, namely at least 17.3%, showed access to Internet connectivity within their homes (Aruleba & Jere, 2022). It is also important to note that having access to the internet does not equate to the use of the internet. The use of mobile devices provided internet access to 67.5% of individuals residing in metropolitan areas and 63.7% of individuals in urban areas whereas a population with internet accessibility in rural areas using mobile devices remained significantly lower at 45% (Pretorius et al., 2022). The relatively slower rate of technology adoption and utilization can be attributed to the comparatively slower spread of technology, along with the lower average levels of education and skills that are more prominent in rural areas. These factors collectively hinder the achievement of equitable technology access and usage (Salemink et al., 2017).

The paradox that exists lies in the fact that rural communities, due to their geographical isolation, are in dire need of enhanced digital connectivity to mitigate their remoteness. Ainslie and Kepe (2016), ascertain that traditional rulers have exhibited greater power over the years, and it may be inferred that when traditional authorities get more involved in governance and assume a formal role in addressing various institutional difficulties, it becomes necessary to raise fresh inquiries regarding their standing, impact, and function in promoting democracy, equality within the context of South Africa rural areas (Ainslie & Kepe, 2016).

The responsibilities of a traditional leader within the context of local government include various aspects. These include assuming the position of the traditional authority's head, presiding over customary law courts, engaging in consultations with traditional communities, providing consultative input to the government on matters about traditional affairs, convening meetings, protecting cultural values, serving as the representative voice of their local rural communities, and demonstrating a symbol of unity (Ndzendze, 2018).

The influence of traditional authority in African politics has persisted since the 1990s in African countries, with a significant development occurring in some African states when traditional chiefs were officially acknowledged and bestowed with legislative authority (Amanor, 2022). The constitutional recognition of traditional authorities in South Africa confers upon them the authority to apply customary law in the passing of legislation within the rural communities they represent. The distinction between traditional communities and standardised procedures and legal codes is in their reliance on internal powers derived from pre-existing community norms and practices (Ndzendze, 2018).

At the local level, traditional leaders are highly regarded for their capacity to deliver essential services and uphold their esteemed position within social and cultural institutions (Boateng & Afranie, 2020). By serving as an intermediary between the local community and the government, traditional leaders have the potential to enhance the legitimacy of local governance and mitigate resistance towards projects (Boateng & Afranie, 2020). Democratic regimes provide opportunities for traditional leaders to engage in government processes and contribute to decision-making (Baldwin, 2019). Traditional leadership structures in South Africa manipulate historical narratives, influence government policies, administer land, and drive mining industry growth. However, state recognition may cause traditional leaders to put government interests ahead of local needs. The South African government must evaluate how well its approach to traditional leadership promotes accountability and rights (Ndzendze, 2018).

Traditional Authorities have the power to bring about change through decision-making and representation for the local rural areas that they look after. The White Paper on Local Government of 1998 introduced a municipal governance framework that emphasized the involvement of traditional leaders in the provision of services to local communities (Ramolobe, 2023). As stated in the White Paper, traditional authorities are authorised to participate in municipal ward committees that adhere to federal legislation, hence facilitating collaborative associations with neighboring municipalities (Ndzendze, 2018). Traditional leaders play a crucial role in ensuring that traditional communities are involved in development decisions, advocating for development initiatives, and land allocation, and advising authorities on trading licenses within their territories. Furthermore, it is important to include traditional communities in the decision-making processes of development initiatives. This may be achieved by actively engaging with the government and other relevant agencies to lobby for development opportunities, especially those related to digital transformation. Additionally, traditional communities can play a crucial role in advising authorities on matters such as land distribution and trading licenses inside their territory, guaranteeing compliance with legal regulations.

Therefore, future research should prioritise the examination of particular geographical locations and rural communities, taking into account both connectivity and digital transformation inclusion concerns to enable the development of tailored policies that address the needs of rural populations who are lacking in digital connectivity and are excluded from digital resources.

The concept of digital transformation has emerged as a crucial subject in several industries, encompassing conventional institutions within the South African context. The concept of digital transformation pertains to the assimilation of digital technologies throughout all facets of an organization's activities, leading to profound alterations in its operational processes and value delivery mechanisms (Hauke-Lopes et al., 2022). In the context of Traditional Authorities, digital transformation involves leveraging digital technologies to enhance governance, service delivery, and community engagement.

Digital transformation can be described as a process of institutional change driven by the adoption and utilization of digital technologies. It is a socioeconomic change that encompasses individuals, organizations, ecosystems, and societies, all shaped by the integration of digital technologies. In this sense, digital transformation is not just about implementing new technologies but also entails a shift in mindset and organizational processes.

2 Understanding Digital Transformation in Traditional Authorities

Numerous scholarly studies have been undertaken to examine the phenomenon of traditional authority in South Africa, which have shed light on the portrayal of traditional leaders as both "decentralised despots" and democratic compromisers. The South African government, however, also recognises them as essential stakeholders within the framework of rural development. Some learnings can be taken from various digital implementations across sectors to link to the digital transformation of areas administered by traditional authorities.

The digital transformation of the postal sector in Southern Africa has yielded valuable insights into the details and obstacles associated with the integration of digital technologies inside traditional industries (Mokgohloa et al., 2022; Sutherland, 2020). Gaining insight into the causal links and influential elements that drive digital transformation in the postal sector can provide valuable guidance for devising plans and ways for digital transformation within traditional authority structures (Mokgohloa et al., 2022).

Effective management of records and digital preservation practices are essential components of digital transformation (Alvarenga et al., 2020; Masenya & Ngulube, 2019; Matlala et al., 2022; Tintswalo et al., 2022). Traditional authorities need to develop strategies for managing digital records and preserving valuable digital resources to ensure transparency, accountability, and accessibility of information (Masenya & Ngulube, 2019).

Traditional authorities in South Africa, which include tribal traditional councils and traditional leadership structures, face unique challenges in embracing digital transformation (Manda & Backhouse, 2017). The preceding problems frequently stem from cultural and historical factors, along with the complex relationships between traditional authorities and the government of South Africa (Ray & van Rouveroy van Nieuwaal, 1996). Digital transformation is still in its early stages in traditional authorities. Although some municipalities have started implementing digital technologies, the majority are still lagging. The main areas of digital transformation identified in the study include e-government services, digital infrastructure, and data management (Davison et al., 2005). However, the adoption of these technologies is often limited by factors such as lack of funding, inadequate skills and knowledge, and resistance to change.

Effective management of records and digital preservation practices are essential components of digital transformation (Tintswalo et al., 2022).

By incorporating digital technologies, traditional authorities can enhance the efficiency and effectiveness of their operations, improve access to information and services, and foster greater participation and engagement among community members.

One of the key aspects of digital transformation is the digitization of information. With digitization, traditional authorities can store and manage vast amounts of data digitally, enabling easier access, analysis, and decision-making. For example, digital databases can be created to store information about land ownership, community demographics, and development projects. This not only streamlines the administration of the traditional authority but also provides challenges in Digital Transformation in Rural South Africa.

Traditional authorities can learn from the experiences of banks in South Africa in adopting digital technologies to improve customer services and operational efficiency. Digitalization strategies in the banking sector provide insights into the challenges and opportunities of digital transformation (Louw & Nieuwenhuizen, 2020). Understanding consumer behavior and resistance to digital-only banking can inform the strategies for engaging the community in the digital transformation process (Nel & Boshoff, 2021).

3   Challenges in Digital Transformation in Rural South Africa

One of the primary challenges highlighted in scholarly literature is the lack of digital infrastructure in rural areas, where many traditional authorities are located (Salemink et al., 2017; Setokoe & Ramukumba, 2020). Without adequate infrastructure; traditional authorities may struggle to implement digital technologies and provide digital services to their communities. Poor infrastructure, including limited access to electricity, can make it difficult to implement digital technologies in rural areas (Kanyane, 2023).

Another challenge is the limited digital skills and knowledge among traditional leaders and their staff. There is a great need for digital skills development in government departments, and this applies to traditional authorities as well. Traditional leaders and their staff need to be equipped with the necessary skills to effectively use digital technologies and leverage their potential benefits. Equipping traditional leaders and their staff with digital technology can entail conducting workshops on the usage of relevant apps, tablets, and smartphones for traditional leaders and their staff. Furthermore, community hub establishment could present guidance and continuous support on the usage of digital tools. In addition; access provision to lessons, programs of mentorship, and online resources will assist with adaptation to technology.

Resistance to change is another significant challenge in traditional authorities (Ademola & Ahiaku, 2023). This resistance can stem from various factors, including cultural norms, fear of job loss, and skepticism toward new technologies. Research has emphasised the significance of employing change management strategies to effectively address resistance encountered during the process of digital transformation inside government agencies. To tackle this difficulty, it may be necessary to implement comparable tactics within conventional governing bodies.

4 Bridging the Digital Divide: Digital Literacy Among Traditional Authorities

The concept of the digital divide relates to the worldwide inequalities in the ability of households, individuals, and enterprises to access the Internet and other Information and Communication Technologies (ICT) that facilitate the process of globalisation (Aruleba & Jere, 2022). One significant factor contributing to this phenomenon is the inherent difficulty faced by rural areas in keeping up with the rapid expansion of digital connectivity. Specifically, the establishment of internet and broadband infrastructures encounters substantial challenges in these particular areas (Aruleba & Jere, 2022).

The issue of digital literacy among traditional authorities in South Africa is a significant subject that necessitates attention to address the disparities between rural and urban areas, as well as socioeconomic disparities (Ainslie & Kepe, 2016; Aruleba & Jere, 2022). Digital literacy plays a pivotal role in fostering sustainable development as individuals residing in rural areas may lack the necessary skills and understanding to proficiently use digital technologies (Aruleba & Jere, 2022). A project has been developed in Kenya to foster digital literacy among economically disadvantaged young adults. This initiative serves as a noteworthy illustration of how digital literacy may effectively empower individuals and stimulate economic advancement in the Sub-Saharan African region (Radovanović et al., 2020). It is important to acknowledge that the digital divide is not just attributable to the fast pace of technological advancements. Hence, it is imperative to comprehend the precise extent of acceptance and utilisation of these technologies before comprehending the impact of digital connectivity (Aruleba & Jere, 2022).

Efforts are being made to address the digital divide and improve digital literacy in South Africa, and initiatives are underway to expand digital infrastructure and improve access to technology. Through sustained investment and comprehensive support, the process of digital transformation holds the capacity to enhance the quality of life for those living in rural areas of South Africa. This can be achieved through facilitating access to better services, education, and economic opportunities.

5 Potential Benefits of Digital Transformation in Traditional Authorities

Despite the difficulties involved in embracing transformation, institutions can yield numerous advantages. These include improved delivery of services, heightened efficiency, increased transparency, and enhanced decision-making (Matheus et al., 2020).

One of the key benefits of digital transformation is seen in the improvement of service delivery (Matheus et al., 2020; Mergel et al., 2019). Digital technologies enable institutions to provide services to their communities efficiently and effectively. For instance, e-government services can streamline processes, and minimize bureaucratic delays resulting in faster and more convenient service provision (Seifert & Chung, 2009).

Increased efficiency is another advantage brought about by transformation. By digitizing processes and automating tasks, traditional institutions can save time and resources which consequently leads to cost savings and enhanced productivity (Shkarlet et al., 2020).

Enhanced transparency is also a benefit derived from transformation. The use of technologies allows traditional institutions to collect data effectively as well as store and analyze it efficiently (Urbinati et al., 2020). This fosters greater transparency in decision-making processes while ensuring accountability, to the community.

Furthermore, better decision-making represents an outcome resulting from digital transformation (Yucel, 2018). By utilizing data analysis and digital tools; traditional authorities can make informed decisions based on evidence and insights (Yucel, 2018). This in turn can result in governance and enhanced outcomes, for the community.

Another crucial aspect of transformation in authorities is the concept of value co-creation (Hauke-Lopes et al., 2022). Through engaging with the community and stakeholders traditional authorities can harness technologies to collaboratively create value, improve service delivery, and foster collaboration. Embracing this approach can lead to effective governance and improved outcomes for the community.

6 Future Perspectives on Digital Transformation in Traditional Areas

Enabling the availability and accessibility of technological infrastructure and connectivity in rural communities is an initial stride toward fostering their growth. However, it is imperative to acknowledge that the subsequent stages of training, adoption, and utilisation must be effectively addressed to ensure that digital connectivity generates significant benefits within these rural areas (Aruleba & Jere, 2022). The White Paper on Traditional Leadership and Governance presents a comprehensive policy framework for the development of national legislation, with a specific focus on traditional leadership. Future legislation will set norms and standards for provincial legislation, addressing peculiarities in various provinces. The document emphasizes the continued existence of National Houses composed of traditional authorities, which promote cooperative relationships, facilitate information flow, and advise governments on matters affecting traditional leadership, communities, and customary law. However, the composition of Provincial Houses varies across provinces, with some provinces having headmen and premiers nominating members (Ndzendze, 2018).

Here are some key points to consider when introducing digital transformation in areas administered by traditional authorities:

In line with benefits, digital transformation can lead to increased public engagement, more transparency, and improved efficiency and productivity.

There are a number of challenges associated with digital transformation. Going digital can be difficult and requires time, effort, and funding. Common obstacles include outdated technology, manual procedures, and resistance to change, training, and maintenance.

Areas that may be a starting point for digital government transformation include automating manual processes and workflows, improving citizen engagement through self-service e-portals, and implementing electronic document management systems.

Team building may assist in building a cross-functional team responsible for driving change and continuously monitoring and improving the digital transformation process is crucial to success.

Culture plays a significant role. A successful digital transformation requires aligning digital efforts with internal values and behaviors to avoid negative effects on organizational culture.

Overall, digital transformation can help traditional authorities provide better support for citizens and employees by improving efficiency and productivity in rural areas. Nevertheless, it is crucial to take into account the prospective difficulties and hindrances and to establish a robust team and culture to guarantee achievement. The successful implementation of digital transformation requires a holistic approach that considers the integration of technology, people, processes, strategies, and structures. Further research is needed to understand the factors that contribute to successful digital transformation and to address the specific needs and challenges of specific rural areas administered by traditional authorities.

7 Key Points

- Traditional authorities in South Africa are only beginning to embrace digital transformation; however, there are numerous obstacles to be addressed.
- By addressing issues such as limited digital infrastructure, lack of digital skills, and resistance to change, traditional authorities can unlock the potential benefits of digital transformation.
- Improved service delivery, increased efficiency, enhanced transparency, and better decision-making are some of the advantages that can be derived from embracing digital technologies.

References

Ademola, O., & Ahiaku, P. K. A. (2023). Prospects for digital transformation in rural South Africa's small and medium-sized enterprises. *International Journal of Trendy Research in Engineering and Technology, 7*(2), 29–35.

Ainslie, A., & Kepe, T. (2016). Understanding the resurgence of traditional authorities in post-apartheid South Africa. *Journal of Southern African Studies, 42*(1), 19–33.

Alvarenga, A., Matos, F., Godina, R., & CO Matias, J. (2020). Digital transformation and knowledge management in the public sector. *Sustainability, 12*(14), 5824.

Amanor, K. S. (2022). Land administration, chiefs, and governance in Ghana. *African Land Reform Under Economic Liberalisation: States, Chiefs, and Rural Communities, 21*–39.

Aruleba, K., & Jere, N. (2022). Exploring digital transforming challenges in rural areas of South Africa through a systematic review of empirical studies. *Scientific African, 16*, e01190.

Baldwin, K. (2019). Elected MPs, traditional chiefs, and local public goods: Evidence on the role of leaders in co-production from rural Zambia. *Comparative Political Studies, 52*(12), 1925–1956.

Boateng, K., & Afranie, S. (2020). All hands on deck: The process and activities of collaboration between chiefs and local government authorities in Ghana. *Ghana Journal of Development Studies, 17*(1), 92–113.

Davison, R. M., Wagner, C., & Ma, L. C. (2005). From government to e-government: A transition model. *Information Technology & People, 18*(3), 280–299.

Hauke-Lopes, A., Ratajczak-Mrozek, M., & Wieczerzycki, M. (2022). Value co-creation and co-destruction in the digital transformation of highly traditional companies. *Journal of Business & Industrial Marketing, 38*(6), 1316–1331.

Kanyane, M. (2023). Digital work–transforming the higher education landscape in South Africa. In *New digital work: Digital sovereignty at the workplace* (pp. 149–160). Springer.

Louw, C., & Nieuwenhuizen, C. (2020). Digitalisation strategies in a south African banking context: A consumer services analysis. *South African Journal of Information Management, 22*(1), 1–8.

Manda, M. I., & Backhouse, J. (2017). Digital transformation for inclusive growth in South Africa. Challenges and opportunities in the 4th industrial revolution. In *Paper presented at the 2nd African conference on information science and technology, Cape Town, South Africa.*

Masenya, T. M., & Ngulube, P. (2019). Digital preservation practices in academic libraries in South Africa in the wake of the digital revolution. *South African Journal of Information Management, 21*(1), 1–9.

Matheus, R., Janssen, M., & Maheshwari, D. (2020). Data science empowering the public: Data-driven dashboards for transparent and accountable decision-making in smart cities. *Government Information Quarterly, 37*(3), 101284.

Matlala, M. E., Ncube, T. R., & Parbanath, S. (2022). The state of digital records preservation in South Africa's public sector in the 21st century: A literature review. *Records Management Journal, 32*(2), 198–212.

Mergel, I., Edelmann, N., & Haug, N. (2019). Defining digital transformation: Results from expert interviews. *Government Information Quarterly, 36*(4), 101385.

Mokgohloa, K., Kanakana-Katumba, M. G., Maladzhi, R. W., & Xaba, S. (2022). A system dynamics approach to postal digital transformation dynamics: A causal loop diagram (CLD) perspective. *South African Journal of Industrial Engineering, 33*(4), 10–31.

Ndzendze, B. (2018). Traditional authorities and customary law in a democratic, constitutional state. *The Thinker, 76.*

Nel, J., & Boshoff, C. (2021). Traditional-bank customers' digital-only bank resistance: Evidence from South Africa. *International Journal of Bank Marketing, 39*(3), 429–454.

Pretorius, A., Kruger, E., & Bezuidenhout, S. (2022). Google trends and water conservation awareness: The internet's contribution in South Africa. *South African Geographical Journal, 104*(1), 53–69.

Radovanović, D., Holst, C., Belur, S. B., Srivastava, R., Houngbonon, G. V., Le Quentrec, E., Miliza, J., Winkler, A. S., & Noll, J. (2020). Digital literacy key performance indicators for sustainable development. *Social Inclusion, 8*(2), 151–167.

Ramolobe, K. S. (2023). The dynamics of traditional leaders' relationship with municipal councillors and service delivery. *Journal of Local Government Research and Innovation, 4*, 95.

Ray, D. I., & van Rouveroy van Nieuwaal, E. A. B. (1996). The new relevance of traditional authorities in Africa: The conference; major themes; reflections on chieftaincy in Africa; future directions. *The Journal of Legal Pluralism and Unofficial Law, 28*(37–38), 1–38.

Salemink, K., Strijker, D., & Bosworth, G. (2017). Rural development in the digital age: A systematic literature review on unequal ICT availability, adoption, and use in rural areas. *Journal of Rural Studies, 54*, 360–371.

Seifert, J. W., & Chung, J. (2009). Using e-government to reinforce citizen citizen relationships: Comparing government reform in the United States and China. *Social Science Computer Review, 27*(1), 3–23.

Setokoe, T. J., & Ramukumba, T. (2020). Challenges of community participation in community-based tourism in rural areas. *WIT Transactions on Ecology and the Environment, 248*, 13–22.

Shkarlet, S., Dubyna, M., Shtyrkhun, K., & Verbivska, L. (2020). Transformation of the paradigm of the economic entities development in the digital economy. *WSEAS Transactions on Environment and Development, 16*(8), 413–422.

Sutherland, E. (2020). The fourth industrial revolution–the case of South Africa. *Politikon, 47*(2), 233–252.

Tintswalo, S., Mazenda, A., Masiya, T., & Shava, E. (2022). Management of records at statistics South Africa: Challenges and prospects. *Information Development, 38*(2), 286–298.

Urbinati, A., Chiaroni, D., Chiesa, V., & Frattini, F. (2020). The role of digital technologies in open innovation processes: An exploratory multiple case study analysis. *R&D Management, 50*(1), 136–160.

Yucel, S. (2018). Estimating the benefits, drawbacks, and risks of digital transformation strategy. In *Paper presented at the 2018 international conference on computational science and computational intelligence (CSCI)* (pp. 233–238).

Digital Transformation and the Process Improvements in General Finance Environment: The Good Governance Perspective

Lethiwe Nzama ⓘ and Sezer Bozkus Kahyaoglu ⓘ

Abstract The finance function is one of the most affected fields of work by digitalization. This is a common feature in all companies, sectors, or various country applications. From this point of view, the basic rule of transformation in financial operations is the strategic importance of digitalization which is creating opportunities. However, this transformation process should be supported by good governance. In this study, the new approaches that take place with digitalization in the financial environment will be discussed and compliance policies will be proposed according to the corporate governance principles, theoretical framework, and international standards based on relevant literature. Due to the digitalization of financial tools and techniques, the fields of change needed in the understanding of corporate management will be put forward. Thus, this work contributed to companies, sectors, and different country applications. In this context, to contribute to the literature and make value-added work, the digital transformation index, corporate governance index, and digital maturity model indicators were used to reveal the interactions and connectedness between finance and corporate governance. Policy recommendations will be made based on new digital business models and good governance perspectives.

L. Nzama
Department of Commercial Accounting, College of Business & Economics, University of Johannesburg, Johannesburg, South Africa
e-mail: lethiwen@uj.ac.za

S. Bozkus Kahyaoglu (✉)
Accounting and Finance Department, Izmir Bakircay University, İzmir, Turkey

Department of Commercial Accounting, College of Business & Economics, University of Johannesburg, Johannesburg, South Africa
e-mail: sezer.bozkus@bakircay.edu.tr

49
T. Moloi (ed.), *Digital Transformation in South Africa*, Professional Practice in Governance and Public Organizations,
https://doi.org/10.1007/978-3-031-52403-5_5

1 Introduction

Considering the recent development in the business world, and specifically in the finance environment, on the one hand, there is increasing competition, rapidly changing stakeholder expectations, financial crises, raw material, and logistics challenges, on the other hand, there are opportunities based on advances and developments in information technologies, as well as the cheapening of these technologies and their purchase and adaptation by every corporation, have led all kinds of organizations to benefit from information technologies by using them more efficiently and effectively. However, when this process is compared with the period until the 2020s, it is observed that the use of these technologies by corporations mostly remains "optional" (Bozkus Kahyaoglu et al., 2023). Corporations and top management who are aware of the benefits and importance of these advanced technologies have quickly adapted them to their organizations and thus gained a significant competitive advantage. It is a fact that the recent COVID-19 pandemic and the consequences of the pandemic have made the adaptation of such technologies and digital transformation in general "obligatory" for every organization (Gardner, 2023; Grant Thornton, 2023).

This obligation is becoming even more strategically important in the finance and general financial environment, which is one of the key business processes of organizations, and it should be considered that even pioneering digital transformation applications are generally carried out in this field. The most obvious example is in financial markets, financial institutions, and new approaches referred to as fintech (FSB, 2019). In fact, every business and transaction related to the field of finance and financial activities, regardless of the sector or country has a structure that is directly dependent on technological developments. The situation is the same regarding the reliability of financial information and management of risks reflected in financial statements. Based on this situation, this study examined the digital transformation in the financial environment, and corporate governance as an integral part of this, focusing on the opportunities and challenges posed by the interaction between the two in process improvement.

The study is designed briefly as follows (Fig. 1): In the first section, the major applied works on finance and the financial environment are examined based on the current literature in the field of digital transformation and corporate governance. In the second section, the structure and success criteria of digital transformation projects and their reflection on the digital business model within the framework of the strategic decision-making mechanism are discussed. The third section analyzed the conceptual framework of digital transformation, corporate governance, and the maturity model assessment approaches that emerge as a result of their interaction. In this respect, the key indicators and basic criteria of the digital maturity model and corporate maturity model are revealed. In the fourth section, good practice recommendations for digital transformation and future expectations specific to finance are examined in the context of current developments in the business world and the impacts of corporate governance principles. Then, in the conclusion, policy

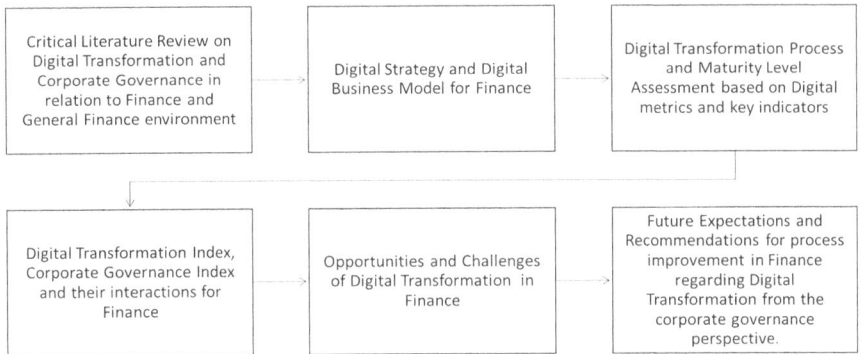

Fig. 1 Organization of work. *Source*: Authors compilation (2023)

recommendations are presented based on all the information discussed in relation to digital transformation in the finance environment from a corporate governance perspective to achieve process improvements and competitive advantages.

2 Critical Literature Review on the Interaction of Digital Transformation and Good Governance in Finance

The increasing importance of digital transformation in the field of finance stems from the fact that financial markets, financial institutions, and financial data are subject to strict regulation and supervision (EBA, 2021; EC, 2018; OECD, 2021). This situation can be expressed as a practice that requires transparency that affects and concerns all stakeholders, whether working in the financial environment or not (di Castri et al., 2020). Due to the effects of regulation and transparency being a necessity, it is important that all financial processes and transactions are based on technological systems, tools, and techniques. When evaluated from this perspective, it cannot be considered a coincidence that the very first projects and applications for digitalization started in the financial sector (OECD, 2020). This is the approach of all businesses that have rational behavior and hope to gain a competitive advantage. Hence, there is a new governance perspective with a new financial environment including emerging digital risks in the new era (Bank of England, 2019). With the contribution of advanced tools and technological infrastructure, significant improvements are taking place in the quality of implementation of corporate governance principles (Fang et al., 2023). In particular, increasing the efficiency of the internal control system of financial transactions, their effective processing, and, in general, ensuring the security of the data generation process can be given as important areas of improvement in the finance environment including macro level, meso level, and micro level (Fig. 2) respectively (Zhang & Jin, 2023).

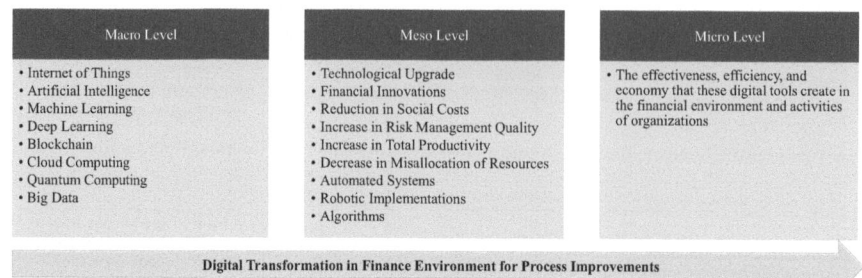

Fig. 2 The Effect of Digital Transformation at the Macro Level, Meso Level, and Micro Level. *Source*: Adapted from Zhang and Jin (2023) and Bozkus Kahyaoglu and Coskun (2022)

Technological development areas covered by digital transformation include technology-supported structures such as artificial intelligence, machine learning, deep learning, blockchain, quantum computing, and cloud computing, which mediate cheaper, more secure, more accessible, and faster processing of big data at the "macro-level" (Zhang & Jin, 2023; Bozkus Kahyaoglu et al., 2023; Bozkus Kahyaoglu & Coskun, 2022). As a result of using these technology-supported approaches in organizations to produce solutions individually or as an integrated, they have mediated the results that accelerate financial innovations. In this context, these technological upgrades are reflected in total productivity as cost reduction or increased profits, and it is possible to address these at the "meso level". The fact that the areas of these technology-driven changes at the macro and meso level become visible and can be observed in organizations and sectors as effective, efficient, and economic transactions and processes can be examined within the framework of the "micro-level".

Whether at the macro, meso, or micro level, this technological change and digital transformation process must be based on an "organization-specific" and pre-planned "digital strategy". Hence, correct understanding and internalization of the digital strategy concept emerge as necessary in successfully managing the digital transformation process. In this context, the importance of "digital strategy" and "digital business models" are explained below, specifically applicable to the finance environment (Gebauer et al., 2020).

3 Digital Strategy and Digital Business Model for Finance Environment

Decisions taken to ensure the effectiveness, efficiency, and economy of organizational resources based on technology can be expressed as "digital strategy". Although it is important to follow technological innovations and necessary for the sustainability of organizations, it is known that the success level of digital transformation projects and decisions taken by management in this regard is relatively low.

The main reason for this is that the change is not based on a digital transformation strategy, and when viewed from the perspective of corporate governance principles, it is revealed that there are problems in internalization and understanding the meaning of digital strategy. The success of the organization is determined within the framework of a strategic management approach. In the rapidly digitalizing era, the basis and priority of this strategic management approach for businesses is closely related to the digital transformation process. When evaluated from this perspective, an organization's digital strategy must be shared with all stakeholders to institutionalize the digitalization process. The point that needs to be considered here is that it may be a wrong approach to see digitalization only as an activity of the IT department and to expect the IT department to be successful. Instead, digital transformation must be managed by creating awareness and getting the contribution of all stakeholders. Research findings have demonstrated that digital transformation projects fail in cases where this is not the case based on the current literature. Accordingly, an approach that includes all stakeholders and where contribution beyond awareness is expected also requires a business model change. This indicates that the traditional business model can be insufficient, so it is important to use the digital business model instead to successfully achieve the digital transformation process (Foss & Saebi, 2017; Christensen, 2016;).

It is a fact that the digital transformation process should start with a proper digital strategy. Since any mistake in the digital strategy will directly affect the result, it is necessary to prepare all aspects of the digital strategy from the perspective of institution-specific and corporate governance principles. It is possible to summarize the factors most frequently encountered in research that cause failure in digital strategy (OECD, 2020; McKinse., 2018;).

The first is that organizations and decision-making units do not fully understand the basic definitions and concepts related to digital, digitalization, and digital transformation and make wrong decisions because they cannot internalize them, or difficulties arise because they cannot make quickly enough or adaptive decisions (Bozkus Kahyaoglu & Coskun, 2022; McKinsey, 2018). Secondly, digitalization is a technological development that provides a significant externality for organizations by reducing transaction and processing costs. Digitalization is a development that impacts every production process in which organizations specialize, from business models to strategic business management. This technological innovation process in business processes creates the second effect of reducing costs by increasing productivity and efficiency. When evaluated from this perspective, failure to take any precautions appears as a development that reduces the effectiveness and efficiency of the labour factor along with the capital and technology in question. What is essential here are the additional costs that may arise from inconvenient investment in increasing digitalization. Therefore, to avoid the destructive effects of technology, it is necessary to adapt to technology and increase the speed of adaptation to sustain digital strategy and digital business model (McKinsey, 2018; Sundberg, 2023).

Thirdly, as a result of digitalization, it is observed that there is a change in sectoral business models and the digital business model of organizations. This situation can be clearly noticed when we look at the world's largest companies: Amazon,

Alibaba, and Facebook. This means that organizations initiate a strategic alignment process in which the digital strategies they determine within the framework of the digital business model can benefit more from the opportunities in digital environments (Campbell & Gutierrez, 2021). This indicates the formation of digital platforms; hence, other organizations, which were previously perceived as competitors, are now in a position to cooperate through digital ecosystems. Parties that would be unimaginable to come together or do business together under physical business conditions can now cooperate through digital ecosystems. We are in a period where sectoral job descriptions and sectoral limitations have disappeared. In other words, the workforce, workplace, and work are all transforming into digital forms, i.e., digital ecosystems (Fig. 3). Businesses that realize this and invest in digital ecosystems can take advantage of digital transformation. It does not seem very easy for those left behind in this vision to be sustainable in the new era (McKinsey, 2018).

Fourthly, the scale of the organizations participating in and leading the digital transformation process is also important regarding the innovations and dynamic structure they bring to the sector. For example, acting by financial institutions, especially banking and insurance giant companies, can increase the devastating effects of digitalization steps for others. In this context, organizations need to think big and not lose sight of what is happening in the digital market and ecosystem when creating digitalization strategies. One of the areas that may be overlooked in digitalization is B2B digital transformations. Although the activities of B2C operators spread faster to the market, the fact that B2B digital transformations are in the background and aim to improve the operations carried out, especially in back-office activities, makes it difficult to notice at first glance. When these B2B business operators increase their digital maturity levels, it may be too late to create contra strategies to compete with them to yield results and gain a competitive advantage (McKinsey, 2018; Sundberg, 2023).

Fifthly, in the digital transformation process, there is a transition in time until the complete change occurs. Meanwhile, organizations' "two-way thinking", i.e., "duality of digital" and the correct construction of their digital strategy and digital business model, contribute to their success. When the opposite situation occurs, and the existing system is slow to integrate digital transformation-based innovations into business processes or harmonize the corporate culture, unsuccessful results occur. In order to manage this process well and make the right decisions, it is necessary to understand the big picture well. This is possible with good teamwork and high awareness of the digital corporate culture. This study focuses on the finance environment and, hence, the nature of the work carried out, and the outputs obtained

Digital Ecosystems

Fig. 3 The Elements of Digital Ecosystem. *Source*: Adapted from StarCIO (2023) and Sundberg (2023)

in the financial environment require high-risk awareness and a high level of control. Therefore, compliance with corporate governance principles is effective in the success of digital transformation projects in finance (Bouwman et al., 2018; McKinsey, 2018).

Even though digital transformation is considered within the framework of technological developments, it also has a human resources and human capital dimension. When evaluated from this perspective, there is a need for trained manpower who can adapt to change and manage innovation. Since the source of technological innovations, the information needed for them is within the framework of statistics, mathematics, and big data analytics. In the new era, technological literacy is also a basic need for employees in the financial environment, as well as financial literacy (OECD, 2022; Sundberg, 2023).

When we consider the human resources and human capital dimension of digitalization, the corporate governance perspective comes into play. Since the managers, employees, and digital transformation project team of an organization are the ones who initiate, carry out, and realize digitalization, the way they handle the issues and the scope of the digital transformation project are the key indicators of the digital maturity level. Accordingly, we are in a period where the level of digital maturity needs to be defined, measured, and monitored. Indices and various model recommendations have been developed to do this in a way that meets the most appropriate and practical needs and with an approach that keeps up with the technological pace. The key features of this digital maturity model issue, which is essential in the finance environment, are discussed in connection with the digital corporate governance perspective in the following sections.

4   Digital Maturity Model from the Digital Governance Perspective in the Finance Environment

Regarding the definition, measurement, and monitoring of digital maturity, although there are different studies, surveys, and index development efforts, there is no single agreed-upon definition and measurement technique yet. When evaluated from this perspective, this study is based on key concepts, definitions, and index criteria in the literature suitable for the financial environment.

The impact of economic shocks is low in organizations that started digital transformation before the 2019 pandemic. However, the most important financial consequence for other organizations that started the digital transformation process as a precaution against post-2019 shocks is that they are negatively affected by the shocks as the cost of being late. Considering ongoing global events shaping the business world, such as the Ukrainian war, the decrease in chip production, the decrease in supply, the increase in energy costs, inflation, and interest rates, and the break in the global supply chain, there is a decrease in the competitiveness and comparative advantage of organizations investing in digital transformation. In general, considering the impact of shocks on the implementation of organizations' forward-looking strategic decisions and the maintenance of their operational activities, the latecomers' financial performances are slow or low in analyses based on the EBIT[1] criterion, which considers the architecture of digital maturity levels (Investopedia, 2023; OECD, 2020; OECD, 2021).

It can be stated that those who started digital transformation before the economic shocks could reduce the negative effects of these shocks and, at the same time, manage them effectively. First of all, the digital transformation process effectively managed the disruptions that occurred in the global supply chain, and the crisis could be managed within the network provided in the global supply chain to the extent of the possibility of a network structure. At this point, depending on the effects of the crisis in world trade, the process of re-establishing a digital supply chain within the countries or among the countries with economic integration will emerge. At this point, the level of digital maturity comes to the fore as a determining factor. Therefore, digitalization necessitates a change in the management approach of organizations to be sustainable in the long term (Bozkus Kahyaoglu et al., 2023).

The most important feature distinguishing the finance environment and the finance function from others is that finance has a structure that is intertwined with all other functions. That information from other functions directly affects the finance function's functioning, agenda, and performance. For this reason, finance functions should have a "business partnering vision" to add value and provide high-quality assistance to their stakeholders (ICAEW & ISCA, 2019). This requires those working in the finance environment to increase their tendency toward technology beyond financial literacy and to take an active role in corporate communication by improving their soft skills. In this context, the technological development level of the financial system, structure, and processes is closely related to both the digital and the corporate maturity level of an organization. The main reason is that the corporate culture is shaped by receiving information from different organizational functions, processing it, and transforming it into value. Suppose the corporate culture is innovative, transparent, and creative. Technological innovations and the production of added value increase. This is a piece of critical information that should be taken into consideration in digital transformation processes. When creating company-specific solutions, the company's employees' business culture and core competencies are decisive for the success of digital transformation projects (Deloitte, 2023; McKinsey, 2018).

Prioritization of work plan for the finance function and managers of an organization that has recently started the digital transformation process and aims to use the digital business model effectively according to corporate governance principles can be presented as follows (ICAEW & ISCA, 2019). Digital transformation can have different meanings and results for different functions, sectors, and business lines. In

---

[1] EBIT stands for "Earnings before interest and taxes" and it is directly related to an organization's operational performance and "operating income". It is a reflection of the results obtained from the core operations of an organization on the financial statements. Please visit the link of Investopedia (2023) for more detailed information: https://www.investopedia.com/terms/e/ebit.asp.

this context, when it comes to digitalization, it is necessary to clarify its meaning in finance. Because it is necessary to know the goals to determine a digital strategy. Accordingly, for a typical finance function, it is important to prioritize and make strategic decisions by considering the benefits of digitalization. The benefits gained from digitalization can also be considered motivational elements and key drivers for digitalization (Gardner, 2023).

The structure of finance functions has changed considerably with the change in the structure of financial markets, especially with the introduction of FinTech organizations. In this context, new payment channels, new funding options, and cryptocurrencies initiated by FinTech can be given as examples. Therefore, finance functions must be faster and activate their decision-making processes to adapt to this digital environment (Deloitte, 2023; Gardner, 2023).

There will be almost no manual transactions or processes left in financial transactions soon. This is ensured by establishing smart systems, reporting, and monitoring mechanisms. Many operations that are considered routine are now carried out with a standard approach with automation support. The structure of the work done in the finance function also changes towards risk management and control activities. The main reason for this is that financial transactions and every issue related to finance are subject to regulation and require legal compliance. The standardization of financial transactions with smart system support, efficient processing, and fast financial reporting options changes the agenda of financial managers (CFOs). Thus, instead of spending time on operational work, there is an opportunity to provide strategic financial information for enterprise resource planning, making market forecasts, and focusing more on value-added investment strategies and sustainability of finance function and organizational success. The way to carry out all these beneficial and value-added tasks depends on the use of advanced analysis and forecasting techniques based on big data accumulated in corporate memory, i.e., data lake. In this respect, those working in the finance function must constantly improve themselves in terms of technical knowledge and be prepared for a new learning process. The consistency of data entries collected from various channels in the corporate memory as creating a data lake and the cleanliness and reliability of the data affect the quality of the data governance process. Data governance structure is becoming as strategically important as human resources management in the new era. Transparency, accountability, and cyber security issues also gain importance in finance, one of the functions most intertwined with data. In this respect, it is necessary to fully implement corporate governance principles for the effectiveness of data governance (Digital Directions Team, 2022; OECD, 2020).

Digital transformation affects all business processes and has some practical implications on the corporate governance principles in the virtual environment within the digitalisation framework (OECD, 2022). Ziniuk et al. (2022) describe this as the "digital transformation of corporate governance". There is a need to define, measure, and monitor these with a similar approach. For this purpose, the corporate governance index is taken as a basis. Considering the corporate governance framework, stakeholder relations should be carried out on an effective, transparent, and, most importantly, ethical basis. Sharing information regarding financial transactions in stakeholder relations and creating a financial reporting system are carried out quickly and effectively with smart technology support in the new era. This is an important best practice in the digital corporate governance process that increases stakeholder satisfaction. However, a source of concern equal to this satisfaction comes from managing cyber risks (Deloitte, 2023; Gardner, 2023; Grant Thronton, 2023). In this context, all activities based on corporate governance principles must be transferred to the digital environment, and assurance must be provided by instant and continuous monitoring. When evaluated from this perspective, smart control and surveillance systems and the use of digital tools and techniques by regulatory and supervisory authorities are becoming widespread. The rapid development process in the field of SupTech and RegTech meets this need and efforts are continuously made to early warning mechanisms that may pose a threat to data privacy violations against cyber-attacks[2] (Unit21, 2022). The reflection of these continuous technological developments and innovations can be monitored more effectively through the digital transformation index and corporate governance index, respectively. Thus, the importance of these indices as leading indicators of valuable knowledge in the decision-making mechanisms for corporate executives, the technical information they contain, their interactions, and the key aspects open to improvement are given below.

5   The Interaction of Digital Transformation Index and Corporate Governance Index

Compared to the past, the most important area of change is now expressed as the first and primary condition for calling an organization corporate, closely related to the extent to which it uses technology. Therefore, a significant interaction and positive linear connection exists between the organization's corporate and digital maturity levels. There are different scientists and researchers who developed the corporate governance index. The prominent ones are presented in the appendix as a summary table. Choosing among indices within the institutional structure, system, and corporate strategy framework is possible. Although the goal is the same, it is observed that there are differences in the approaches (Tipurić et al., 2014). Different indices and their contents are presented in Appendix 1, and the areas they generally measure are based on the perspective of accountability, regulatory compliance, and ethics within the framework of stakeholders' expectations. Here, technological innovations are used to measure, monitor, and report the metrics in each index. Therefore, it can be stated that indexes are intertwined and interact in their practical use (Dell Technologies, 2020; Deloitte, 2023).

The difference in the level of gap between countries and regions regarding readiness for digital transformation started to close during the COVID-19 pandemic. At

---

[2] For detailed information visit the link: https://www.unit21.ai/blog/fintech-regtech-suptech.

the same time, the resistance to digitalization caused by age differences has also been broken WEF (2023a, 2023b). In the new era, institutions and countries need to consider this information when developing policies and determining a strategy appropriate to the realities of the new era. Detailed information on this subject can be clearly seen by looking at the current reports of the indexes in Appendix 2.

6 Key Points

- Digital transformation should start with a well-defined digital strategy and be implemented within the framework of a digital business model. Although this practice is for organizations at the micro level, it is also a relevant approach that should be followed at the macro level based on sectors and countries.

- When evaluated from this perspective, special attention should be paid to international policy coordination and effective interdisciplinary cooperation to manage the digital transformation process well and avoid wasting resources. Thus, it will be possible to carry out transactions based on mutual trust, which is the most essential feature of financial markets and institutions. For this sustainability, relying on corporate governance principles emerges as the only rational solution. Since the only constant is change, corporate governance principles are always needed but in a suitable form. In this context, corporate governance principles must be adapted to changing field conditions, i.e., digital platforms, digital ecosystems, and blockchain-based transactions. This can be expressed as digital corporate governance principles. We are in a period where technological support, infrastructure, and cybersecurity systems are being used to protect the rights of investors, shareholders, and minorities. Presenting financial transactions, financial statement information, and all kinds of corporate information to the public in a real-time, reliable, and transparent manner is not a choice but a basic obligation for organizations. This is possible with digital transformation based on a good digital strategy, business model, and culture. As a result of the digital transformation of the financial environment, it may be possible to improve financial activities, processes, and transactions by standardizing data, ensuring data security, and creating a process based on a corporate governance perspective to produce reliable financial information.

- No matter how widespread digital transformation and technological innovations become, it is important to consider the human factor at every stage. It should be noted as a sensitive issue of critical importance, especially in the context of the ethical application of technology. Although there are changes in the area of authority and responsibilities where the human factor comes into play, compared to the past, with the influence of technology, needs will always continue. Therefore, although the need for humans will continue in the future, those who do not know artificial intelligence, coding, data analytics, and, in short, technology literacy will not have much of a chance in business life. In order to avoid this situation, finance professionals need to educate themselves and follow and internalize innovations constantly.

Appendix 1: The Comparison of Major Corporate Governance Indexes

Governance Index Name	Dimensions of Governance Index
G-Index	"Delay"—consists of four provisions for delaying hostile takeover bidders "Voting"—deals with shareholder voting rights "Protection"—refers to six provisions protecting directors and officers from legal liability or compensating them for termination "State"—refers to incorporation in a state with one of six state takeover laws "Other"—other takeover defenses
Bebchuk, Cohen and Ferell's "Entrenchment" Index E-Index	staggered boards limits to shareholder bylaw amendments poison pills Golden parachutes supermajority requirements for mergers charter amendments.
Brown and Caylor's Gov-Score Index	Audit—consists of four factors regarding the overall audit process of the firm as well as the powers and accountability of the audit committee. Board of Directors—consists of seventeen factors analyzing the board of directors as a mechanism of corporate governance. Charter/bylaws—consists of seven factors regarding shareholders' rights Director education—represented with one factor: participation of directors in ISS-accredited director education program Executive and director compensation—consists of ten factors dealing with the compensation system in a firm Ownership—consists of four factors dealing with directors' ownership Progressive practices—consists of seven factors which represent progressive corporate governance practices State of incorporation—consists also of one factor: incorporation in state with no takeover statutes
Standard and Poor's GAMMA: Governance, Management, Accountability Metrics and Analysis	Ownership Influences Shareholders' Rights Transparency, Audit and Enterprise Risk Management Board Effectiveness, Strategic Process Compensation Practices

Governance Index Name	Dimensions of Governance Index
ISS Governance QuickScore	Board Structure Compensation/Remuneration Shareholder Rights Audit Practices
ISS Corporate Governance Quotient	Board Structure and Composition Audit Issues Charter and Bylaw Provisions Laws of the State of Incorporation Executive and Director Compensation Qualitative Factors Director and Officer Stock Ownership Director Education
FTSE ISS Corporate Governance Index	Structure and Independence of the Board Equity Structure Compensation Systems for Executive and Non-Executive Directors Executive and Non-Executive Stock Ownership Independence and Integrity of the Audit Process
OECD Principles of Corporate Governance	Rights of Shareholders Protection and Equitable Treatment of Shareholders Role of Stakeholders in Corporate Governance Disclosure and Transparency Responsibilities of the Board
The SEECGAN Index of Corporate Governance	Structure and Governance of Boards Transparency and Disclosure of Information Shareholders' Rights Corporate Social Responsibility Audit and Internal Control Corporate Risk Management Compensation/Remuneration

Source: Adapted from Tipurić et al. (2014)

Appendix 2: The Key Variables and Types of Digital Transformation Indexes (DTI)

Household based DTI variables	Information equipment in households: desktop computer, portable computer, tablet computer, mobile phone, game console, TV connected to the internet; Household internet access status, household internet usage status, types of internet connections used at home; Fixed broadband connection, mobile broadband connection, dial-up connection, dial-up connection or ISDN connection, narrowband connection over the mobile phone; Household monthly total income, literacy status, education level, internet usage, portable devices used to connect to the internet; Mobile phone, portable computer, wireless network, other devices; Obtaining information from public institutions' websites, downloading forms from e-government platforms, sending forms, purchasing goods or services via e-commerce, downloading over the internet; Movies-music, books, magazines-newspapers, computer software; Transferring files between computers and other devices, installing software or mobile applications, copying files and folders, using ready-made programs, editing photos, videos, or audio files using the software.
Organization based DTI variables	Cloud strategy Microservices Strategy Kubernetes Strategy NoSQL Usage Automation and Artificial Intelligence Cyber security Digital transformation and technology trends
WEF Global Competitiveness Index	*ICT adoption* Mobile-cellular telephone subscriptions Mobile-broadband subscriptions Fixed-broadband internet subscriptions Fibred internet subscriptions Internet users
WEF Networked Readiness Index	This index is used to measure the degree of readiness of countries to exploit opportunities offered by information and communications technology.
WEF Technological Readiness Index	This is a composite index based on various layers, i.e., technology, people, governance, impact.
The UN Global E-Government Development Index	This is a composite index based on three major dimensions of e-government implementations, namely provision of online services, telecommunication connectivity and human capacity.
Digital Economy and Society Index	This index is based on human capital, connectivity, digital public services, integration of digital technology.
ICT Development Index	This index is used for monitoring and comparing developments in information and communication technology (ICT) between countries.

The Web Index	This index is used for measuring the World Wide Web's contribution to social, economic, and political progress in countries across the world.

Source: Adapted from Kabakuş and Yorulmaz (2023); EY (2020); WEF (2023a, 2023b); EU (2023); UN (2023a, 2023b); Webindex (2023)

References

Bank of England. (2019). New economy, new finance, new Bank: The Bank of England's response to the van Steenis review on the Future of Finance. Retrieved October 9, 2023, from https://www.bankofengland.co.uk/media/boe/files/report/2019/response-to-the-future-offinance-report.pdf

Bouwman, H., Nikou, S., Molina-Castillo, F. J., & de Reuver, M. (2018). The impact of digitalization on business models. *Digital Policy, Regulation and Governance, 20*(2), 105–124. https://doi.org/10.1108/DPRG-07-2017-0039

Bozkus Kahyaoglu, S., & Coskun, E. (2022). *University Auditing in the Digital Era.* Taylor and Francis Publications. ISBN: 9781003093008. Retrieved October 9, 2023, from https://www.taylorfrancis.com/books/mono/10.1201/9781003093008/university-auditing-digital-era-sezer-bozkus-kahyaoglu-erman-coskun

Bozkus Kahyaoglu, S., Durst, S., & Coskun, E. (2023). To digitalize or not? Covid effect in medium sized companies based on three cases. *EDPACS Journal, 68*(4), 1–25. Retrieved October 9, 2023, from https://www.tandfonline.com/doi/abs/10.1080/07366981.2023.2260612

Campbell, A., & Gutierrez, M. (2021). Why you need an operating model: To align your people and deliver your strategy. *Management and Business Review, 1*(2), 66.

Christensen, C. M. (2016). *The innovator's dilemma: When new technologies cause great firms to fail (Management of Innovation and Change).* Harvard Business Review Press.

Dell Technologies. (2020). Measuring digital transformation progress around the world. Accessed 9 Oct 2023.

Deloitte. (2023). Digital Maturity Index Survey 2023. Retrieved October 9, 2023, from https://www2.deloitte.com/content/dam/Deloitte/de/Documents/industry-operations/Deloitte-Digital-Maturity-Index-Survey-2023.pdf

di Castri, S., Grasser, M., & Kulenkampff, A. (2020). The 'DataStack': A data and tech blueprint for financial supervision, innovation, and the data commons (May 7, 2020). BFA Global, 2020. Retrieved October 9, 2023, from https://ssrn.com/abstract=3595344

Digital Directions Team. (2022). 45 digital transformation KPIs: The ultimate list. Retrieved October 9, 2023, from https://digitaldirections.com/digital-transformation-kpis/

EBA. (2021). EBA Analysis of RegTech in the EU Financial Sector. Accessed 9 Oct 2023.

EC. (2018). FinTech Action plan: For a more competitive and innovative European financial sector. Accessed 9 Oct 2023.

EY. (2020). Digital Transformation Index. By EY Poland. Retrieved November 15, 2023, from https://www.ey.com/en_pl/technology/digital-transformation-index

Fang, Q., Yu, N., & Xu, H. (2023). Governance effects of digital transformation: From the perspective of accounting quality. *China Journal of Accounting Studies, 11*(1), 77–107. https://doi.org/10.1080/21697213.2023.2148944

Foss, N. J., & Saebi, T. (2017). Business models and business model innovation: Between wicked and paradigmatic problems. *Long Range Planning, 50*(3), 249–258. https://doi.org/10.1016/j.lrp.2017.07.006

FSB. (2019). FinTech and market structure in financial services: Market developments and potential financial stability implications. Retrieved October 9, 2023, from https://www.fsb.org/wp-content/uploads/P140219.pdf

Gartner. (2023). Top Priorities for Audit Executives in 2023. White paper. Retrieved October 25, 2023, from https://www.gartner.com/en/audit-risk/trends/audit-agenda-polls

Gebauer, H., Fleisch, E., Lamprecht, C., & Wortmann, F. (2020). Growth paths for overcoming the digitalization paradox. *Business Horizons, 63*(3), 313–323. https://doi.org/10.1016/j.bushor.2020.01.005

Grant Thonton. (2023). Financial services internal audit report 2022/23. Retrieved October 25, 2023, from https://www2.grantthornton.co.uk/financial-services-internal-audit-report-2022-23.html

ICAEW & ISCA. (2019). Digital transformation in finance functions: ASEAN and UK perspectives. Retrieved October 9, 2023, from https://www.icaew.com//media/corporate/files/technical/technology/thought-leadership/digital-transformation-in-finance-functions.ashx

Investopedia. (2023). Corporate finance: Earnings before interest and taxes (EBIT): Formula and example. Retrieved October 9, 2023, from https://www.investopedia.com/terms/e/ebit.asp

Kabakuş, A. K., & Yorulmaz, M. (2023). Calculating digital transformation index with geographically weighted regression. *Current Perspectives in Social Sciences, 27*(1), 76–85. Retrieved November 15, 2023, from https://dergipark.org.tr/tr/pub/atasobed/issue/78317/1320704

McKinsey. (2018). *Why digital strategies fail*. McKinsey Quarterly. Retrieved October 9, 2023, from https://www.mckinsey.com/~/media/mckinsey/business%20functions/mckinsey%20digital/our%20insights/why%20digital%20strategies%20fail/why-digital-strategies-fail.pdf?shouldIndex=false

OECD. (2020). *OECD business and finance outlook 2020: Sustainable and resilient finance*. OECD Publishing. https://doi.org/10.1787/eb61fd29-en

OECD. (2021). The use of SupTech to enhance market supervision and integrity. In *OECD Business and Finance Outlook 2021*. OECD Publishing. https://doi.org/10.1787/d478df4c-en

OECD. (2022). *Digitalization and corporate governance*. OECD Publishing. Retrieved October 9, 2023, from https://www.oecd.org/corporate/ca/Background-note-Asia-roundtable-digitalisation-and-corporate-governance.pdf

StarCIO. (2023). Defining Digital Transformation, Strategy and other Digital Terminology. Retrieved October 9, 2023, from https://blogs.starcio.com/2016/07/defining-digital-transformation.html

Sundberg, L. (2023). Towards the Digital Risk Society: A Review. *Human Affairs*. https://doi.org/10.1515/humaff-2023-0057

Tipurić, D., Dvorski, K., & Delić, M. (2014). Measuring the quality of corporate governance – A review of corporate governance indices. *EJEM- European Journal of Economics and Management., 1*(1) Retrieved October 9, 2023, from https://core.ac.uk/download/pdf/343512521.pdf

Unit21. (2022). Risk and compliance operations blog. Retrieved November 15, 2023, from https://www.unit21.ai/blog/fintech-regtech-suptech

Zhang, Y., & Jin, S. (2023). How does digital transformation increase corporate sustainability? The moderating role of top management teams. *Systems, 11*(7), 355. https://doi.org/10.3390/systems11070355

Ziniuk, M., Dyeyeva, N., Bogatyrova, K., Melnychenko, S., Fayvishenko, D., & Shevchun, M. (2022). Digital transformation of corporate governance. *Financial and Credit Activity: Problems of Theory and Practice, 5*, 46. Retrieved October 9, 2023, from https://fkd.net.ua/index.php/fkd/issues

References from Internet Pages

EU. (2023). Digital economy and society index (DESI). Retrieved November 15, 2023, from https://digital-strategy.ec.europa.eu/en/policies/desi

UN. (2023a). The UN Global E-Government Development Index. Retrieved November 15, 2023, from https://publicadministration.un.org/egovkb/en-us/About/Overview/-E-Government-Development-Index

UN. (2023b). ICT Development Index. Retrieved November 15, 2023, from https://www.itu.int/en/ITUD/Statistics/Pages/IDI/default.aspx

Webindex. (2023). Worldwide web's global impact index. Retrieved November 15, 2023, from https://thewebindex.org/

World Economic Forum (WEF). (2023a). WEF Global Competitiveness Index. Retrieved November 15, 2023, from https://www.weforum.org/publications/top-10-emerging-technologies-of-2023/

World Economic Forum (WEF). (2023b). WEF Networked Readiness Index. Retrieved November 15, 2023, from https://networkreadinessindex.org/

Digital Transformation in Corporate Reputation

Lindie Grebe (iD)

Abstract This chapter described the development of corporate reputation into e-reputation against the background of a global digital transformation as part of the Fourth Industrial Revolution, based on the theories of legitimacy and signalling. The importance of corporate reputation in the long-term sustainability and success of organisations was illustrated, and the effects of digital transformation on reputation management were highlighted. The chapter proposed that organisations should be more proactive in managing their e-reputation in a digitally transformed environment. Specifically, it was proposed that e-reputation be perceived in three important new ways, namely what forms e-reputation, how it is formed, and who forms e-reputation. Firstly, in the digital age, it was proposed that corporate reputation is becoming increasingly impersonal. This is a significant trend that implies that practitioners and researchers should realise that the reputational landscape is a multifaceted field with various potential challenges. Secondly, how e-reputation is formed must be perceived in a new way that moves from the traditional paradigm of reputation development, which relies on perceptions of past and expected future interactions between organisations and their stakeholders, to the inclusion of digitally transformed systems. For practitioners and researchers to be able to manage and understand corporate reputation, they must redefine the dimensions, components, and items of corporate reputation within a unique digitally transformed organisational context. Finally, a shift in who forms an e-reputation was also proposed, to include other entities. Stakeholders and organisations, as well as corporate reputation practitioners and researchers, rely on a digitally transformed system of designers, information providers, and data holders who underpin digital interactions and information from which reputations are formed.

L. Grebe (✉)
Department of Financial Governance, School of Applied Accountancy, College of Accounting Sciences, Unisa, Pretoria, South Africa
e-mail: grebel@unisa.ac.za

T. Moloi (ed.), *Digital Transformation in South Africa*, Professional Practice in Governance and Public Organizations,
https://doi.org/10.1007/978-3-031-52403-5_6

1   Introduction

The extant academic literature widely acknowledges the positive relationship between corporate reputation and sustained competitive advantage. Scholars and practitioners agree that good corporate reputations are valuable assets that can influence organisational functioning and profitability (Edi & Wati, 2022). Research has further demonstrated strong correlations between corporate reputation and organizational performance (Batrancea et al., 2022; Frare & Beuren, 2022; Gomez-Trujillo et al., 2020; Maaloul et al., 2023; Roberts & Dowling, 2002; Singh & Misra, 2021).

The digital transformation of organisations, characterised by a shift towards online and social channels, has had a profound impact on corporate reputation. In the online context, reputation is more important than ever, as it can be easily and quickly shaped by a wide range of stakeholders, including customers, employees, competitors, and the media. As a result, business organisations can no longer ignore the role of digitally transformed online platforms in reputation management (Veh et al., 2019; Zhang et al., 2021).

While there is no single, universally accepted definition of e-reputation, it is generally understood to be an extension of offline reputation to the online context (Chun & Davies, 2001; Dutot & Castellano, 2021). While e-reputation might be considered an extension of offline reputation to an online context, a need exists for a deeper understanding of how digital transformation influences corporate reputation and how to manage e-reputations accordingly. More theoretical development is needed to fully understand the unique dynamics of e-reputation and the extent to which it is influenced by the distinctive features of the online environment (Gomez-Trujillo et al., 2020; Zhang et al., 2021).

The sections that follow discussed digital transformation, the development of corporate reputation into e-reputation from legitimacy theory and signalling theory perspectives, and present propositions and implications for practitioners and researchers of corporate reputation alike.

2   Digital Transformation

A global digital transformation as part of the Fourth Industrial Revolution affects all aspects of everyday business, from how organisations transact to how they communicate and share information. This digital transformation is a seminal event for all organisations across all sectors, involving the adoption of disruptive digital technologies to create or modify existing business processes, increase productivity, and generate value (Zaoui & Souissi, 2020). These disruptive, technological advancements differ from earlier technologies in their ability to create interconnections between humans and machines.

In the context of digital transformation, Stafie and Grosu (2022) asserted that technological evolution drives organisations to adapt to an ever-evolving landscape.

Digital transformation in organisations uses technology to develop new business processes, models, software, and systems with the goal of enhancing competitiveness, efficiency, and profitability. Organisations across all industries and sectors are innovating to transform and improve their business models, processes, workforce efficiency, customer personalisation, and innovation (Schwertner, 2017). While digital transformation is projected to experience rapid annual growth, it has already led to new trends such as artificial intelligence (Barr-Pulliam et al., 2022).

Digital transformation has positively impacted the value proposition of organisations, as Schwertner (2017) noted that companies strive to maintain corporate flexibility in a favourable business environment, and the ability to adapt to digital transformation effectively is a key factor for success.

3   Corporate Reputation

Organisations must deal with the increasing visibility of their activities to a wider range of stakeholders, facilitated by digital and social technologies. Stakeholders are more interconnected than in the past, meaning that an issue that poses reputational risks on one continent, can become a concern to investors on another (Baah et al., 2020).

The relationship between corporate reputation and a sustained competitive advantage is widely acknowledged in the literature (Batrancea et al., 2022; Frare & Beuren, 2022; Gomez-Trujillo et al., 2020; Maaloul et al., 2023; Roberts & Dowling, 2002; Singh & Misra, 2021). The consensus is that good corporate reputations are valuable assets, which can influence the functioning and profitability of organisations. Corporate reputation is based on an organisation's historical actions but can quickly change if new opinions about the organisation's actions are formed.

Fombrun (1996) notes in one of the most widely used definitions, that a corporate reputation is a collective representation of a firm's past actions and results that describe the firm's ability to deliver valued outcomes to multiple stakeholders. The main components emphasised in this definition are that reputations are based on perceptions, that reputations are collective judgements of all stakeholders, and that reputations are comparative. Adding to Fombrun's (1996) definition that illustrates the interconnectedness between identity, image and reputation, Walker (2010) suggested an additional two components, namely that reputations could be positive or negative, and that reputations are stable and enduring.

As such, a corporate reputation develops from the different related images that stakeholders have of an organisation. An organisation's reputation, and changes in its reputation, influence its relationship with stakeholders (Carroll, 2016; Mohd Sofian et al., 2023). Not being reputable as seen by stakeholders can, in turn, have immediate and long-lasting consequences, as a weak corporate reputation may affect the future actions of stakeholders towards an organisation. Stakeholders have the power to hold organisations accountable for their actions and a good corporate reputation increases the likelihood that stakeholders will enter a contract with a given organisation.

A Legitimacy Theory Perspective on Corporate Reputation
Accordingly, legitimacy theory takes a social constructivist perspective of organisations as being part of a bigger social network (Bourdieu, 1990), and these organisations are considered not to have an inherent right to operate. A right to operate must be earned (Mathews, 1997) and legitimate organisations can sustain their rights to operate through a social contract with its stakeholders (Bunduchi et al., 2023; Marco-Lajara et al., 2022; Veh et al., 2019). It is from this view that legitimacy, and therefore corporate reputation can be regarded as a resource that is necessary for an organisation's sustainability. Thus, legitimacy and corporate reputation can be seen as resources that can be created, managed, and manipulated through various actions.

From the above discussion, it is clear that both organisations, whose corporate reputations are formed, and their stakeholders, who form opinions and corporate reputations about organisations, play an important role. These organisations are described as social entities with their structures, actions, and ideas whose acceptability is being assessed (Suchman, 1995). This description again confirms that legitimacy is socially constructed, based on social norms within a larger social construct. It also implies that legitimacy is subjective, for example within a competitive environment and sector context. The assumption can then be made those subjects of legitimacy, organisations, are not passive, but active creators of organisational legitimacy that adapt to their unique environments to manage their corporate reputations and social acceptance (Bunduchi et al., 2023; Suchman, 1995; Veh et al., 2019).

4   E-Reputation

The digital transformation of organisations, characterised by a shift towards online and social channels, has expanded the range of stakeholders that can influence corporate reputation. In the online context, reputation is more important than ever, as it can be easily and quickly shaped by a variety of sources, including customers, employees, competitors, and the media. It is no longer possible for organisations to ignore the role of digital transformation in reputation management (Dutot & Castellano, 2021; Veh et al., 2019).

Both e-reputation and corporate reputation are the perceptions of the firm by its audience. It is also sometimes referred to as cyber reputation, web reputation, digital reputation, or online reputation. While there is no single agreed-upon definition of e-reputation, it is generally understood to be an extension of offline reputation to the online context (Elmada et al., 2022; Moccia et al., 2021). Previous research on reputation has identified a number of key attributes, such as trustworthiness, competence, performance, and attractiveness (Fombrun, 1996; Walker, 2010, as discussed in the definition of corporate reputation above. However, it is important to note that the digital transformation may have a different impact on each of these attributes.

E-reputation refers to the elements of corporate reputation that are specifically derived from online interactions. For example, the ease with which information can be shared online can make it more difficult for organisations to maintain a positive reputation. On the other hand, the digital transformation with its online platforms can also provide organisations with new opportunities to build and manage their reputations, such as through social media engagement and customer reviews. Overall, the digital transformation of organisations has had a significant impact on corporate reputation. E-reputation is now a critical component of any organisation's overall reputation management strategy.

Corporate reputation communications as digital signals that create an e-reputation, are key to corporate reputation management. e-Reputation therefore further refers to corporate reputation derived from digital interconnection, consisting of two elements, namely reputation and online digital platforms, and is derived from electronic contacts. This means that corporate reputation is seen as the signals that organisations send out about their attractiveness. (Dutot & Castellano, 2021; Elmada et al., 2022). Signalling theory provides a lens through which e-reputation and its online signals can be understood.

A Signalling Theory Perspective of E-Reputation

Signalling theory relates to the information signals about organisations that are sent to stakeholders. Signalling theory enables scholars to describe the behaviour when two parties, for example, organisations and online stakeholders have access to different information (Drover et al., 2018; Plummer et al., 2016; Seth & Bayne, 2022). Typically, one party is the sender of information and must decide on whether and how to signal the information. The other party is the receiver of information and must decide how to interpret the signal (Connelly et al., 2011; Seth & Bayne, 2022).

Signalling theory relates to the efforts made by organisations to influence stakeholders' perceptions in order to build support for preferred initiatives and interests. These efforts include actions such as lobbying and marketing to convey a desirable image of the organisation (Carroll, 2016; Dutot & Castellano, 2021; Elmada et al., 2022), as well as messages through integrated reporting which is the focus of this study. Reputations as signals are based on observations of organisations' actions over time and under particular conditions (Dutot & Castellano, 2021; Elmada et al., 2022).

This perspective therefore means that reputations create value by providing information about otherwise unobservable organisational actions and characteristics. This information improves the predictability of economic interchanges between organisation and stakeholders who are interested in measuring and predicting the behaviour of the organisation against societal standards and norms (Fombrun, 1996; Mohd Sofian et al., 2023).

Signalling theory views organisations as having reputations about specific characteristics with different stakeholder groups, based on their past actions measured against societal standards and norms. An organisation can as such have different reputations for different characteristics or actions with different stakeholder groups, based on the values and norms of those different stakeholders. From this perspective, the economic value of corporate reputation depends on the specific perceptions held within a stakeholder group that is concerned with a specific characteristic along which e-reputation is deduced from prior behaviours. Signalling theory suggests that the locus of control over an organisation's corporate reputation lies mainly with the organisation as it decides on the reputational signals that it sends to its stakeholders (Dutot & Castellano, 2021; Elmada et al., 2022; Gardberg et al., 2019).

Managing E-Reputation

Organisations globally are fast adopting corporate reputation management as an essential function. Organisations need to manage their reputations in ways that can contribute to their ability to attract the support of their stakeholders. They must manage risks that stem from their need for social acceptance; a social license to operate. In order to create and manage corporate reputation successfully, organisations need to develop clear corporate reputation value frameworks that signal their desired organisational corporate reputation to their sources of legitimacy. These sources are the complex network of internal and external stakeholders that observe organisations and make legitimacy assessments (Fuhrmann, 2019; Mohd Sofian et al., 2023; Ruef & Scott, 1998). Organisations should live up to their envisaged values (London, 2019; Veh et al., 2019). Reputation systems have developed as devices that organisations use to position themselves in terms of corporate reputation (Dutot & Castellano, 2021; Mohd Sofian et al., 2023; Nath, 2019).

e-Reputation management takes place in a digitally transformed environment where transactions and interactions are performed online. In today's digital world, e-reputation management is essential for organisations and stakeholders alike. The global digital transformation has had a significant impact on how reputation is perceived and managed, both online and offline. The digital environment can pose significant threats to reputation. For example, negative reviews and ratings can be easily found and shared online, and can have a lasting impact on a business's reputation. This environment has made it easier for competitors to target and undermine an organisations' reputation (Dutot & Castellano, 2021; Zhang et al., 2021).

Simultaneously, digital transformation offers new opportunities for organisations to manage their reputations in new and innovative ways. Organisations can use social media to interact with stakeholders, build relationships of online trust, and develop high-quality websites to communicate important information to stakeholders through digital signals to increase e-reputations. Additionally, organisations can use online reputation monitoring tools to track their reputation and to respond to negative feedback quickly and effectively (Dutot & Castellano, 2021; Zhang et al., 2021).

It is important to note that the impact of digital transformation on e-reputation management varies depending on the specific technology used. These technologies are aimed at specific stakeholder groups, for example, discussion groups and brand communities can help businesses to build relationships with customers and to get feedback on their products and services. However, anonymous consumer profiling and communication systems can also pose a threat to reputation, as they can be used to spread negative information about a business (Kaur & Kaur, 2020). Digital transformation has created a more complex and dynamic environment for reputation management. Modern organisations are required to be more aware of the potential threats and opportunities that face their e-reputation, and to develop strategies to manage their reputation effectively (Dutot & Castellano, 2021; Veh et al., 2019; Zhang et al., 2021).

5 Propositions and Practical Implications

Prior research on corporate reputation has identified a number of key attributes as described by Fombrun (1996) and Walker (2010), but it is important to note that the recent global digital transformation may have a differential impact on each of these traditional attributes. Digital transformation has given rise to new reputation channels, such as social media and customer review platforms. These channels have become increasingly important in influencing how stakeholders perceive organisations.

New opportunities created by digital transformation to build and manage e-reputations, such as through social media engagement and artificial intelligence customer engagement, have made it easier for stakeholders to access information about organisations, both positive and negative. This has led to increased transparency and accountability on the part of organisations.

The digital transformation has also made it easier for stakeholders to engage with organisations directly, to provide them with a greater voice in shaping corporate reputations. The digital transformation of organisations has made e-reputation a critical component of any organisation's overall reputation management strategy.

As a result of these changes, organisations need to be more proactive in managing their e-reputation. This includes developing and implementing e-reputation management strategies, monitoring online conversations about the organisations, and responding to negative feedback promptly and effectively. In addition, further research is needed to better understand the nature of e-reputation and the best practices for managing it in the digital age.

Specifically, this chapter proposes that e-reputation be perceived in three important new ways, namely *what* forms e-reputation, *how* it is formed, and *who* forms e-reputation. Firstly, in the digital age, corporate reputation is becoming increasingly impersonal. This is due to the shift away from traditional interpersonal collaboration, where reputation was built on shared history or mutual acquaintances among stakeholders. Today, stakeholders increasingly engage in transactions with individuals that are unfamiliar, and they must therefore rely on broader systems to form an opinion and e-reputation of an organisation.

One example of this is blockchain technology. In a blockchain-based system, a reputation is not formed of the other party to the transaction, but rather an e-reputation is formed of blockchain itself. This is because the blockchain is a distributed ledger that is tamper-proof and transparent. As a result, participants in a blockchain system can be confident that the information on the ledger is accurate and that no party can unilaterally change it. The shift to impersonal trust is not unique to blockchain technology. It is also evident in other digital platforms, such as online marketplaces and social media. In these platforms, trust is often mediated by algorithms and reputation systems. For example, when online commerce takes place, customers may rely on other customer reviews to assess the e-reputation of an organisation. This shift to an impersonal e-reputation has a number of implications. On the one hand, it can make it easier for people to engage in transactions with organisations that they do not know well, which can create new opportunities for economic and social interaction. On the other hand, it also raises concerns about the potential for fraud and abuse. As a result, it is important to develop new mechanisms for establishing and maintaining reputations in impersonal environments.

Overall, the shift to impersonal e-reputation is a significant trend in the digital age. It has the potential to both expand and contract opportunities for obtaining and managing corporate reputation. It is therefore important for both practitioners such organisational reputation managers, and researchers to understand the implications of this trend. Corporate reputation practitioners and researchers should realise that the reputational landscape is a multifaceted field where various potential challenges exist that relate to, for example, the interconnectedness of technology, information, knowledge, and opinions.

Secondly, *how* e-reputation is formed must be perceived in a new way. The traditional paradigm of reputation development, which relies on perceptions of past and expected future interactions between organisations and their stakeholders, is being challenged by the rise of machine learning algorithms and other technological systems. In the digital age, e-reputation is increasingly formed based on the characteristics of the organisation within its operational contexts, as opposed to the interpersonal relationships between customers and personnel.

Artificial intelligence machine learning algorithms are a prime example of this trend. These algorithms are being used in a variety of industries, including insurance, investments and assurance, to ascribe trust and corporate reputation scores to organisations based on a number of pre-determined corporate reputation dimensions. This process is often opaque and discriminatory, and it can lead to individuals being denied access to services or being charged higher prices. For an organisation to be able to manage corporate reputation, the dimensions, components, and items of corporate reputation must be identified within their organisational context (Dutot & Castellano, 2021; Van Riel, 2019). In short, the shift towards impersonal and institution-based e-reputation has a number of implications for corporate reputation practitioners and researchers. An institution-based e-reputation can facilitate new opportunities for both individuals and organisations by making it easier to interact with strangers and unknown organisations. However, it also raises concerns about the potential for discrimination, abuse, and loss of control. It is important to be aware of these challenges and to develop new mechanisms for ensuring that e-reputation is fair and reliable in the digital age. For practitioners and researchers to be able to manage and understand corporate reputation, the dimensions, components, and items of corporate reputation must redefined and identified within a unique digitally transformed organisational s context (Dutot & Castellano, 2021; Van Riel, 2019).

Finally, there is also a proposed shift in *who* forms an e-reputation. Despite the increasingly impersonal nature of e-reputation in the digital age, traditional stakeholders of an organisation remain the key group that assigns legitimacy and thereby a license of social acceptance to operate, to an organisation. Although it is important to understand how specific stakeholder groups view an organisation based on specific actions and characteristics, criticism is raised around a disregard for the transferal of reputations from one stakeholder group to another, as well as interference effects that may result from different reputations from different entities. Therefore, an e-reputation implies the inclusion of other entities than individuals when sending corporate reputational signals. For example, system designers as the developers and architects of digital systems are key to ensuring the integrity and fairness of these systems. They pose a reputational risk of introducing loopholes or personal biases in these systems that influence corporate reputation, whether intentionally or unintentionally.

Information providers play an important role in ensuring the quality and accuracy of the data that feeds these algorithms, as this has a direct impact on the opinions that are formed about an organisation based on the resultant output information. The individuals and organisations, other than the organisations in which e-reputation is at stake, that provide information to the algorithms that power stakeholders' digital experiences, are further important role players. This includes the likes of social media platforms or news reporters. Data holders that aggregate, analyse, and profit from the information they control in a digital era, such as data brokers and cloud computing providers, have a responsibility to use data in a responsible and ethical manner so as not to falsely influence a corporate reputation.

It is clear that e-reputation is no longer simply a matter of trusting the other party in a transaction. Stakeholders and organisations, as well as corporate reputation practitioners and researchers, rely on a digitally transformed system of designers, information providers, and data holders who underpin digital interactions and information from which reputations are formed. This is because our everyday business is increasingly mediated by complex algorithms and digital systems that are often complex and difficult to understand. To manage e-reputations in the digital age, these important role players must be transparent about their practices, accountable for their decisions, and committed to providing true information that would affect opinions about the reputations of organisations.

Although stakeholder groups will remain essential for forming and managing a reputation, corporate reputation practitioners and researchers must recognise the impact of increasing digital transformation on the dynamics of reputation. Misunderstanding these trends could lead to misjudged reputation, wasted efforts to manage reputation and an underestimation of its enduring significance.

In the digital age, stakeholders and organisations, as well as practitioners and researchers, increasingly need to rely on entities that they have never met, which necessitates a new set of skills for making accurate corporate reputation decisions based on different types of reputational signals. For example, stakeholders may need to rely on online reviews, social media presence, or other digital signals to assess the reputations of organisations. Stakeholders and organisations inevitably cede a degree of control over reputation to computer algorithms that automate reputational assessments. Practitioners and researchers must understand the logic behind these algorithms and how they are used to evaluate corporate reputation. For example, reputation managers and researchers may need to consider the criteria used by the algorithm, the quality of the data it is trained on, and its potential for bias to ensure the validity, credibility, and trustworthiness of reputational data.

For organisations to be regarded as reputable and legit by society, they may need to adapt their e-reputation management approach to consider these new dynamics. Organisations may need to be more transparent about their data collection and usage practices, or they may need to invest in new technologies to send reputational signals to stakeholders. In summary, the digital transformation of business operations is transforming the dynamics of corporate reputation. Corporate reputation practitioners and researchers who fail to understand these trends risk making poor reputational decisions that could damage their organisation's reputations.

6   Key Points

- This chapter described the development of corporate reputation into e-reputation against the background of a global digital transformation as part of the Fourth Industrial Revolution, based on the theories of legitimacy and signalling. The importance of corporate reputation in the long-term sustainability and success of organisations was illustrated, and the effects of digital transformation on reputation management were highlighted.
- The chapter proposed that organisations should be more proactive in managing their e-reputation in a digitally transformed environment. Specifically, it was proposed that e-reputation be perceived in three important new ways, namely *what* forms e-reputation, *how* it is formed, and *who* forms e-reputation. Firstly, in the digital age, it was proposed that corporate reputation is becoming increasingly impersonal. This is a significant trend that implies that practitioners and researchers should realise that the reputational landscape is a multifaceted field with various potential challenges. Secondly, *how* e-reputation is formed must be perceived in a new way that moves from the traditional paradigm of reputation development, which relies on perceptions of past and expected future interactions between organisations and their stakeholders, to the inclusion of digitally transformed systems. For practitioners and researchers to be able to manage and understand corporate reputation, they must redefine the dimensions, components, and items of corporate reputation within a unique digitally transformed organisational context. Finally, a shift in *who* forms an e-reputation was also proposed, to include other entities. Stakeholders and organisations, as well as corporate reputation practitioners and researchers, rely on a digitally transformed

system of designers, information providers, and data holders who underpin digital interactions and information from which reputations are formed.

- By offering suggestions for a distinct, broader agenda for corporate reputation practice and research, this chapter contributes to the development and management of e-reputation. These propositions and practical implications for corporate reputation practitioners and researchers, require them to adapt their e-reputation management approach to consider new dynamics in a digitally transformed era. Future research could test these propositions and practical implications to further the debate towards corporate reputation and digital transformation. However, the timing of this chapter is important—this knowledge could add to organisations' corporate reputations at a time when all aspects of everyday business are affected by digital transformation.

References

Baah, C., Jin, Z., & Tang, L. (2020). Organizational and regulatory stakeholder pressures friends or foes to green logistics practices and financial performance: Investigating corporate reputation as a missing link. *Journal of Cleaner Production, 247*, 119–125.

Barr-Pulliam, D., Brown-Liburd, H. L., & Munoko, I. (2022). The effects of person-specific, task, and environmental factors on digital transformation and innovation in auditing: A review of the literature. *Journal of International Financial Management & Accounting, 33*(2), 337–374.

Batrancea, L. M., Nichita, A., & Cocis, A. D. (2022). Financial performance and sustainable corporate reputation: Empirical evidence from the airline business. *Sustainability, 14*(20), 13567.

Bourdieu, P. (1990). *The logic of practice*. Polity Press.

Bunduchi, R., Smart, A. U., Crisan-Mitra, C., & Cooper, S. (2023). Legitimacy and innovation in social enterprises. *International Small Business Journal, 41*(4), 371–400.

Carroll, C. E. (2016). *The SAGE encyclopaedia of corporate reputation*. Sage.

Chun, R., & Davies, G. (2001). E-reputation: The role of mission and vision statements in positioning strategy. *The Journal of Brand Management, 8*(4), 315–333.

Connelly, B. L., Certo, S. T., Ireland, R. D., & Reutzel, C. R. (2011). Signalling theory: A review and assessment. *Journal of Management, 37*(1), 39–67.

Drover, W., Wood, M. S., & Corbett, A. C. (2018). Toward a cognitive view of signalling theory: Individual attention and signal set interpretation. *Journal of Management Studies, 55*(2), 209–231.

Dutot, V., & Castellano, S. (2021). E-reputation in web entrepreneurship. In *Research anthology on strategies for using social media as a service and tool in business*. IGI Global.

Edi, E., & Wati, E. (2022). Measuring intangible asset: Firm reputation. *Business: Theory and Practice, 23*(2), 396–407.

Elmada, M. A. G., Elmaresa, M. V., Wardhani, S., & Putri, W. A. N. (2022). Online reputation management with an electronic word of mouth approach. *Jurnal Komunikasi Profesional, 6*(2), 119–128.

Fombrun, C. J. (1996). *Reputation: Realizing value from the corporate image*. Harvard Business School Press.

Frare, A. B., & Beuren, I. M. (2022). Effects of corporate reputation and social identity on innovative job performance. *European Journal of Innovation Management, 25*(5), 1409–1427.

Fuhrmann, S. (2019). A multi-theoretical approach on drivers of integrated reporting-uniting firm-level and country-level associations. *Meditari Accountancy Research, 28*(1), 168–205.

Gardberg, N. A., Zyglidopoulos, S. C., Symeou, P. C., & Schepers, D. H. (2019). The impact of corporate philanthropy on reputation for corporate social performance. *Business and Society, 58*(6), 1177–1208.

Gomez-Trujillo, A. M., Velez-Ocampo, J., & Gonzalez-Perez, M. A. (2020). A literature review on the causality between sustainability and corporate reputation: What goes first? *Management of Environmental Quality: An International Journal, 31*(2), 406–430.

Kaur, P., & Kaur, N. (2020). The impact of social media on reputation management in the hotel industry: A systematic literature review. *International Journal of Contemporary Hospitality Management, 32*(12), 3121–3141.

London, T. (2019). The role of values in the creation and maintenance of an organization's reputation. In D. Deephouse, N. Gardberg, & W. Gardberg (Eds.), *Global aspects of reputation and strategic management*. Emerald.

Maaloul, A., Zéghal, D., Ben Amar, W., & Mansour, S. (2023). The effect of environmental, social, and governance (ESG) performance and disclosure on cost of debt: The mediating effect of corporate reputation. *Corporate Reputation Review, 26*(1), 1–18.

Marco-Lajara, B., Zaragoza-Sáez, P., Falcó, J. M., & Millan-Tudela, L. A. (2022). Corporate social responsibility: A narrative literature review. *Frameworks for Sustainable Development Goals to Manage Economic, Social, and Environmental Shocks and Disasters, 1*, 6–34.

Mathews, M. R. (1997). Twenty-five years of social and environmental accounting research: Is there a silver jubilee to celebrate? *Accounting, Auditing and Accountability Journal, 10*(4), 481–531.

Moccia, S., García, M. R., & Tomic, I. (2021). Fintech strategy: e-reputation. *International Journal of Intellectual Property Management, 11*(1), 38–53.

Mohd Sofian, F. N. R., Abdullah, K. H., & Mohd-Sabrun, I. (2023). Research on corporate reputation: A bibliometric review of 43 years (1977–2020). *International Journal of Information Science and Management (IJISM), 21*(2), 31–54.

Nath, S. (2019). Praemia virtutis honores? The making of global reputations and the false promise of meritocracy. In D. Deephouse, N. Gardberg, & W. Gardberg (Eds.), *Global aspects of reputation and strategic management*. Emerald.

Plummer, L. A., Allison, T. H., & Connelly, B. L. (2016). Better together? Signaling interactions in new venture pursuit of initial external capital. *Academy of Management Journal, 59*(5), 1585–1604.

Roberts, P. W., & Dowling, G. R. (2002). Corporate reputation and sustained superior financial performance. *Strategic Management Journal, 23*(12), 1077–1093.

Ruef, M., & Scott, W. R. (1998). A multidimensional model of organizational legitimacy: Hospital survival in changing institutional environments. *Administrative Science Quarterly, 43*, 877–904.

Schwertner, K. (2017). Digital transformation of business. *Trakia Journal of Science, 15*(1), 388–393.

Seth, A. K., & Bayne, T. (2022). Theories of consciousness. *Nature Reviews Neuroscience, 23*(7), 439–452.

Singh, K., & Misra, M. (2021). Linking corporate social responsibility (CSR) and organizational performance: The moderating effect of corporate reputation. *European Research on Management and Business Economics, 27*(1), 100139.

Stafie, G., & Grosu, V. (2022). Digital transformation of accounting as a result of the implementation of artificial intelligence in accounting. *Revista Romana de Economie, 54*(1).

Suchman, M. C. (1995). Managing legitimacy: Strategic and institutional approaches. *Academy of Management Review, 20*(3), 571–610.

Van Riel, C. (2019). Why do people love museums so much? Empirical evidence about the stellar reputations of art museums and what companies can learn from it. In D. Deephouse, N. Gardberg, & W. Gardberg (Eds.), *Global aspects of reputation and strategic management*. Emerald.

Veh, A., Göbel, M., & Vogel, R. (2019). Corporate reputation in management research: a review of the literature and assessment of the concept. *Business Research, 12*, 315–353.

Walker, K. (2010). A systematic review of the corporate reputation literature: Definition, measurement, and theory. *Corporate Reputation Review, 12*(4), 357–387.

Zaoui, F., & Souissi, N. (2020). Roadmap for digital transformation: A literature review. *Procedia Computer Science, 175*, 621–628.

Zhang, L., Wang, Y., & Wang, Y. (2021). The impact of online reviews on brand reputation: A meta-analysis. *Journal of Business Research, 131*, 9–20.

Lessons on Digital Transformation in the Marketing Environment

Khuliso Mapila and Tankiso Moloi (ⓘ)

Abstract Digital technologies are shaping the industrial revolution, extending beyond industry and influencing markets and customer experiences. Their transformative power is noticeable, particularly in the field of marketing. In this chapter, we discuss the concept of digital transformation in the marketing environment. Digital transformation in the marketing environment includes the incorporation of technological advancements across all dimensions of marketing tactics, aiming to foster growth while retaining relevance within a constantly changing digital landscape. Digital transformation has had a significant impact on the marketing landscape, particularly digital marketing. It has driven changes in marketing practices and markets, necessitating a deep understanding of the consumer value chain and adaptation to evolving business practices. The integration of marketing and sales departments has been affected, leading to changes in organizational performance. Digital transformation has also improved the interaction between firms and customers, emphasizing the importance of integrated communication. However, the digital transformation of marketing is not without its challenges, including barriers to change and a skills gap. Nonetheless, digital marketing has become critical for firms to remain competitive and respond to changing market landscape. As emerging economies advance technologically, the digital landscape confronts marketers with both challenges and possibilities. This chapter aims to identify the challenges and opportunities of incorporating digital transformation into marketing activities, by examining existing knowledge and real-world examples that evaluate the adoption and use of digital technology for marketing in selected emerging economies. Leveraging technological capabilities is critical for organisations to compete and thrive in both domestic and international markets. However, emerging economies, particularly in Africa have reported low rates of technological adoption, limiting their ability to compete and grow. As a result, emerging economies are confronted with a rapidly evolving digital transformation process that has a profound impact on

K. Mapila · T. Moloi (✉)
Johannesburg Business School, University of Johannesburg, Johannesburg, South Africa
e-mail: tankiso.moloi@jbs.ac.za

© The Author(s), under exclusive license to Springer Nature Switzerland AG 2024
T. Moloi (ed.), *Digital Transformation in South Africa*, Professional Practice in Governance and Public Organizations,
https://doi.org/10.1007/978-3-031-52403-5_7

marketing practices. Organisations can position themselves advantageously in emerging economies through effective digital transformation by understanding the discussed strategies, challenges, and opportunities. This chapter proposes to contribute towards the existing knowledge on the adopting digital technology, specifically within the marketing environment towards building sustainable and better emerging economies.

1 Introduction

The current technology landscape is rapidly evolving, making it vital for marketers to understand and embrace digital transformation. It is important for marketers to possess an in-depth understanding of and completely adopt digital technologies. The process entails more than simply adoption of digital tools and platforms; it necessitates a fundamental transformation in mindset, strategy and approach.

Digital transformation refers to transformation and changes that technology brings through its integration into organisations, their products, customer engagement approach, manufacturing operations, business models, products or organisational structures (Chawla & Goyal, 2022; Nadkarni & Prügl, 2021; Vial, 2019). This goes beyond adopting tools and platforms; it requires a fundamental shift, in mindset and approach. This is to facilitate key organisational improvements including enhancing customer experience, create new business operating models and streamlining operations (Chawla & Goyal, 2022). According to Yablonsky (2020), digital transformation includes the use of digital technologies to improve operational performance as well as the introduction of innovative approaches to successfully address the implications of such transformation (Yablonsky, 2020).

Digital transformation can be defined as a continual and iterative advancement towards greater levels of digital expertise (Ivančić et al., 2019). This is the utilisation of digital technology, alongside various organisational tactics, to cultivate the growth of a culture that is centred around digitalization. Upon thorough examination, the achievement of this particular stage of maturity will enable the organisation to improve its service offerings, establish a competitive advantage, and effectively tackle issues within a complex environment (Ivančić et al., 2019). Morakanyane et al. (2017), identified the following: digital technologies, digital capabilities, strategies, business models and value chain as some of the drivers of digital transformation (Morakanyane et al., 2017).

Numerous researchers and experts have attempted to understand digital transformation (DT) from various perspectives, including strategic, business model innovation, and organisational impacts (Chawla & Goyal, 2022; Morakanyane et al., 2017). Furthermore, extensive research on the topic of digital transformation has been undertaken across a variety of business sectors, including healthcare, retail, manufacturing, finance, mining, automobile, telecom, and experiential computing (Chawla & Goyal, 2022). The field of marketing, similar to various other industries, is undergoing a digital transformation. The implementation of digital transformation has resulted in a wide array of digital marketing approaches that are designed to offer value to customers (Miklosik & Evans, 2020). A crucial aspect of transformation involves understanding individuals and effectively connecting with them through technology. This includes analyzing customer data utilizing intelligence and machine learning and harnessing the power of media. By comprehending the preferences, behaviors, and needs of their target audience (Ma & Sun, 2020).

Digital transformation has generated numerous opportunities across various industries. The term "Fourth Industrial Revolution" (4IR) describes a time of rapid technical development and shifts in society brought about by automation and digital technologies (Petrillo et al., 2018). Businesses can collect data and use it to get the customer insights, preferences, and purchase behaviours within the context of the fourth industrial revolution (4IR) (Kruger & Steyn, 2023). This is made possible by the advancements in technology, which enable seamless integration across various corporate divisions and activities.

2   Digital Transformation in Emerging Markets

Emerging markets, encompassing numerous economically disadvantaged nations, are presently utilising basic forms of artificial intelligence to tackle significant developmental issues, particularly in the provision of financial services for vulnerable and marginalised populations (Imran, 2023). Market dynamics, such as competition and market orientation, play a crucial role in shaping marketing strategies and outcomes (Nenonen et al., 2019). Nonetheless, emerging economies frequently face challenges that prevent them from fully participating in the global digital transformation revolution. Numerous challenges remain in the digital transformation process. These economies are confronted with challenges such as limited technological integration, a lack of access to available digital technologies, and slow adoption rates. Overcoming these challenges is critical for emerging economies to achieve long-term growth. To that end, technological initiatives should concentrate on marketing long-term benefits. Only 40% of the world's population lacks even the most basic internet connection, despite the fact that the UN has declared internet access to be a human right (Imran, 2023).

Individuals with little financial resources may not be able to purchase digital technology or intelligence equipment, but they can profit from AI-as-a-service solutions by using their mobile devices (Jayashree et al., 2022). With the advent of mobile technology and the industrial revolution 4.0, digital marketing has emerged as a way to advance technological advancement and make all necessary information readily available. There are limitations associated with digital marketing. Digital marketing depends upon the use of the internet (Desai & Vidyapeeth, 2019). Several factors are accelerating digital transformation in these markets. The rapid expansion of the internet and widespread mobile phone penetration have resulted in an increase in online activities, with consumers devoting more time to digital platforms. By the beginning of 2022, there were 5.31 billion unique mobile phone users globally, accounting for more than two-thirds (67.1%) of the global population, and internet penetration rate is 62.5 percent of the global population (We Are Social, 2022). The number of people using social media worldwide has seen an increase by more than 10% in the last 12 months. As of January 2022, there were 424 million new users who began using social media, making up 4.62 billion (58.4%) of all users worldwide (We Are Social, 2022). However, due to the absence of internet infrastructure or insufficient connectivity in certain regions, access to online resources may be limited or unreliable (Desai & Vidyapeeth, 2019). Research shows that 17% of South Africans use voice assistance, 29% image recognition, and 33% online translation tools to find information (Deloitte, 2022). The existence and current use of some applications allows for South Africa to adopt modern technology, including artificial intelligence (Dimitrieska et al., 2018).

While digital transformation presents a lot of challenges, it also presents a number of benefits for businesses. Digital technologies are being used in emerging economies to reach new customers, cultivate relationships with existing customers, and develop innovative products and services (Imran, 2023).

Most emerging economies, such as Nigeria, are experiencing a growing population, which serves as a market opportunity and a catalyst for the spread of digital marketing (Jayashree et al., 2022). Businesses that embrace digital transformation successfully will be well-positioned to succeed in such marketplaces.

The ongoing digital revolution is exerting a disruptive influence on global economy, thereby affecting emerging markets. A few studies have been conducted in digital transformation, across different emerging markets on marketing or digital marketing: digital transformation in the retail industry in China to understand how businesses react to changing customer demands while saving money during strategic renewal (Wang et al., 2023); digital transformations using blockchain technology within retail in India, to grow sales through permission marketing (Nigam et al., 2023); digital marketing transformation process for SMEs in Turkey during the pandemic (Meydanoglu et al., 2022); the significance of digital marketing in India through the application of machine learning (Jayashree et al., 2022); digital transformation, the use of digital platforms, and digital marketing by SMEs in Bangladesh during Covid-19 (Hossain et al., 2022); digital marketing and sales transformation in India (Gupta et al., 2021); consumer behaviour changes trigger on digital transformation in Romania (Brumă et al., 2021).

Based on the above, one may safely assume that digital transformation gained traction during the pandemic which encouraged businesses, especially in emerging markets to start developing tools, adapting technology strategies to survive (Hossain et al., 2022). The significance of technology adoption has been reinforced by the COVID-19 epidemic, as businesses have been driven to change their strategies in response to the evolving environment (Imran, 2023; Omer, 2021).

3 Understanding Digital Transformation in the Marketing Environment

Similar to other industries and business functions, marketing has shifted and evolved over the years and has changed now more than ever because of the digital revolution. Marketing is a necessary activity that can be defined as the strategic process of identifying, forecasting, and fulfilling consumer demands and wants employing the development, promotion, and distribution of goods or services to both current and new customers (Bist et al., 2022; Grover, 2023). The transition towards digital marketing is an important part of marketing evolution. The development of technology and the internet has completely changed the marketing environment, with digital marketing outperforming old tactics in terms of effectiveness (Nesterenko et al., 2023).

Due to shifts in consumer behaviour, technology, and market dynamics, marketing techniques, and approaches have evolved with each period. Marketing can be divided into four distinct periods: Marketing 1.0, to Marketing 4.0, which represent the stages in the evolution of marketing. Over time, marketing transformed from being products centred (Marketing 1.0) which focused on selling products; to the customer-centric era (Marketing 2.0), which emphasised the importance of understanding customer needs and preferences; values-driven era (Marketing 3.0), which pushed businesses to align their marketing strategies with societal values and focused on building emotional connections with customers; lastly, digitally driven (Marketing 4.0), which combines online and offline engagements between businesses and their customers (Fuciu & Dumitrescu, 2018; Kotler et al., 2016; Vassileva, 2017). The 4.0 strategy employs human-to-human connectivity to improve consumer interaction and productivity leveraging machine learning, artificial intelligence, and other ITC technologies (Fuciu & Dumitrescu, 2018, pp. 43–48). According to Fuciu and Dumitrescu (2018), "marketing 4.0" refers to a "marketing approach that combines the online and offline interaction between companies and customers (Bintaro et al., 2022; Fuciu & Dumitrescu, 2018; Kotler et al., 2016; Vassileva, 2017). The complex shifts brought about by market volatility, strong global competition, demanding consumers, the rapid growth and development of new technology, and disruptive innovation give rise to marketing 4.0 (Vassileva, 2017; We Are Social, 2022). This new wave of marketing called Marketing 4.0 is being achieved by the constant or disruptive integration of digital technologies with marketing operations (Vassileva, 2017; We Are Social, 2022).

Customer value creation is an important aspect of the marketing value chain. The development of a complete framework focused on generating, sharing, and acquiring customer value is important to every business's strategy (Keiningham et al., 2020). In this process, the marketing function creates customer value by evaluating the needs of the target customers, designing product or service offerings that are appealing to the target customers, distributing and promoting these offerings through various channels, and devising innovative pricing strategies to capture customer value (Keiningham et al., 2020; Sánchez-Gutiérrez et al., 2019).

4 The Concept of Digital Marketing

The process of integrating digital technologies and strategies into marketing practices to adapt and thrive in today's digital world. The drivers of digital transformation in marketing are multifaceted, including the need to understand the consumer value chain and adapt to changing business practices (Gillpatrick, 2019). The implementation of digital transformation generates positive results in the field of customer engagement, emphasising the importance of integrated marketing communication within marketing (Bist et al., 2022).

Digital marketing includes the utilisation of different developments in technology, such as artificial intelligence (AI) and the Internet of Things (IoT), to effectively achieve marketing goals in both consumer-to-consumer and business-to-consumer environments, enhance products and services, improve operational efficiency, automate processes and transform business models (Krishen et al., 2021). Digital marketers are responsible for promoting brand recognition and generating leads across all digital platforms, including paid and unpaid ones (Desai & Vidyapeeth, 2019).

Digital transformation and digital marketing are different concepts that are interlinked and complement each other. Both digital transformation and digital marketing analyse the utilisation of Information Technologies (IT) within the industry to enhance service delivery, modify organisational processes, influence organisational culture, and affect value creation (Melović et al., 2020). However, Digital transformation is a comprehensive and strategic approach that involves the transformation of business activities, organizations, processes, competencies, and models. On the other hand, digital marketing focuses specifically on the use of digital channels and technologies for marketing purposes (Gillpatrick, 2019; We Are Social, 2022).

Digital marketing is a commonly employed strategy for the promotion of products or services, as well as to engage with consumers, using various digital channels (Melović et al., 2020). It can be defined as "the use of digital technologies to create an integrated, targeted and measurable communication which helps to acquire and retain customers while building deeper relationships with them" (Melović et al., 2020). The presence of excessive visual and informational elements within advertising spaces poses a challenge for marketers, as they encounter difficulties in effectively differentiating their advertisements and initiating meaningful discussions pertaining to a certain brand or product (Desai & Vidyapeeth, 2019).

The concept of digital transformation in marketing refers to the utilisation of technologies to enhance and reconfigure traditional marketing approaches and techniques (Dash & Chakraborty, 2021; Gupta et al., 2021). Traditional marketing is predominantly based on offline strategies, covering a range of conventional means that can be broadly classified into four categories: print, broadcast, direct mail, and telephone (Bist et al., 2022). Unlike the majority of traditional methods of marketing, digital marketing enables marketers to view accurate results in real time and measure impact (Desai & Vidyapeeth, 2019).

Therefore, a comprehensive and inclusive definition of digital marketing can be formulated as follows: the application of data, information and communication technology (ICT) tools such as artificial intelligence, various platforms including social networks, different media channels, and devices to expand the reach of marketing activities across physical and virtual domains (Krishen et al., 2021). The primary objective of digital marketing is to enhance customer relationships by enabling, educating, persuading, and engaging consumers (Krishen et al., 2021).

The marketing approach discussed involves the combination of historical context, statistical analysis, and advertising and marketing strategies, to develop a marketing strategy that is more focused on the needs and preferences of customers and is characterised by a systematic approach (Grover, 2023). The rapid changes in the digital marketing environment necessitate a practical understanding of digital marketing tools.

The implementation of tools such as SEM/SEO, display advertising, and E-CRM strategies has had a substantial influence on customer satisfaction levels and the likelihood of customers making a purchase. Additionally, a mediation-moderation strategy was employed. The purchase intention of consumers is significantly influenced by customer satisfaction, which serves as an effective mediator in the relationship between digital marketing practices and buy intention. Furthermore, the extent of consumer interaction played a moderating role in the association between content marketing and communication and purchase intention (Dash & Chakraborty, 2021).

5   Priorities for Digital Transformation in the Marketing Environment

For marketing to successfully undergo digital transformation, it is vital to comprehend the customer value chain and the evolving company practises. The following are some of the core elements that need to be prioritised when undergoing digital transformation within the marketing environment.

5.1   *Focus on the Customer "Customer First" and Their Needs*

Marketers need to focus on understanding and meeting the needs of their customers in the digital age. The development of digital technologies has facilitated the ability of businesses collect, analyse, and harness vast amounts of data in order to customise their marketing efforts, hence fostering a more customer-centric strategy (Grover, 2023). The concept of "Customer First" was created as the key principle driving the organisation's management philosophy to effectively address the difficulties that evolved from their traditional structure, leaders of China Overseas Land &

Investment Ltd (COLI), began offering real estate-related products and services, which resulted in increased market presence, improved customer satisfaction, and the promotion of wise and sustainable development practices (Wang et al., 2023). In another example, in its sales and marketing initiatives for digital transformation, Tata Steel developed a customer-focused structure that enabled the digital transformation of the company (Gupta et al., 2021).

Consumers express a need for enhanced access to supplementary information regarding the products they intend to purchase, as well as the ability to conduct information searches and place purchases (Brumă et al., 2021). It can be concluded that consumers are looking for and possess a keen interest in a distribution system that is best able to accommodate the digital transformation of modern society (Bonnet & Westerman, 2020; Sánchez-Gutiérrez et al., 2019). This means using data and analytics to understand customer behavior, and developing personalized marketing campaigns.

5.2   Embrace New Technologies

New technologies are constantly emerging that can help marketers to reach and engage their customers in more effective ways. Marketers need to be willing to embrace new technologies and to learn how to use them effectively. This includes technologies such as artificial intelligence, machine learning, and big data analytics. The case study of COLI revealed that the managers of the organisation successfully implemented a transformative organisational restructuring within the marketing and customer service divisions through the development and implementation of a management information system known as the Whole Life Cycle Management System (Wang et al., 2023).

New technologies such as Blockchain technology can be used in marketing to gain consumer trust. This can be done through this technology which makes it easier to keep track of how things are made and where they come from for consumers. By giving customers access to safe technology that lets them access information, you can ease their worries about fake goods, which can change their decision to buy (Nigam et al., 2023). Blockchain technology has the potential to enhance consumers' confidence in the realm of in-home purchasing, thereby fostering an upsurge in both spontaneous and suggested impulse purchases, ultimately leading to heightened levels of customer satisfaction (Nigam et al., 2023).

5.3   Build a Strong Digital Culture and Capabilities

Digital transformation is not just about technology, it is also about the culture and people who will use the technology. It is also about creating a culture within the organization that is open to change and innovation. Marketers need to work with other departments to ensure that the organization is aligned on its digital strategy. Policymakers must recognise the inherent capacity of digital transformation and strategic renewal programmes to handle the dual dilemma of changing business landscapes and cost containment. As a result, they should take actions to facilitate the effective implementation of digital transformation and strategic renewal practises in state-owned enterprise governance (Wang et al., 2023).

In a comprehensive case study of Zhejiang Meorient Commerce and Exhibition Inc, a company that was compelled to adopt a novel strategic approach in response to the disruptive impact of the pandemic on their conventional exhibition tactics. A novel method was devised and executed, involving the utilisation of a digital exhibition product known as Webshow Max. This product seamlessly incorporated five distinct service modules, namely digital information, digital exhibiting, digital buyer-exhibitor pairing, big data mining, and digital negotiating. The main points to be emphasised are as follows: When developing its digital platform strategy, and effectively implementing a digital platform strategy, firms must have robust and adaptable skills to seize or generate opportunities while concurrently reconfiguring existing resources (Bai et al., 2022).

6   Challenges in Implementing Digital Transformation in Marketing

Digital transformation in marketing faces several challenges that organizations need to overcome to successfully implement it. One of the main challenges is the resistance to change and the need for a shift in mindset (Lei et al., 2023). Nevertheless, the presence of numerous competitor products and services employing similar digital marketing strategies can be a disadvantage and drive technology adoption (Desai & Vidyapeeth, 2019). Many organizations are accustomed to traditional marketing methods and may be hesitant to adopt digital strategies. This resistance can be due to a lack of understanding or fear of the unknown (Mani & Chouk, 2018). To address this challenge, organizations need to invest in training and education to help employees understand the benefits and opportunities that digital transformation can bring.

Another challenge is the requirement for cooperation and coordination across several organisational divisions, particularly marketing, and sales (Hauer et al., 2021). For digital transformation, an all-inclusive plan involving numerous departments and services is required. Differences in goals, priorities, and communication styles may make this collaboration difficult. Businesses must foster efficient communication and cooperation by establishing a collaborative culture and allocating suitable resources and tools (Hauer et al., 2021).

Despite the challenges posed by the pandemic, Meorient has shown a notable commitment to research and development by increasing its expenditure in this area. In the year 2020, the corporation allocated a sum of 13.6708 million RMB yuan towards research & development activities, constituting approximately 14.49% of the overall revenue. As of December 31, 2020, the company has acquired a total of 21 legally recognised copyrights for its software products and had submitted applications for four patents (Bai et al., 2022).

Additionally, the rapid pace of technological advancements presents a challenge in keeping up with the latest trends and technologies (Hauer et al., 2021). Digital marketing is constantly evolving, and organizations need to stay updated with the latest tools, platforms, and strategies. This requires continuous learning and adaptation. Organizations can address this challenge by investing in research and development, staying connected with industry trends, and fostering a culture of innovation (Kutnjak, 2021).

Furthermore, the digital divide can make it difficult to undertake digital transformation in marketing (Imran, 2023). Not all organisations, particularly small and medium-sized firms, have equal access to digital technologies and resources. This can lead to inequities in the ability to implement and leverage digital marketing tactics. To solve this issue, governments and industry associations should provide assistance and resources to assist SMEs in overcoming digital transformation challenges (Imran, 2023).

Another challenge comes as a consequence of the proliferation of false advertising on the internet and social media platforms, certain consumers may develop a negative perception of certain companies (Desai & Vidyapeeth, 2019).

7 Key Steps to Achieve Digital Transformation in Marketing

Digital transformation is a crucial process for businesses to adapt to the changing market landscape and meet customer expectations. Marketing practice and markets have been significantly impacted by the digital transformation of marketing. It necessitates a thorough understanding of the consumer value chain as well as the implementation of new business practices. Tata Steel (India) has outlined a framework for achieving digital transformation, which involves several key steps (Gupta et al., 2021). Firstly, it is crucial to establish a consensus within the organisation regarding the need for action. This entails garnering agreement and support from all relevant stakeholders and incorporating one of the key steps to achieve digital transformation in marketing, which is the adoption of an omnichannel approach to marketing communications (Radchenko et al., 2021). Secondly, high-potential initiatives should be carefully selected and implemented, taking into account the strategic directive of the company. These would include the development of new business models that leverage digital technologies (Yanovska et al., 2019). These initiatives should be aligned with the overall goals and objectives of the organisation which need to be defined through a clear strategy. Thirdly, a governance mechanism should be established to monitor and evaluate the performance of digital initiatives. This mechanism will ensure that progress is regularly reviewed and any necessary adjustments are made. Lastly, it is important to view digital transformation as an ongoing process, rather than a one-time event. This entails creating a virtuous cycle where continuous improvement, culture change and innovation are embraced, leading to sustained digital transformation (Cozmiuc & Pettinger, 2021; Gupta et al., 2021).

8 Key Points

- Digital transformation in the marketing environment is driven by various factors, including the need to understand the consumer value chain, changing business practices, and the development of digital skills and competencies. It involves the integration of online and offline channels, the incorporation of digital technologies into business processes, and the adoption of digital marketing strategies.
- Digital transformation has significant implications for marketing practices, markets, and the larger economy. Digital marketing is constantly evolving, making it essential for marketers to stay current. to thrive in the rapidly changing digital landscape, marketers must stay updated with the latest trends and technologies implementing digital transformation.
- The integration and availability of online and offline channels in marketing communications have been identified as important aspects of digital transformation in the service marketing industry and marketing faces several challenges, including resistance to change, the need for collaboration and coordination, keeping up with technological advancements, data privacy and security, and the digital divide.
- Organizations need to address these challenges by investing in training and education, fostering a culture of collaboration, staying updated with industry trends, ensuring data privacy and security, and providing support to SMEs.
- By overcoming these challenges, organizations can successfully implement digital transformation and leverage its benefits to enhance their marketing strategies.

References

Bai, O., Yang, X., Hunter, K. O., & Wang, B. (2022). Meorient: A pioneer of the digital exhibition industry. *Emerald Emerging Markets Case Studies, 12*(3), 1–27.

Bintaro, B. K., Sokibi, P., Amsyar, I., & Sanjaya, Y. P. A. (2022). Utilizing digital marketing as a business strategy: Utilizing digital marketing as a business strategy. *Startupreneur Business Digital (SABDA Journal), 1*(1), 63–71.

Bist, A. S., Agarwal, V., Aini, Q., & Khofifah, N. (2022). Managing digital transformation in marketing: "Fusion of traditional marketing and digital marketing". *International Transactions on Artificial Intelligence, 1*(1), 18–27.

Bonnet, D., & Westerman, G. (2020). The new elements of digital transformation. *MIT Sloan Management Review, 62*(2).

Brumă, I. S., Vasiliu, C. D., Rodino, S., Butu, M., Tanasă, L., Doboş, S., Butu, A., Coca, O., & Stefan, G. (2021). The behavior of dairy consumers in short food supply chains during COVID-19 pandemic in the Suceava area, Romania. *Sustainability, 13*(6), 3072.

Chawla, R. N., & Goyal, P. (2022). Emerging trends in digital transformation: A bibliometric analysis. *Benchmarking: An International Journal, 29*(4), 1069–1112.

Cozmiuc, D. C., & Pettinger, R. (2021). Consultants' tools to manage digital transformation: The case of PWC, Siemens, and Oracle. *Journal of Cases on Information Technology (JCIT), 23*(4), 1–29.

Dash, G., & Chakraborty, D. (2021). Digital transformation of marketing strategies during a pandemic: Evidence from an emerging economy during COVID-19. *Sustainability, 13*(12), 6735.

Deloitte. (2022). *2022 connectivity and mobile trends.* Available at https://www.deloitte.com/an/en/our-thinking/insights/industry/media-telecommunications/connectivity-mobile-trends-survey.html

Desai, V., & Vidyapeeth, B. (2019). Digital marketing: A review. *International Journal of Trend in Scientific Research and Development, 5*(5), 196–200.

Dimitrieska, S., Stankovska, A., & Efremova, T. (2018). Artificial intelligence and marketing. *Entrepreneurship, 6*(2), 298–304.

Fuciu, M., & Dumitrescu, L. (2018). *From marketing 1.0 to marketing 4.0–The evolution of the marketing concept in the context of the 21 century.* Paper presented at the International Conference Knowledge-Based Organization, Vol. 24(2), pp. 43–48.

Gillpatrick, T. (2019). The digital transformation of marketing: Impact on marketing practice & markets. *Economics-Innovative and Economics Research Journal, 7*(2), 139–156.

Grover, Y. (2023). Digital transformation in marketing: Prospects and challenges. *IUJ Journal of Management, 11*(1).

Gupta, P., Steward, M., Narus, J., & Seshadri, D. (2021). Pursuing digital marketing and sales transformation in an emerging market: Lessons from India's tata steel. *Vikalpa, 46*(4), 197–208.

Hauer, G., Naumann, N., & Harte, P. (2021). Digital transformation challenges successful enterprises–An exploration of the collaboration of marketing and sales department in German organizations. *Innovation & Management Review, 18*(2), 164–174.

Hossain, M. R., Akhter, F., & Sultana, M. M. (2022). SMEs in COVID-19 crisis and combating strategies: A systematic literature review (SLR) and a case from emerging economy. *Operations Research Perspectives, 9*, 100222.

Imran, A. (2023). Why addressing digital inequality should be a priority. *The Electronic Journal of Information Systems in Developing Countries, 89*(3), e12255.

Ivančić, L., Vukšić, V. B., & Spremić, M. (2019). Mastering the digital transformation process: Business practices and lessons learned. *Technology Innovation Management Review, 9*(2).

Jayashree, S., Sidana, N., Pham, L. T., Kunju, L. M., Ratnavalli, B., & Gangodkar, D. (2022). *The progressive role of machine learning in enhancing the effectiveness of digital marketing in emerging economies.* Paper presented at the 2022 2nd International Conference on Advance Computing and Innovative Technologies in Engineering (ICACITE), pp. 1640–1645.

Keiningham, T., Aksoy, L., Bruce, H. L., Cadet, F., Clennell, N., Hodgkinson, I. R., & Kearney, T. (2020). Customer experience-driven business model innovation. *Journal of Business Research, 116*, 431–440.

Kotler, P., Kartajaya, H., & Setiawan, I. (2016). *Marketing 4.0: Moving from traditional to digital.* John Wiley & Sons.

Krishen, A. S., Dwivedi, Y. K., Bindu, N., & Kumar, K. S. (2021). A broad overview of interactive digital marketing: A bibliometric network analysis. *Journal of Business Research, 131*, 183–195.

Kruger, S., & Steyn, A. A. (2023). Leveraging technology adoption to navigate the 4IR towards a future-ready business: A systematic literature review. *Engineering Reports*, e12762.

Kutnjak, A. (2021). COVID-19 accelerates digital transformation in industries: Challenges, issues, barriers and problems in transformation. *IEEE Access, 9*, 79373–79388.

Lei, J., Indiran, L., & Haiyat Abdul Kohar, U. (2023). Barriers to digital transformation among MSME in the tourism industry: Cases studies from Bali. *International Journal of Academic Research in Business and Social Sciences, 13*(3), 844–858.

Ma, L., & Sun, B. (2020). Machine learning and AI in marketing–Connecting computing power to human insights. *International Journal of Research in Marketing, 37*(3), 481–504.

Mani, Z., & Chouk, I. (2018). Consumer resistance to innovation in services: Challenges and barriers in the Internet of things era. *Journal of Product Innovation Management, 35*(5), 780–807.

Melović, B., Jocović, M., Dabić, M., Vulić, T. B., & Dudic, B. (2020). The impact of digital transformation and digital marketing on brand promotion, positioning, and electronic business in Montenegro. *Technology in Society, 63*, 101425.

Meydanoglu, E. S. B., Nayır, D. Z., Klein, M., & Öztürk, R. (2022). *Digital challenges and strategies in a post-pandemic world*. Peter Lang GmbH.

Miklosik, A., & Evans, N. (2020). Impact of big data and machine learning on digital transformation in marketing: A literature review. *Ieee Access, 8*, 101284–101292.

Morakanyane, R., Grace, A. A., & O'reilly, P. (2017). Conceptualizing digital transformation in business organizations: A systematic review of the literature.

Nadkarni, S., & Prügl, R. (2021). Digital transformation: A review, synthesis and opportunities for future research. *Management Review Quarterly, 71*, 233–341.

Nenonen, S., Storbacka, K., & Windahl, C. (2019). Capabilities for market-shaping: Triggering and facilitating increased value creation. *Journal of the Academy of Marketing Science, 47*, 617–639.

Nesterenko, V., Miskiewicz, R., & Abazov, R. (2023). Marketing communications in the era of digital transformation. *Virtual Economics, 6*(1), 57–70.

Nigam, A., Behl, A., Pereira, V., & Sangal, S. (2023). Impulse purchases during emergency situations: Exploring permission marketing and the role of blockchain. *Industrial Management & Data Systems, 123*(1), 155–187.

Omer, M. (2021). Pandemic COVID-19: Impact on digital marketing. *Journal of Contemporary Issues in Business and Government, 27*(4), 131–138.

Petrillo, A., De Felice, F., Cioffi, R., & Zomparelli, F. (2018). Fourth industrial revolution: Current practices, challenges, and opportunities. *Digital Transformation in Smart Manufacturing, 1*, 1–20.

Radchenko, Y., Marenych, V., Marchenko, O., Kryvosheeva, N., Guzenko, H., & Shcheblykina, T. (2021). Digital transformations of service marketing: Theoretical fundamentals and directions. *ScienceRise, 2*, 37–43.

Sánchez-Gutiérrez, J., Cabanelas, P., Lampón, J. F., & González-Alvarado, T. E. (2019). The impact on the competitiveness of customer value creation through relationship capabilities and marketing innovation. *Journal of Business & Industrial Marketing, 34*(3), 618–627.

Vassileva, B. (2017). Marketing 4.0: How technologies transform marketing organization. *Óbuda University E-Bulletin, 7*(1), 47.

Vial, G. (2019). Understanding digital transformation: A review and a research agenda. *The Journal of Strategic Information Systems, 28*(2), 118–144.

Wang, K., Zhang, Z., Xiong, J., Li, H., Liu, H., & Ma, H. (2023). Balancing strategic renewal, cost and efficiency: A case study in digital transformation. *Journal of Business Strategy, 44*(5), 266–276.

We Are Social. (2022). *Global overview report*. Available at https://datareportal.com/reports/digital-2022-global-overview-report

Yablonsky, S. A. (2020). AI-driven digital platform innovation. *Technology Innovation Management Review, 10*(10).

Yanovska, V., Levchenko, O., Tvoronovych, V., & Bozhok, A. (2019). *Digital transformation of the Ukrainian economy: Digitization and transformation of business models*. Paper presented at the SHS Web of Conferences, 67 05003.

Digital Transformation in the Finance and Banking Sector

Pulane Modiha

Abstract The finance and banking sector must embrace digital transformation more now than ever, to stay competitive. Implementation of digital transformation initiatives and strategies could unlock costs and processes efficiencies and ensure sustainable growth, and improved service delivery which ensures improved customer experiences. In this chapter, we discuss digital transformation in finance and banking with a specific focus on servicing customers' changing behaviors, the use of big data and analytics to make informed decisions as well as operational efficiencies required when customer-centric models are adopted.

Finance and banking institutions need to adjust their strategy to take into account the changing requirements and behaviors of their customers as the financial landscape changes along with technological improvements. The backbone of this evolution is digital transformation, which is supported by big data analytics and operational efficacy. A shift towards customer-centric models, supported by data-driven insights and operational efficiencies, is essential for financial institutions to thrive in this digital era. In the drive to meet and surpass customer expectations, those who can successfully combine the human factor with the technology component will emerge as frontrunners.

1   Introduction

The term "digital transformation" describes the process of integrating digital technology into various business processes, radically changing how business function and provide value to their consumers (Westerman et al., 2011). At its core, it is a cultural and operational transformation that supports new business models, improves the customer experience, and streamlines processes (Berman, 2012). For many years, the financial and banking industries have been at the forefront of numerous

P. Modiha (✉)
Johannesburg Business School, University of Johannesburg, Johannesburg, South Africa

© The Author(s), under exclusive license to Springer Nature   95
Switzerland AG 2024
T. Moloi (ed.), *Digital Transformation in South Africa*, Professional Practice in Governance and Public Organizations,
https://doi.org/10.1007/978-3-031-52403-5_8

technological developments, from the advent of automated teller machines (ATMs) to internet banking channels. Expectations for smooth, quick, and secure services have increased as the percentage of people who are "digital aware," or those who were born in the internet and smartphone era, has increased worldwide (Palfrey & Gasser, 2008). Therefore, the need for innovation and adaptation in the finance and banking sector has become critical, making digital transformation more than just a choice.

The importance of digital transformation in finance and banking is validated by a number of factors such as, customer experience, data and analytics which enables data driven insights and decisions, processes efficiencies, not excluding regulatory and risk considerations. The financial and banking sector must embrace digital transformation as an ongoing strategy rather than a one-time project due to the continual growth of the digital ecosystem. Banks and financial institutions must continue to lead innovation if they want to compete and stay relevant as digital technologies continue to influence consumer behavior and market dynamics.

2 Customer Experience

Customer experience (CX) redesign is a key component of digital transformation in the financial and banking industry. It goes beyond simply advancing technology. The customer's journey must be understood and given top priority as banks and other financial organisations manage this digital change. In this regard, the following are important customer experience considerations:

2.1 Personalisation

These days' customers anticipate banking services that are catered to their interests and financial habits. The ability to provide personalised product recommendations and guidance is made possible by banks using advanced analytics and AI-driven insights, which improves client engagement (Hosanagar et al., 2014).

2.1.1 Personalisation Value in Banking

Historically, banks have been viewed as monolithic organisations that frequently provide services that are one size fits all. However, traditional banks are under pressure to innovate and stand out in the face of accelerating technological advancement and rising competition from fintech businesses (Kapoor et al., 2018). This is when personalization becomes crucial. Banks may create personalised services that not only meet but also surpass consumer expectations by studying the particular demands, behaviors, and preferences of each customer.

2.1.2 The Advantages of Personalisation

Enhanced Customer Experience
A more intuitive and seamless banking experience is made possible by personalisation. Customer loyalty and trust in the business rise when they feel heard and catered to (Li et al., 2015).

Increased Revenue Streams
Banks can capitalize on untapped revenue potential by providing specialised financial products and services. For example, a customised loan offer based on a customer's spending patterns might lead to a quicker conversion than a general campaign (Xu et al., 2019).

Operational Efficiency
Banks may streamline their processes, cut back on unneeded expenses, and improve their services by having a better grasp of the demands of their customers (Ngai et al., 2009).

2.1.3 Challenges with Personalisation

Despite its advantages, the path to effective personalisation is paved with difficulties:

Concerns About Data Privacy
Data privacy and security are seriously questioned when using client data for personalisation. Banks must strike a balance between providing customised services and protecting the privacy of client data (Romanosky et al., 2011).

Integration with Legacy Systems
Many traditional banks use outdated/legacy IT systems, which might make it difficult to integrate modern personalisation tools seamlessly (Verhoef et al., 2015).

Relevance and Accuracy
The precision and applicability of the insights discovered determine how effective personalisation is. Inaccurately predicting a customer's need might result in discontent and mistrust (Huang & Rust, 2018).

Banks should use cutting-edge technologies like artificial intelligence and machine learning to forecast customers' requirements even before they arise in the hyper-personalised banking of the future (Kannan & Li, 2017). Along with improving personalisation accuracy, the integration of these technologies will allow banks to provide customers with proactive solutions.

Finally, personalisation in banking represents a significant transition from standard banking encounters to unique financial journeys. Although personalisation has many advantages, banks must be aware of its drawbacks, particularly those relating to data protection. As a result of technological improvements, the future promises a banking experience that is even more personalised.

2.2 Omnichannel Experience

Customers want the same experience regardless of the channel they use to access services, whether it is mobile apps, online banking, or even in-branch. Consistency and smooth transitions between different platforms are guaranteed by an integrated omnichannel approach (Lemon & Verhoef, 2016).

2.2.1 Relevance of Omnichannel in Banking and Finance

Banks and financial institutions are at a turning point as a result of the growth of digital technologies and changing consumer behavior. Customers no longer connect with their bank exclusively through one channel; instead, they now demand and expect a variety of channels, each of which provides a consistent experience (Lemon & Verhoef, 2016).

2.2.2 The Advantages of Omnichannel Experiences

A Higher Level of Customer Satisfaction
Regardless of the channel customers choose, an omnichannel strategy guarantees that clients have a smooth experience. This reliability promotes more confidence and contentment (Neslin et al., 2006).

Efficiency in Operations
When different channels are integrated, financial institutions can improve resource allocation, streamline operations, and minimise operational expenses (Cao & Li, 2015).

Growth in Sales and Engagement
Banks may successfully cross-sell and up-sell their goods and services through a variety of integrated channels, which boosts sales (Verhoef et al., 2015).

2.2.3 Omnichannel Experiences: Implementation Challenges

Integration Difficulties
Significant technical and practical difficulties arise when synchronizing several channels, particularly when combining older (legacy) digital platforms with newer ones (Beck & Rygl, 2015).

Data Privacy and Security
With various platforms being used to handle customers data, there is a higher chance of security breaches and more regulatory challenges (Romanosky et al., 2011).

Branding and Messaging Consistency
Consistency in branding and messaging across media can be challenging, but it is essential to prevent customer confusion (Herhausen et al., 2019).

2.2.4   Banking's Future with Omnichannel

An even higher level of integration will define banking in the future. The omnichannel experience will be improved by the use of technologies like artificial intelligence (AI) and machine learning (ML), which will play crucial roles in providing predictive personalisation across channels (Kannan & Li, 2017).

Virtual Reality (VR) and Augmented Reality (AR) technologies may also develop into additional channels that can be incorporated into the omnichannel banking matrix as they advance.

In conclusion, the omnichannel experience, which promises an integrated and seamless customer journey, is the next step in banking and finance. The potential benefits are enormous for both customers and financial institutions as they work through the implementation hurdles. An even richer, more immersive omnichannel experience is promised for the future, powered by technological improvements.

3   Simplicity and Usability

Traditional banks must place a higher priority on the usability of their digital interfaces in light of the rise of FinTech firms that place a focus on user-centric design. The whole customer experience can be significantly enhanced by streamlining processes and improving user interfaces.

3.1   *The Value of Simplicity and Usability*

The financial and banking industry is characterised by complex processes and goods, such as complicated financial derivatives and insurance contracts with numerous terms. However, digital platforms have the ability to simplify these complexities.

Customers' top expectation is for financial platforms to be simple and easy to use (Zhou et al., 2010). This idea emphasises how crucial it is to create digital banking interfaces that put simplicity and usability first.

3.2 Advantages of Simple and Usable Digital Platforms

Higher Customer Trust

Customer trust can be increased by a platform's ease of use and simplicity, which increases transparency in how it operates (Kim et al., 2008).

Increased Engagement

The platform's ease of use fosters frequent customers interaction, which boosts transaction rates and expands service usage (Venkatesh & Davis, 2000).

Reduced Support Costs

Platforms that are simple and intuitive decrease the chance of user errors and the corresponding customer support requests (Lee & Kozar, 2006).

A Better Customer Acquisition and Retention Strategy

A positive user experience can significantly entice new customers and increase user loyalty among current ones (Herrero & Rodriguez del Bosque, 2008).

Problems in Achieving Simplicity and Usability

Combining Simplicity and Functionality:

It might be difficult to provide a full range of capabilities while keeping an interface clear of clutter (Cyr et al., 2009).

Multifaceted User Demographics:

Digital banking is used by a wide range of consumers, including elder generations and tech-savvy millennials. Designing for such a diverse customer base can be challenging (Pikkarainen et al., 2004).

Technological Changes That Are Rapid:

It can be difficult for banks to continually meet usability standards given how quickly digital technology is evolving (DeLone & McLean, 2004).

Future of Usability and Simplicity in Banking

Artificial intelligence and machine learning, promise to push the boundaries of simplicity and usability. In order to ensure a more personalised and straightforward experience, predictive analytics can help adjust user interfaces depending on individual preferences (Li et al., 2019b).

In addition, the development of voice-activated banking via smart assistants and augmented reality interfaces opens up new opportunities to improve usability.

In conclusion, simplicity and usability continue to be crucial as the financial and banking digital landscape develops. They are the cornerstone for creating loyalty among customers, ensuring engagement, and establishing trust. They go beyond simple design concepts. Financial institutions must put these principles first if they want to stay current and competitive as technology develops.

4   Security and Trust

Concerns regarding fraud and data breaches grow along with the growth of digital transactions. Increasing security precautions and educating users about them promotes client trust in digital platforms.

While providing unprecedented convenience, digital channels also carry significant vulnerabilities that could erode the basis of trust that traditional banks have worked so hard to establish over the years.

4.1   Security and Trust: The Dual Challenge

Worries About Security
Digital platforms are vulnerable to fraud, data breaches, and cyberattacks. Sensitive client data is increasingly being collected and stored in digital formats, making them attractive targets for malicious actors (Böhme & Moore, 2009).

Issues with Trust
When customers believe their financial institution is not sufficiently protecting their data or when they personally encounter security breaches, trust, the foundation of banking relationships, may be challenged (Richards & Hartzog, 2015).

4.2   Advantages of Maintaining Security and Trust

Client Loyalty
Customer loyalty is increased by a secure and reliable digital banking experience since people are more likely to continue with businesses they believe will protect their money and data (Crosman, 2017).

Continuity of Operations
Banks can guarantee continuous service, maintain customer confidence, and avoid the reputational and financial penalties associated with security incidents by preventing cyberattacks and data breaches (Biener et al., 2015).

Compliance with Regulations
By ensuring security, banks can comply with changing regulatory demands and avoid significant fines and legal implications (Basel Committee on Banking Supervision, 2018a, 2018b).

4.3   Techniques to Strengthen Security and Trust

Advanced Authentication and Encryption

Banks can increase the security of customer's transactions and data by utilising sophisticated encryption techniques and multi-factor authentication (Ali et al., 2023).

Customers Education

Financial institutions should proactively inform their clients about security best practices and the safeguards they have put in place to strengthen customer confidence (Vatanasombut et al., 2008).

Openness in Business Practices

Banks can align with customers expectations and regulatory requirements by being open and honest about their data usage rules. This promotes a trusting environment (Awad & Krishnan, 2006).

While the banking industry is undergoing a digital transition, this not only offers many benefits but also exposes substantial security and trust-related concerns. These elements need to be given top priority by financial institutions, not just as compliance exercises but also as fundamental tactics for preserving client relationships and ensuring long-term success. The next era of reliable digital banking will be characterised by the fusion of cutting-edge technology with open and moral business practices.

5   Instantaneous Services

Digital transformation has caused a paradigm shift in the financial and banking industry, which was formerly defined by outdated processes, conventional face-to-face encounters, and paper-based transactions. Customers' expectations for quick, effective, and real-time services in banking have increased as they become more acclimated to using digital interfaces in other aspects of their lives.

Customers now expect instant responses in the digital era. Implementing technology that allow for rapid loan approvals, real-time transaction updates, or immediate customer support can greatly improve CX (Foroudi et al., 2018). The financial and banking sector is going through its own digital renaissance, and as a result, it is dealing with clients who are getting impatient and wanting services right away (Shaikh & Karjaluoto, 2015).

5.1 Factors That Encourage a Need for Speed

Natives of the Digital Age (Internet-Born Individuals)
A generation that was raised with the internet and smartphones expects their banking interactions to be as quick and easy as their interactions on social media (Palfrey & Gasser, 2008).

A Threat from FinTech
Traditional banks are under pressure to produce solutions as quickly as FinTech firms, which frequently outperform them by utilising agile techniques and cutting-edge technologies (Zavolokina et al., 2016).

Globalisation
The demand for real-time banking solutions has increased as both business and personal matter become more globally interconnected, particularly in areas like cross-border transactions (Hann et al., 2016).

5.2 Consequences of Instantaneous Services

Customer Retention and Satisfaction
Improving customer satisfaction by providing immediate services could result in increased customer retention rates (Hossain & Prybutok, 2008).

Efficiency of Operations
Automated, real-time operations frequently result in fewer errors and an operating framework that is more efficient (Rogers, 2016).

Strategic Alignment
Banks that meet the demand for prompt services can establish themselves as market leaders by maintaining an advantage over both established competitors and up-and-coming FinTech rivals (Gomber et al., 2017).

5.3 Challenges and Things to Think About

Security Issues
Extended security checks can occasionally be bypassed by real-time processes, particularly in transactions, which could expose vulnerabilities (Li et al., 2019a).

Infrastructure Restrictions
It may be expensive and technically difficult for traditional banks with legacy systems to switch to real-time operations (Bátiz-Lazo, 2018).

Regulatory Challenges
Instantaneous services could run into regulatory obstacles that require navigation, especially in cross-border transactions (Arner et al., 2016a).

The financial and banking landscape is changing quickly as institutions are pushed to provide instantaneous services by the winds of digital change. Banks need to adapt if they don't want to become obsolete as customers expectations match the immediacy of the larger digital ecosystem. The key issue in the next stage of digital banking will be to balance speed with security, functionality, and regulatory compliance.

6 Feedback and Continuous Improvement

Establishing avenues for consumer feedback and actively implementing this feedback into digital transformation initiatives ensures that banks remain aware of the requirements and expectations of their customers (Rust & Huang, 2014).

6.1 The Role of Customers Feedback in Digital Banking

Product Development
Customer wants can be catered for through the development of additional features, improvements, or even totally new goods (Rogers, 2016).

Determine Pain Points
Direct feedback can bring to light bugs, usability problems, or other obstacles that obstruct the best possible user experience (Zhou et al., 2010).

Determine Strategic Direction
Aggregated input over time can help with strategic choices, from market positioning to cooperation opportunities (Oestreicher-Singer & Zalmanson, 2013).

6.2 The Need for Constant Improvement

The digital environment is always changing. What is novel today could not be relevant tomorrow. As a result, financial institutions must adhere to the principle of continual improvement:

Maintain Competitiveness
Traditional banks need to constantly improve if they want to stay ahead of or even remain relevant given that FinTech startups and internet giants are eyeing the financial services market (Gomber et al., 2017).

Be Flexible with Regulatory Changes
The banking industry struggles a lot with regulatory changes. Digital platforms can remain compliant without sacrificing user experience if they adopt a constant improvement approach (Arner et al., 2016a).

Utilise Technological Progress
Emerging technology, like blockchain and AI, can be used more effectively when a company is committed to ongoing improvement (Tapscott & Tapscott, 2016).

6.3   Continuous Improvement and Feedback Are Linked

In order for feedback to be transformative, it needs to be methodically incorporated into a loop of continuous improvement:

Feedback Gathering
Utilise digital tools to collect real-time feedback, such as chatbots powered by AI, feedback widgets, and in-app surveys (Kaplan & Haenlein, 2019).

Data Evaluation
Utilise data analytics to analyse the collected input and identify patterns, trends, and areas for concern (Chen et al., 2012).

Implementation
Prioritise feedback-based action items and incrementally enhance digital platforms or services (Deshpandé & Farley, 2004).

Communication
Customers' trust will be strengthened, and you'll encourage more interaction, if you let them know about the adjustments done in response to their comments (Mangold & Faulds, 2009).

In the financial and banking industry, digital transformation is not simply about deploying the newest technologies; it is essentially about improving customer service. Customer input becomes a compass in this situation, and constant improvement becomes the way forward. Financial institutions may create a responsive, adaptable, and future-ready digital ecosystem by fusing these features.

7   Accessibility and Inclusion

For many, the unparalleled convenience provided by the growing digitalisation of banking services is welcome. But it unintentionally runs the risk of leaving out particular groups of individuals, like the elderly, those with disabilities, or those who lack computer literacy (Servon & Kaestner, 2008). Therefore, even while digital transformation has the potential to change access, it must be approached from an inclusive perspective.

Accessibility for all users, including those with disabilities, should be a priority when designing digital platforms. Digital solutions should also strive to include underbanked or unbanked communities into the financial ecosystem (World Bank, 2022).

7.1 Accessibility and Inclusion: How Important Are They?

Increased Customer Base
By making sure that digital banking platforms are accessible, banks are able to serve a wider range of customers, including individuals who may have disabilities or other restrictions (Wilson et al., 2020).

Banks Have an Ethical Duty
Banks have an ethical duty to ensure that their services are fair and do not target any group of people unfairly, independent of their commercial interests (Rozas & Klein, 2010).

Regulatory Compliance
It is now a need for banks to comply with regulations that many jurisdictions now place on digital platforms with regard to accessibility standards (Ellis & Kent, 2011).

7.2 Strategies to Make Digital Banking More Accessible

User-Centric Design
By adopting the universal design principles, banks may make sure that everyone can use their digital platforms, regardless of their physical or mental capabilities (Seelman, 2001).

Assistive Technology
Using screen readers, voice commands, and other technology can increase accessibility for digital banking platforms (Jaeger, 2012).

Digital Literacy Programs
Digital literacy programs can close the accessibility gap, ensuring that everyone can use digital services. These programs provide training and support for customers who are unfamiliar with digital platforms (Gee, 2012).

7.3   Promoting Inclusion in the Ecosystem of Digital Banking

Localised Content

According to Warschauer and Matuchniak (2010), offering content in a variety of languages and dialects can make digital banking more inclusive for linguistically varied groups.

Cultural Sensitivity

By comprehending and taking into account cultural nuances in digital platforms, it is possible to assure greater acceptance among various socioeconomic groups (Leong & Sung, 2018).

Financial Literacy Programs

Digital platforms can provide resources and tools to improve financial literacy for underprivileged communities or individuals who have traditionally been excluded from formal banking (Huston, 2010).

The values of accessibility and inclusiveness must stay at the heart of the banking and finance sector as it advances toward full digitalisation. This strategy not only makes good commercial sense, but it also demonstrates a dedication to social responsibility and justice. It's critical that no one is left behind in this transformational journey as the digital world becomes synonymous with everyday banking.

8   Transparency

In the digital context, transparency refers to the openness, honesty, and clarity with which institutions govern, disclose, and report their operations, particularly to stakeholders and customers.

It is essential to express terms, conditions, and any modifications to services or costs in clear language. Transparent business processes not only increase customers confidence but also make them feel valued and respected.

It is essential to put the customers at the heart of the digital transformation taking place in the financial and banking sector. Institutions that emphasize and improve the customer experience as part of their digital initiatives are more likely to cultivate a culture of loyalty, maintain their competitive edge, and prosper in the changing financial landscape.

Transparency is increasingly desired in the age of digital natives. Given the complexity of the digital environment, stakeholders, customers, and regulators want financial institutions to be open and honest about their business practices (Basel Committee on Banking Supervision, 2018a, 2018b).

8.1 Transparency in Digital Banking: Its Increasing Importance

Trust Among Stakeholders

In light of the 2008 financial crisis's increased suspicion toward powerful financial institutions, openness is essential to establishing and maintaining trust (Mishkin, 2009).

Regulatory Compliance

As a result of new fintech applications and digital operations, regulatorys are progressively requiring higher degrees of disclosure (Zetzsche et al., 2017).

Operational Clarity

As banking operations become more digital, maintaining openness ensures that the internal teams can easily interact and address possible concerns quickly (Urbinati et al., 2020).

8.2 Transparency in Digital Banking: Different Aspects

Transparent Fee Structures

With the rise of digital services, consumers now expect to understand transaction fees, service fees, and any additional prices that may be there. According to Hann et al. (2007), financial institutions that use transparent pricing models frequently have an advantage in attracting and keeping customers.

Data Usage and Privacy

As banks use enormous amounts of data, it is crucial to be open and honest about how this data is used, stored, and safeguarded. Customer trust can be increased by communicating clearly about data privacy regulations (Martin, 2015).

Algorithmic Transparency

As Artificial Intelligence and machine learning become more and more integrated into banking operations, it is crucial to explain how these algorithms function, especially in situations where decisions must be made quickly, like when approving a loan (Pasquale, 2015).

8.3 Techniques to Increase Transparency in the Digital Transformation

Open Banking

This idea is a beacon of openness, allowing users to have control over their data and understand how it's used (Chiu & Ko, 2019). It entails safely and in-real-time sharing of consumer data with third-party developers.

Clear Communication Channels

Customers' questions about digital banking services may be answered by implementing platforms like chatbots, FAQ sections, and round-the-clock customer care (Gursoy et al., 2019).

Reporting Transparency

Regular publication of reports on an institution's financial standing, data breaches (if any), and other related issues helps solidify that institution's commitment to reporting transparency (Holland, 2009).

In the era of digital transformation, transparency is not only a catchphrase; it also serves as a guiding principle for the banking and finance industry.

Being transparent will help these institutions meet legal requirements, ethical obligations, and customer trust as they progress farther into the digital world.

In a time of information asymmetry, the financial and banking industry has a unique opportunity to establish new standards for accountability and openness.

The Use of Data-Drive Insights by Banks as Part of Digital Transformation

The utilisation of data-driven insights has become crucial as a cornerstone of banks' digital transformation. We examine how banks use these findings, their ramifications, and the benefits.

8.4 Data-Driven Banking

Due to a growth in online transactions, digital interactions, and the spread of internet-connected gadgets, the digital era has given rise to an abundance of data. According to Bholat et al. (2016), banks have realised the potential of using this data to streamline operations, improve client experiences, and generate new revenue sources.

8.5 Utilising Customer Data to Personalise Experience

Enhancing client experiences through personalisation has been one of the banking industry's most immediate uses of data insights. By examining consumers' transaction histories, online interactions, and feedback, banks can forecast their financial requirements, preferences, and behaviors (Servon & Kaestner, 2008). This makes it possible for banks to provide specialised financial products, specialised marketing, and even specialised financial advice, significantly increasing customer engagement.

8.6 Fraud Detection and Risk Management

The transformation of risk assessment and fraud detection processes within banks depends critically on data-driven insights. Banks can examine large databases to find abnormalities, examine patterns, and anticipate future fraudulent activity using machine learning and artificial intelligence models (Jagtiani & Lemieux, 2017). This safeguards the integrity of financial systems in addition to preventing financial loss.

8.7 Efficiency in Operations and Cost Reductions

For internal operations streamlining, banks have started embracing data analytics. They can forecast peak transaction times, automate repetitive processes, and optimise staff allocation by looking for trends in data. Data insights can potentially save millions of dollars in operational costs by assisting in the decision-making process for physical infrastructure choices such as branch locations, ATM placements, and other physical infrastructure (Awan et al., 2021).

8.8 Strategic Decision-Making

Banks are now able to make decisions based on facts rather than just intuition. Banks can decide strategically regarding product launches, mergers, and other big investments by examining market trends, customer feedback, and competitive landscape data (Amenu-Tekaa, 2022).

8.9   Challenges and Consequences

Although the benefits are clear, banks must proceed with caution. Challenges can include data breaches, ethical issues with data usage, and possibly regulatory repercussions (Zetzsche et al., 2017). Additionally, primarily relying on data-driven insights without human supervision may lead to over-optimisation and potential blind spots.

8.10   Conclusion

A big change in the operational strategy of the sector has been made with banks' adoption of data-driven insights. Banks must make sure they handle the complexity of digital transformation with a mix of technological innovation and ethical considerations, even while the benefits in terms of personalisation, efficiency, and risk management are significant.

Process Efficiencies in Finance and Banking Brought by Digital Transformation

Due to the digital revolution, the banking and finance industries have seen extraordinary progress in recent years. This transformation has brought about tremendous process efficiencies across multiple banking services, driven mostly by technological developments and customers needs for ease. The characteristics of these efficiencies and their effects on the industry are discussed below.

8.11   Digital Context

The banking industry has traditionally relied primarily on manual procedures, in-person encounters, and paper-based paperwork. However, with the advent of the digital age, these processes underwent a significant transformation, opening the door for quicker, more practical, and more effective processes (Tapscott & Tapscott, 2016).

8.12   Chatbots and Automated Customer Service

Numerous banks have introduced chatbots and virtual assistants to answer consumer questions in real time as a result of advances in artificial intelligence and machine learning. With fewer human interventions required, wait times have decreased, and service quality has increased. The extent of this efficiency is highlighted by a study by Arner et al. (2016b), which claims that chatbots can answer up to 80% of common consumer inquiries.

8.13   Processes for Digital Onboarding and KYC

The time-consuming Know Your Customer (KYC) and onboarding processes have been reduced by digitalisation. Instant identity verification is now possible because of biometrics, optical character recognition (OCR), and blockchain, which greatly shortens onboarding times and improves accuracy (Zavolokina et al., 2019).

8.14   Trading and Investment Using Algorithms

Algorithms have been used effectively in the financial sector to execute high-frequency trades and make investment decisions based on real-time data analysis. Such algorithms examine enormous databases in milliseconds, enabling investors to profit from minute market fluctuations (Chaboud et al., 2014).

8.15   Digital Wallets and Mobile Banking

Mobile banking and the use of digital wallets have increased dramatically as a result of the widespread use of smartphones. Customers may now perform a variety of banking tasks on the go, such as paying bills and transferring money, which speeds up transactions and improves convenience (Liébana-Cabanillas et al., 2018).

8.16   Challenges and Potential Future Effects

Despite these advantages, there are also challenges, such as regulatory ramifications, cybersecurity dangers, and data privacy issues. Additionally, infrastructure improvements and worker upskilling are continuing need as banks continue to innovate (Philippon, 2016).

9 Conclusion

Unquestionably, the advent of digital transformation has ushered in a new era of efficiency in banking and finance. The benefits, which range from better customer service to greater risk management, imply a bright trajectory for the industry's future, even though the sector must remain attentive to potential dangers.

10 Key Points

- Implementation of digital transformation initiatives and strategies could unlock costs and processes efficiencies and ensure sustainable growth, and improved service delivery which ensures improved customer experiences. In this chapter, we discuss digital transformation in finance and banking with a specific focus on servicing customers' changing behaviors, the use of big data and analytics to make informed decisions as well as operational efficiencies required when customer-centric models are adopted.
- Finance and banking institutions need to adjust their strategy to take into account the changing requirements and behaviors of their customers as the financial landscape changes along with technology improvements. The backbone of this evolution is digital transformation, which is supported by big data analytics and operational efficacy.
- A shift towards customer-centric models, supported by data-driven insights and operational efficiencies, is essential for financial institutions to thrive in this digital era. In the drive to meet and surpass customer expectations, those who can successfully combine the human factor with the technology component will emerge as frontrunners.

References

Ali, R., Jamil, M. K., Alali, A. S., Ali, J., & Afzal, G. (2023). A robust S box design using cyclic groups and image encryption. *IEEE Access, 11*, 135880–135890.

Amenu-Tekaa, K. S. (2022). Examining the survival strategies of banks in Ghana in the post-2017 banking crisis. *Research Journal of Finance and Accounting, 13*(2), 47–58.

Arner, D. W., Barberis, J., & Buckley, R. P. (2016b). The evolution of Fintech: A new post-crisis paradigm? *Georgetown Journal of International Law, 47*(4), 1271–1319.

Arner, D. W., Barberis, J. N., & Buckey, R. P. (2016a). FinTech, RegTech, and the reconceptualization of financial regulation. *Northwestern Journal of International Law & Business, 37*(3), 371–413.

Awad, N. F., & Krishnan, M. S. (2006). The personalization privacy paradox: An empirical evaluation of information transparency and the willingness to be profiled online for personalization. *MIS Quarterly*, 13–28.

Awan, U., Shamim, S., Khan, Z., Zia, N. U., Shariq, S. M., & Khan, M. N. (2021). Big data analytics capability and decision-making: The role of data-driven insight on circular economy performance. *Technological Forecasting and Social Change, 168*, 120766.

Basel Committee on Banking Supervision. (2018a). *Cyber-resilience: Range of practices*. Bank for International Settlements.

Basel Committee on Banking Supervision. (2018b). *Sound practices: Implications of fintech developments for banks and bank supervisors*. Bank for International Settlements.

Bátiz-Lazo, B. (2018). The emergence and evolution of digital banking. *Business History, 60*(5), 771–775.

Beck, N., & Rygl, D. (2015). Categorization of multiple channel retailing in multi-, cross-, and omni-channel retailing for retailers and retailing. *Journal of Retailing and Consumer Services, 27*, 170–178.

Berman, S. J. (2012). Digital transformation: Opportunities to create new business models. *Strategy & Leadership, 40*(2), 16–24.

Bholat, D., Lastra, R. M., Markose, S. M., Miglionico, A., & Sen, K. (2016). Non-performing loans: Regulatory and accounting treatments of assets.

Biener, C., Eling, M., & Wirfs, J. H. (2015). Insurability of cyber risk: An empirical analysis. *The Geneva Papers on Risk and Insurance Issues and Practice, 40*(1), 131–158.

Böhme, R., & Moore, T. (2009). The iterated weakest link: A model of adaptive security investment. In *WEIS* (Vol. 2009).

Cao, L., & Li, L. (2015). The impact of cross-channel integration on retailers' sales growth. *Journal of Retailing, 91*(2), 198–216.

Chaboud, A. P., Chiquoine, B., Hjalmarsson, E., & Vega, C. (2014). Rise of the machines: Algorithmic trading in the foreign exchange market. *The Journal of Finance, 69*(5), 2045–2084.

Chen, H., Chiang, R. H., & Storey, V. C. (2012). Business intelligence and analytics: From big data to big impact. *MIS Quarterly, 36*(4), 1165–1188.

Chiu, J. S., & Ko, R. K. (2019). Regulatory challenges and approaches to digital financial innovations. *Journal of Financial Regulation and Compliance*.

Crosman, P. (2017). Can banks rebuild public trust through digital advice? *American Banker, 182*(77), 1.

Cyr, D., Head, M., & Ivanov, A. (2009). Perceived interactivity leading to e-loyalty: Development of a model for cognitive–affective user responses. *International Journal of Human-Computer Studies, 67*(10), 850–869.

DeLone, W. H., & McLean, E. R. (2004). Measuring e-commerce success: Applying the DeLone & McLean information systems success model. *International Journal of Electronic Commerce, 9*(1), 31–47.

Deshpandé, R., & Farley, J. U. (2004). Organizational culture, market orientation, innovativeness, and firm performance: An international research odyssey. *International Journal of Research in Marketing, 21*(1), 3–22.

Ellis, K., & Kent, M. (2011). *Disability and new media*. Routledge.

Foroudi, P., Gupta, S., Sivarajah, U., & Broderick, A. (2018). Investigating the effects of smart technology on customer dynamics and customer experience. *Computers in Human Behavior, 80*, 271–282.

Gee, J. P. (2012). The old and the new in the new digital literacies. *The Educational Forum, 76*(4), 418–420.

Gomber, P., Koch, J. A., & Siering, M. (2017). Digital Finance and FinTech: Current research and future research directions. *Journal of Business Economics, 87*, 537–580.

Gursoy, D., Chi, O. H., Lu, L., & Nunkoo, R. (2019). Big data analytics capability and decision-making: The role of data-driven insight on circular economy performance. *Technological Forecasting and Social Change, 168*, 120766.

Hann, I. H., Hui, K. L., Lee, S. Y., & Png, I. P. (2007). Will the global village fracture into tribes? Recommender systems and their effects on consumer fragmentation. *Management Science, 60*(4), 805–823.

Hann, I. H., Koh, B., & Niculcea, R. (2016). The extent and evolution of standardization in the banking industry. In *Proceedings of the 37th International Conference on Information Systems (ICIS 2016)*.

Herhausen, D., Binder, J., Schoegel, M., & Herrmann, A. (2019). Integrating bricks with clicks: Retailer-level and channel-level outcomes of online–offline channel integration. *Journal of Retailing, 95*(1), 70–90.

Herrero, Á., & Rodriguez del Bosque, I. (2008). The effect of innovativeness on the adoption of B2C e-commerce: A model based on the theory of planned behaviour. *Computers in Human Behavior, 24*(6), 2830–2847.

Holland, J. B. (2009). Banks, knowledge, and crisis: A case of knowledge and learning failure. *Journal of Financial Regulation and Compliance, 17*(3), 294–308.

Hosanagar, K., Fleder, D., Lee, D., & Buja, A. (2014). Will the global village fracture into tribes? Recommender systems and their effects on consumer fragmentation. *Management Science, 60*(4), 805–823.

Hossain, M. A., & Prybutok, V. R. (2008). Consumer acceptance of RFID technology: An exploratory study. *IEEE Transactions on Engineering Management, 55*(2), 316–328.

Huang, M. H., & Rust, R. T. (2018). Artificial intelligence in service. *Journal of Service Research, 21*(2), 155–172.

Huston, S. J. (2010). Measuring financial literacy. *Journal of Consumer Affairs, 44*(2), 296–316.

Jaeger, P. T. (2012). *Disability and the internet: Confronting a digital divide*. Lynne Rienner Publishers.

Jagtiani, J., & Lemieux, C. (2017). Fintech lending: Financial inclusion, risk pricing, and alternative information. Risk Pricing, and Alternative Information (December 26, 2017).

Kannan, P. K., & Li, H. A. (2017). Digital marketing: A framework, review, and research agenda. *International Journal of Research in Marketing, 34*(1), 22–45.

Kaplan, A. M., & Haenlein, M. (2019). Siri, Siri, in my hand: Who's the fairest in the land? On the interpretations, illustrations, and implications of artificial intelligence. *Business Horizons, 62*(1), 15–25.

Kapoor, K. K., Tamilmani, K., Rana, N. P., Patil, P., Dwivedi, Y. K., & Nerur, S. (2018). Advances in social media research: Past, present and future. *Information Systems Frontiers, 20*(3), 531–558.

Kim, D. J., Ferrin, D. L., & Rao, H. R. (2008). A trust-based consumer decision-making model in electronic commerce: The role of trust, perceived risk, and their antecedents. *Decision Support Systems, 44*(2), 544–564.

Lee, Y., & Kozar, K. A. (2006). Investigating the effect of website quality on e-business success: An analytic hierarchy process (AHP) approach. *Decision Support Systems, 42*(3), 1383–1401.

Lemon, K. N., & Verhoef, P. C. (2016). Understanding customer experience throughout the customer journey. *Journal of Marketing, 80*(6), 69–96.

Leong, L. Y., & Sung, B. L. (2018). Digital banking: Enhancing customer experience via E-service quality. *Management Research Review*.

Li, T., He, Q., & Wu, D. (2019a). The impact of digital finance on household consumption: Evidence from China. *Economic Modelling, 83*, 345–358.

Li, T., Luo, X., Zhang, X., & Xu, H. (2015). Personalized online banking service quality, satisfaction, and loyalty in an oriental culture. *Service Business, 9*(3), 507–528.

Li, T., Xu, L., & Zhao, D. (2019b). How do technology readiness, platform functionality, and trust influence C2C user loyalty? *Journal of Retailing and Consumer Services, 48*, 69–78.

Liébana-Cabanillas, F., Sánchez-Fernández, J., & Muñoz-Leiva, F. (2018). Predictive and explanatory modeling regarding adoption of mobile payment systems. *Technological Forecasting and Social Change, 126*, 14–23.

Mangold, W. G., & Faulds, D. J. (2009). Social media: The new hybrid element of the promotion mix. *Business Horizons, 52*(4), 357–365.

Martin, K. D. (2015). Privacy notices as tabula rasa: An empirical investigation into how complying with a privacy notice is related to meeting privacy expectations online. *Journal of Public Policy & Marketing, 34*(2), 210–227.

Mishkin, F. S. (2009). Why we shouldn't turn our backs on financial globalization. *IMF Staff Papers*, 1–7.

Neslin, S. A., Grewal, D., Leghorn, R., Shankar, V., Teerling, M. L., Thomas, J. S., & Verhoef, P. C. (2006). Challenges and opportunities in multichannel customer management. *Journal of Service Research, 9*(2), 95–112.

Ngai, E. W., Xiu, L., & Chau, D. C. (2009). Application of data mining techniques in customer relationship management: A literature review and classification. *Expert Systems with Applications, 36*(2), 2592–2602.

Oestreicher-Singer, G., & Zalmanson, L. (2013). Content or community? A digital business strategy for content providers in the social age. *MIS Quarterly*, 591–616.

Palfrey, J., & Gasser, U. (2008). *Born digital: Understanding the first generation of digital natives*. Basic Books.

Pasquale, F. (2015). *The black box society: The secret algorithms that control money and information*. Harvard University Press.

Philippon, T. (2016). *The fintech opportunity*. National Bureau of Economic Research Working Paper, No. w22476.

Pikkarainen, T., Pikkarainen, K., Karjaluoto, H., & Pahnila, S. (2004). Consumer acceptance of online banking: An extension of the technology acceptance model. *Internet Research, 14*(3), 224–235.

Richards, N., & Hartzog, W. (2015). Taking trust seriously in privacy law. *Stanford Technology Law Review, 19*, 431.

Rogers, D. L. (2016). *The digital transformation playbook: Rethink your business for the digital age*. Columbia University Press.

Romanosky, S., Telang, R., & Acquisti, A. (2011). Do data breach disclosure laws reduce identity theft? *Journal of Policy Analysis and Management, 30*(2), 256–286.

Rozas, L. W., & Klein, W. C. (2010). The value and purpose of the traditional qualitative literature review. *Journal of Evidence-Based Social Work, 7*(5), 387–399.

Rust, R. T., & Huang, M. H. (2014). The service revolution and the transformation of marketing science. *Marketing Science, 33*(2), 206–221.

Seelman, K. D. (2001). *Universal design, usability, and accessibility: A review of concepts, principles, projects, and research*. Assistive technology and information technology use and need by persons with disabilities in the United States, 2.

Servon, L. J., & Kaestner, R. (2008). Consumer financial literacy and the impact of online banking on the financial behavior of lower-income bank customers. *Journal of Consumer Affairs, 42*(2), 271–305.

Shaikh, A. A., & Karjaluoto, H. (2015). Mobile banking adoption: A literature review. *Telematics and Informatics, 32*(1), 129–142.

Tapscott, D., & Tapscott, A. (2016). *Blockchain revolution: How the technology behind bitcoin is changing money, business, and the world*. Penguin.

Urbinati, A., Chiaroni, D., Chiesa, V., & Frattini, F. (2020). The role of digital technologies in open innovation processes: An exploratory multiple case study analysis. *R&d Management, 50*(1), 136–160.

Vatanasombut, B., Igbaria, M., Stylianou, A. C., & Rodgers, W. (2008). Information systems continuance intention of web-based applications customers: The case of online banking. *Information & Management, 45*(7), 419–428.

Venkatesh, V., & Davis, F. D. (2000). A theoretical extension of the technology acceptance model: Four longitudinal field studies. *Management Science, 46*(2), 186–204.

Verhoef, P. C., Kannan, P. K., & Inman, J. J. (2015). From multi-channel retailing to omnichannel retailing: Introduction to the special issue on multi-channel retailing. *Journal of Retailing, 91*(2), 174–181.

Warschauer, M., & Matuchniak, T. (2010). New technology and digital worlds: Analyzing evidence of equity in access, use, and outcomes. *Review of Research in Education, 34*(1), 179–225.

Westerman, G., Calméjane, C., Bonnet, D., Ferraris, P., & McAfee, A. (2011). *Digital transformation: A roadmap for billion-dollar organizations.* MIT Center for Digital Business and Capgemini Consulting.

Wilson, F., Tillotson, J., & Harwood, T. (2020). Algorithmic (re) ordering and digital inclusion: Cash, fintech, and the geographies of payday lending. *Geoforum, 114,* 10–18.

World Bank. (2022). *Financial inclusion.* World Bank Group. https://www.worldbank.org/en/topic/financialinclusion/overview

Xu, L., Li, D., & Liu, Z. (2019). The effect of online service quality of internet-only banks on user behavior: A comparison of the SEM and fsQCA models. *Information & Management, 56*(1), 45–58.

Zavolokina, L., Dolata, M., & Schwabe, G. (2016). The FinTech phenomenon: Antecedents of financial innovation perceived by the popular press. *Financial Innovation, 2*(1), 1–16.

Zavolokina, L., Dolata, M., & Schwabe, G. (2019). The landscape of blockchain adoption in the financial services. *Business & Information Systems Engineering, 61*(6), 741–749.

Zetzsche, D. A., Buckley, R. P., Arner, D. W., & Barberis, J. N. (2017). From FinTech to TechFin: The regulatory challenges of data-driven finance. *New York University Journal of Law and Business, 14,* 393.

Zhou, T., Lu, Y., & Wang, B. (2010). Integrating TTF and UTAUT to explain mobile banking user adoption. *Computers in Human Behavior, 26*(4), 760–767.

Digital Transformation in the Auditing Environment

Varaidzo Denhere (ID)

Abstract Digital transformation (DT) is contemporary and has been a buzzword in recent years. The concept has gripped most economic sectors and regulatory bodies including the International Auditing and Assurance Standards Board (IAASB) to the extent that the board had to call for a research study to examine digital transformation in the external audit space. The purpose of the study was to inform the initiatives of setting standards to guide the employment of technology in audit engagements. One of the things that DT has done in auditing is to change the nature of the data that auditors work with. This stemmed from the soaring digitalisation of business processes. Among other things, auditors found themselves having to work with larger volumes of data than they did before digitalisation. This had a ripple effect on the auditing procedures. The auditing space is highly regulated hence the outset of digital transformation had a destructive effect on the traditional way of doing things in this space. The digital transformation had implications for the regulation of auditing and meant that the existing International Standards on Auditing (ISA) had to be revisited and reviewed. Against this backdrop, this chapter sought to examine the adoption of digital technologies in the auditing environment through the lenses of Technology Task Fit Theory (TTF). The chapter will give a brief background and a definition of digital transformation before describing the audit process. Furthermore, the chapter will describe the factors that affect the adoption of digital transformation in auditing engagements. It will also examine the adoption of digital technologies in the auditing space as well as how auditing has been transformed by digital technologies including implications of DT on International Standards on Auditing (ISA). The chapter ends with a focus on the benefits and challenges of employing digital transformation in auditing.

V. Denhere (✉)
Johannesburg Business School, University of Johannesburg, Johannesburg, South Africa
e-mail: vdenhere@uj.ac.za

© The Author(s), under exclusive license to Springer Nature Switzerland AG 2024
T. Moloi (ed.), *Digital Transformation in South Africa*, Professional Practice in Governance and Public Organizations,
https://doi.org/10.1007/978-3-031-52403-5_9

1   Introduction

Digital transformation (DT) has a long history that dates back to the late 1970s but has been lying low almost for three decades. However, the continuous increase in the usage of digital technologies bringing forth innumerable changes in business saw the digital transformation concept bouncing back in the year 2000 (Van Veldhoven & Vanthienen, 2022). Furthermore, a renewed focus on the concept has been observed during the past decade with a new urgency witnessed specifically during the COVID-19 period (OECD, 2020). Reis et al. (2018) asserted that the popularity of DT by both researchers and practitioners rapidly grew after 2014. The concept has gripped most industrial sectors and regulatory bodies including the International Auditing and Assurance Standards Board (IAASB) to an extent that in 2021 the board had to call for a literature review research study to examine digital transformation in the external audit space (Davies, 2022). The research was conducted by members of the International Association for Accounting Education and Research (IAAER) and the results revealed a growing interest in the publication of digital transformation-related research observed over recent years. Furthermore, the study also observed that research on external auditors' use of emerging technologies was still in its genesis. Against this backdrop, this chapter sought to examine the adoption of digital technologies in the auditing environment through the Technology Task Fit Theory lenses, and also to investigate how the auditing sector has been transformed by digital technologies.

Extant literature indicates that there is no consensus on a common definition of digital transformation. According to McKinsey & Company (2023), the concept has become a catchall term because it is perceived differently by different people. This is a challenge because business leaders would lack a clear understanding of DT and would not be able to align their organisation around relevant digital transformation programs. Due to the different perceptions of the concept, DT has numerous definitions. One of the definitions is by Plekhanov et al. (2022) who refer to DT as "*the use of digital technologies to create new or to reform existing business models and processes or to support the transformation of organizational structures, resources, or relationships with internal and external players.*" McKinsey & Company (2023) also defined digital transformation as "*the rewiring of an organization, with the goal of creating value by continuously deploying technology at scale*". DT brings total transformation to a firm's business model, and this should be aligned with the firm's business strategy.

Unlike the adoption of traditional technologies, DT is a radical change which aims at enabling new business models, improving operational efficiency, and enhancing customer experiences for a firm (Gertzen et al., 2022). In its function DT combines technical systems, which are the advanced digital technologies, and social systems which are the organisational practices to enable major business enhancement, improved customer services, and competitive advantage (Imran et al., 2021). To fit into the DT agenda, firms need to re-orient their business strategies in terms of the value creation paths from what they relied on in the past and adopt a variety of relevant digital technologies to remain competitive (Vial, 2019). The impact of adopting DT by any modern firm is spread across but not limited to the organisational chain of command, production, and relationships with clients, suppliers, and other crucial stakeholders (Plekhanov et al., 2022).

Verhoef et al. (2021) identified three external drivers for DT. These are digital technology, digital competition, and digital customer behaviour. Digital technology as a driver emanates from the continuous worldwide emergence of digital technologies that have reinforced the development of e-commerce. The outset of these technologies signalled the need for business organisations to digitally transform their businesses. The substantial rise of digital firms dramatically changed the business competition landscape. The competition sprung to a global level with increased intensity as big global firms with a lot of information began to dominate the global market. Other firms would realise that they are trailing and would find means to close the gap between those leading companies. This would prompt the trailing firms to also digitalise their businesses. Consumer behavior is also responding to the digital revolution. According to Verhoef et al. (2021), emerging technologies that support online search and social media tools, have enabled consumers to be connected hence they are kept informed and empowered to actively participate in the digital economy. DT is not going to end in the near future because the drivers behind it are constantly evolving. Therefore, digital transformation in business organisations is long-term as efforts to rewire organisations through technologies are continuous to enable competitiveness. Consequently, firms ought to adapt to these changes to leverage the digital technologies so that they remain competitive and attractive to customers. In the same light, the audit industry finds itself having to service these digitalised firms, and this leaves them without an option except to adopt digital technologies in order to remain relevant and competitive.

Against all this, business organisations are left with no option except to embrace digital technologies. However, the adoption of DT involves prevailing over some challenges. Gehrke et al. (2016) identified the following challenges faced by firms in their DT: absence of tools, methods, and concepts; obscure migration scenarios; absence of structure and direction for the management of the transformation; organizational structure; lack of collaboration and cooperation; time and budget constraints; lack of understanding; an unsupportive culture; and absence of competencies. Firms would need to develop a DT strategy for their businesses before adopting digital technologies. The strategy should include the creation of a culture that accepts change, willing to experiment, and continually learning for improvement. It is believed that transformations do succeed when they are cost-effective, incremental, and sustainable (Zhang, 2022).

The remainder of this chapter is structured in the following sections: Theoretical framework; The external auditing process; Factors affecting the adoption of DT for the audit engagements; Adoption of digital technologies in auditing; The transformation of auditing by digital technologies; Implications of adopting DT on International Auditing Standards (ISAs); Benefits and challenges of employing DT in auditing; and it folds with Key points.

2 Theoretical Framework

Digital transformation brings a profusion of opportunities to turnaround the auditing environment, but it also comes with its own challenges. This chapter looks at the adoption of digital technologies by the auditing sector through the lenses of the Technology Task Fit (TTF) theory which was developed by Goodhue and Thompson in 1995 to explain the utilisation of technology by examining the fit of technology to users' tasks or requirements (Marikyan & Papagiannidis, 2023). According to Andersone et al. (2021), the theory proposes the relationship between digital technology and the tasks that it aims to support. The objective of the TTF theory was to examine and validate the assumption that the utilisation of technologies causes heightened performance only on condition that technology functionality is consistent with the users' task requirements (Goodhue & Thompson, 1995). The TTF has a conceptual version called the Technology-to-Performance Chain (TPC) model which explains the relationships between the three main components of the chain, namely task-technology fit, utilisation and performance impact.

The founders of the TTF theory proposed it as an evaluation construct that assesses certain facets of technology seeking to understand how the use of technology impacts performance (Andersone et al., 2021). Consequently, according to the theory, a better performance and more efficient task accomplishment results from a higher fit between technology, task requirements, and individual abilities (Andersone et al., 2021; Goodhue, 1995). A higher adoption of technology would be a result of an acknowledgement by users that the technology indeed improves the execution of a task at hand and hence improved performance. Regarding utilisation, which is the state of being useful or beneficial, an assessment of user experience is conducted based on various aspects such as usability, data quality, and reliability of the technology. In this regard, the theory assumption is that users assess both the technology functionality and the extent to which the technology assists them in task accomplishment and suits their abilities (Andersone et al., 2021; Dishaw, 1999). With regards to performance, the improved performance is registered at an optimal TTF, a point where technology matches the characteristics that it intends to support and the individual abilities of the users (Andersone et al., 2021). At an optimal TTF, users may execute their tasks flawlessly (Spies et al., 2020).

The relevance of the technology task fit theory in this chapter lies in its conceptual version, the Technology-to-Performance chain. The components explained in this chain are very relevant as measures that anyone who is considering adopting digital technologies would consider. Before auditors decide on adopting any technology, they would want to establish whether the technology fits their tasks, and its utilisability i.e., whether it is beneficial to them, and whether it will improve their performance. Therefore, the TTF theory informs the intending user about what to check for on any technology before they adopt it. According to the TTF theory, it is only when the audit firms establish these three facts about a technology that they would consider adopting it. As described earlier on, a higher adoption of technology would result from an acknowledgment by users that the technology indeed improves the execution of a task at hand and hence achieving an improved task performance.

3   The External Auditing Process

The term auditing has various definitions from different scholars. Ajao et al. (2016, p. 33) defined it as *"a systematic and independent examination of books, accounts, documents and vouchers of an organization to ascertain how far the financial statements present a true and fair view of the concern."* Extant literature describes it as a financial review carried out to objectively obtain and assess evidence concerning assertions about economic actions and events to establish the extent of conformity between those assertions and established standards and communicate findings to the organisation. The process of auditing is conducted within a defined set of rules and standards and is about reliability, security, and confidence regarding the accounts being audited (Wallberg, 2017). The need for auditing to be conducted within a defined set of rules and standards shows that the industry is highly regulated.

The auditing process has been evolving over a long period due to technological evolution. The original purpose of auditing was to establish if certain accounting duties were honestly met, properly met, and if they were met according to the specific instructions and regulations (Wallberg, 2017). Furthermore, traditional audits were based on inquiry, observance, and reperformance, with auditors having had to be physically based on the client's premises over time to get an opportunity to interact and observe management's actions (Mupanguri, 2021). This setup has existed for centuries, but technology has revolutionised the auditing industry. Auditing has been described as a systematic process, implying that there are laid down phases that are followed in conducting audits. The audit process consists of four major phases namely: preliminary planning; field work; reporting; and post audit follow-up. These are illustrated in Fig. 1.

Out of the four phases of the audit process, the fieldwork phase has the greatest number of activities. It is in this phase that the auditor assesses the identified audit risks for the client business processes as well as evaluates the effectiveness of internal controls. Some of the fieldwork activities include walkthroughs of processes and systems, data collection, sample testing, observing workers carrying out certain transactions, and staff interviews. All the processes conducted in the field work one way, or another make use of data analytics in the era of digital auditing. Upon completion of the fieldwork, and before the reporting phase, a preliminary exit is conducted. This involves validation and feedback where the auditors present significant findings and preliminary observations as well as advisory and assistance services recommendations. It is after the preliminary exit that the auditors go and prepare a report which will communicate the findings. Finally, a post-audit follow-up will be made to determine the outcome of actions taken by a client as well as obtaining client feedback on the audit.

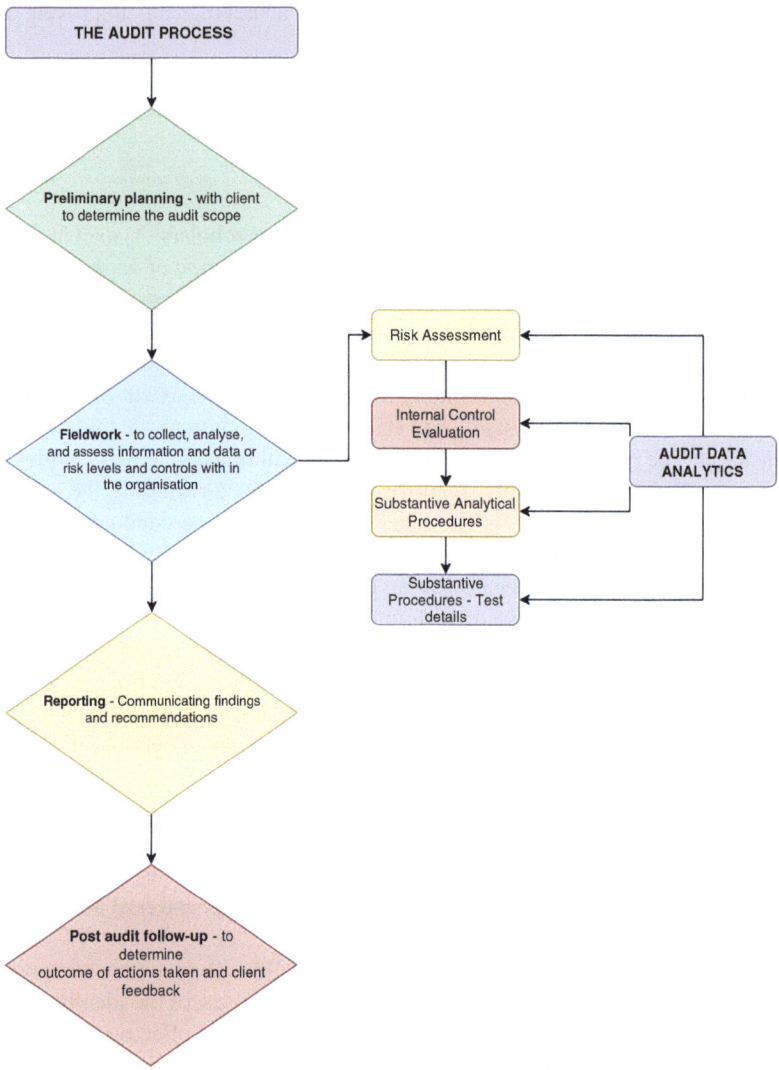

Fig. 1 The audit process. Source: Author's compilation

Before the advent of digital transformation, all the above audit phase activities would be done manually. However, DT has seen some changes from the arduous manual processes to automation and the use of other technological systems to conduct the audit process.

4 Factors Affecting Adoption of DT for the Auditing Engagements

A literature review study that was called for by the Auditing and Assurance Standards Board (IAASB) in 2021 to examine digital transformation in the external audit space and conducted by Barr-Pulliam et al. (2022) identified three categories of factors that affect the adoption of DT in the audit engagements (Davies, 2022). These are personal related factors, task-related factors, and environmental factors. Personal related factors affect the enthusiasm and willingness to adopt technology in the auditing environment. The task-related factors have to do with audit task complexity and how it affects adoption of technology, while environmental factors involve the regulatory issues, operating environment, geopolitical issues, and clientele influence. The following is an outline of the factors.

Personal Factors
- Training and skills—The accounting practice is lagging due to the inadequate university accounting curriculum which lacks components of the information lifecycles and the technologies of the information system. Hence tool specific training is critical.
- Auditor characteristics and behaviour—Certain auditor behaviours, among them agility, and critical thinking, are conceded to positively influence reliance and support for technology in the audit.
- Stakeholder/external attitudes—Varying views from peers and regulators might influence auditors' willingness to adopt technology.

Task Related Factors
- Task complexity—Task complexity moderates the effectiveness of technology used in the audit. For example, the increased complexity of descriptive analytics caused by voluminous data creates challenges for the auditor in understanding and interpreting this data and making appropriate judgments.

Environmental Factors
- A regional and global shift towards digitalisation, automation, and business intelligence—Government influence, competition of audit firms, regulation, the furtherance of technology, and availability of requisite talent significantly affect the adoption of technology.
- Influence of the audit client on adoption of emerging technologies—The audit client's expectation of auditor adoption of emerging technology as well as client support for data access influences how the auditor can deploy emerging technology and the regularity of use. Issues like the impact of the use of technology on audit fees may be critical. Furthermore, an expectation gap may exist regarding the level of assurance achieved from testing full populations of transactions.
- Business drive to achieve or maintain competitive advantage—Digital technologies present opportunities to increase audit efficiency and effectiveness. Larger accounting firms tend to have innovation leaders or get professional assistance to

identify, develop, and facilitate the digital transformation process whilst smaller firms tend to use off-the-shelf tools, a situation which puts them at a disadvantage in competing for both clients and human capital.

- Regulator response to adoption of emerging technologies—Regulators' uncertain response and acceptance of the emerging technologies may hamper their adoption. The uncertainty stems from the fear of a perceived breach of audit independence which consequently impacts on audit quality.

5 Adoption of Digital Technologies in Auditing

According to Tulinayo et al. (2018), digital technologies refer to a wide range of technologies, tools, services, and applications employing various types of hardware and software to facilitate services or activities by electronic means in the process creating, storing, processing, transmitting, and displaying information. These technologies have proved to improve productivity and efficiency when integrated with different production processes in various industries. Examples of digital technologies that can be employed in digital auditing include machine learning (ML), natural language processing (NLP), machine vision, speech recognition, internet of things (IoT), robotic process automation (RPA), smart analytics, the cloud, and blockchain. These examples can be classified under one of the following applications of artificial intelligence (AI): Assisted intelligence which automates simple tasks such as inventory counts; Augmented intelligence which supports human decisions such as performing risk assessments and fraud detections; and Autonomous intelligence which operates on its own without any human intervention such as automated transactions entry and automated tests of controls (Vasarhelyi, 2019).

Pizzi et al. (2021) described the digitalisation of auditing and accounting as a paradigm shift that has been ongoing during the last years. The shift has seen auditing evolving from an administrative to a strategic approach to operate more effectively within a complex and dynamic scenario. DT has introduced a new audit ecosystem that is implanted into Enterprise Resource Planning (ERP), a type of software used by organisations to manage daily business activities such as accounting and auditing (Vasarhelyi, 2019). The new audit ecosystem produces audit evidence and evaluation frequently through the implementation of audit heuristics at process levels. In this audit ecosystem the cloud is used for tapping information at all locations. Furthermore, the new audit ecosystem delivers evidence on an alert basis with scores and frequent indicators.

The coming of technological changes in the twentieth and twenty-first centuries witnessed the transformation of auditing but just like any other changes, auditors were hesitant to embrace the technologies though the changes had the potential to improve audit efficiency and effectiveness (Barr-Pulliam et al., 2022). However, with time and getting acknowledgment by users that the technology indeed improves the execution of a task at hand resulting in their improved performance as indicated by the TTF theory (Andersone et al., 2021), auditors began to embrace digital technologies for auditing. This is where the TTF theory applies. Before auditors decide on adopting any technology, they would want to establish whether the technology fits their tasks, whether it is beneficial to them, and whether it will improve their performance. This results in varying rates of digital technology adoption resulting in auditors, accounting firms, and their clients being at different stages of the digital transformation journey (Grant Thornton 2020; Barr-Pulliam et al., 2022).

5.1 Examples of Digital Technologies That Could Be Used in Auditing

The accounting processes which provide data and information that is subject to auditing are now generating big volumes of data resulting in data now labelled the new business currency (Vasarhelyi, 2019). The voluminous data has become too big for human analysis and requires auditors to employ relevant digital technologies at each phase of auditing. Table 1 illustrates some of the digital technologies that could be employed in digital auditing.

6 The Transformation of Auditing by Digital Technologies

The transformation of auditing was inevitable because business organisations which are the audit firms' clients had changed the way of doing businesses due to digital transformation leading to some changes introduced in their accounting processes. Consequently, the auditing industry found itself having to work with a new nature of data from the audit clients. Besides the changed nature of data, auditors found themselves having to work with larger volumes of data than they did before digitalisation. This automatically had implications on the auditing procedures. Particularly with the rampant remote working witnessed during and post-COVID pandemic period, most of the auditor's clients are also most likely to work remotely thereby calling for new interactive methods between the auditor and the audit clients (Mupanguri, 2021).

Mupanguri (2021) argued that auditors will continue to get pressure to be innovative in the ways they will conduct audits for the client who is working in an environment facing continuous technological advancements. The auditors would be pressured to conduct technology-powered and data-driven audits so as to deliver timely and reliable audits. Table 2 summarised the difference between traditional auditing and digital auditing.

Table 1 Digital technologies used in digital auditing

Digital technology	How the technology is used in auditing
Natural Language Processing	• Enables auditors to analyse unstructured data. • Text classification—NLP's text classification ability can be used in identifying negative and positive sentiments of news for the KYC about key personnel in the client firm. • Informational retrieval—Through optical character recognition (OCR) which converts hard copies into machine-readable formats, NLP retrieves key information from documents, such as invoices and delivery orders, and helps in vouching documentary evidence to verify the accuracy and occurrence of a transaction. • Synthesis of text—e.g., review of contracts, supplier invoices, and transcribed conversations.
Machine Vision	• Extraction of data from images—ML with the combination of OCR scans through extensive financial data, and swiftly detects anomalies such as duplicate payments and fraud indicators. • Inventory inspection—the combination of OCR and ML enables drones and IoT to perform inventory inspection.
Machine Learning	• Making predictions—ML understands patterns and makes predictions. This enables deep analysis of big data within a short space of time, in the reviewing of full population. • Fraud detection. • Classification of transactions
Blockchain	• Reduces risk of management override in systems—There is no 'super user' role in blockchain hence it is difficult to alter records. • It reduces the risk of manipulation of audit workpapers. • It ensures the reliability and integrity of the audit-related data collected. • It is a proactive inspection process to detect deficiencies in real-time.
Big AI or Smart Analytics	• Large-scale data analysis—structured data found in spreadsheets and ledgers. • Discovery of facts and relations that are difficult for the human mind.
Robotic Process Automation	• This can automate repetitive and manual tasks—availing more time for auditors to focus on higher-value activities. RPA can generate standard reports, update records, prepare documents, send emails, review general ledger, bank confirmation, and test transactions.
Sensors	• These collect real-time accounting information such as employee working hours and quality of inventory. • Assists in energy auditing.
The Cloud	• Storage of data and information to enable real-time access and data sharing from different locations.

Source: Author's compilation

7 Implications of Adopting DT on International Audit Standards (ISAs)

The disruptive nature of digital technologies requires the auditing regulatory body to understand how these technologies influence the industry. As such the International Auditing and Assurance Standards Board (IAASB) did not just watch and fold their hands but instead envisaged an ultimate impact on auditing standards from the

Table 2 Traditional versus digital auditing

Dimension	Traditional auditing	Digital auditing
Working Methods	Manual/Large number of manual integrated data collection and analysis modes, based on inquiry, observance, and reperformance. Less flexible and less efficient.	Automated/Technological/data-driven, computer-based data collection, storage, and analysis procedures. More flexible and efficient.
Audit phases	Characterized by regular and continuous phases, with poor overall audit effect.	Real-time auditing achieves the ultimate goal of auditing.
Standard processes	Standard audit processes are followed each time resulting in wasted time and energy on the same issues.	Digital audits achieve more value by revealing common issues from big data measurement, as well as quantifying and classifying possible problems.
Audit evidence and audit conclusions	Auditors rely on their subjective judgement to select audit evidence resulting in human bias errors.	Digital auditing can reduce human bias errors.
Audit sample	Auditors select an audit sample based on their expertise, making the sample unrepresentative, thereby increasing audit risk.	The whole population can be tested thereby reducing audit risk and increasing sample credibility.
Auditor's work focus	Auditors focus on collecting audit evidence and organizing information.	Digital audit searches for problems by setting up procedures in advance, thereby freeing time to focus more on analysing and dealing with problems, ultimately improving the efficiency and effectiveness of the audit.
Audit Location	Onsite/Client's premises	Remotely
Time Spent on an Audit	More time	Less time
Handling of Information	More errors/Less accurate	Fewer errors/More accurate
Data/information Storage	Hard copies of documents/Physical files/Paper Documents	Digital data on the cloud/Paperless
Audit Findings	Limited insights	Better insights
Auditor Skills Set	Traditional financial accounting qualification and finance.	Financial accounting and finance, digital technological skills, Big data Analytical skills, Critical thinking, etc.

Source: Author's compilation

digital transformation in the accounting and auditing fields. This led them to ask the members of the International Association for Accounting Education and Research (IAAER) to carry out a literature review research study to examine DT in the external auditing environment in 2021 (Davies, 2022).

The current auditing standards do not rule out the use of digital technologies and this is worrisome for accountants as they perceive that this clear lack of focus on using technology could result in regulatory scrutiny (Barr-Pulliam et al., 2022). Furthermore, some audit firms are hesitant to employ the data analytic techniques because their functionality could impact the perceived persuasiveness of audit evidence and hence have the potential to spiral their legal liability if an audit failure happens (Barr-Pulliam et al., 2021). As a result of these concerns, it is not clear whether there is need for completely new audit evidence standards that specifically address the use of technology in audit or the modification of existing audit standards to focus on the disruptive aspects of digital transformation in auditing (Barr-Pulliam et al., 2022).

With all these concerns, in late 2016, the board issued a Consultation Paper titled "Exploring the Growing Use of Technology in the Audit, with a Focus on Data Analytics." The board provided an awareness of both challenges and opportunities related to the adoption of technology in auditing with special mention of data analytics. The intention was to get feedback from stakeholders on whether there was a need for new or revised audit standards in light of the impact of technologies in auditing. The responses indicated that the regulatory board *'should consider whether the use of audit data analytics automatically addresses the sufficiency and appropriateness of audit evidence'*. From this conversation between the regulatory board and the stakeholders on the issue of audit evidence sufficiency, it emerged that standard setters and regulators need to take charge in addressing the impact of the disruptive technologies on traditional forms of audit evidence since they were perceived to be no longer adequate (Barr-Pulliam et al., 2022).

The concerns raised by auditors that the current ISAs did not prohibit the use of data analytics in auditing was acknowledged in the Consultation Paper and in response to these concerns the IAASB Technology Working Group (TWG) in 2020 issued several nonauthoritative support materials meant to guide auditors in understanding the relevant consideration for the use of automated tools and techniques (ATT) on audit engagements. These non-authoritative materials addressed the "*adoption of ATT related to audit documentation, identifying, and evaluating the risk of material misstatement, performing audit procedures, as well as addressing the risk of overreliance on technology and information generated by a client's information systems according to ISA 230, Audit Documentation, and the documentation requirements of other relevant ISAs*", (IAASB, 2020).

Summarily, the adoption of the digital technologies had an impact on the issue of audit evidence through the use of data analytics in particular and the use of automated tools and techniques. This warranted some deviation from the traditional convention stance on audit evidence and saw the IAASB as the regulatory board providing some non-authoritative materials to guide auditors. Currently literature indicates that there has been no reviewing nor formulation of new audit standards as a result of adopting the disruptive digital technologies.

8   Benefits and Challenges of Employing DT in Auditing

Being disruptive and ongoing, DT necessitates both challenges and benefits for the audit industry (Wallberg, 2017). Furthermore, being a buzz word with a lot of marketing going on, businesses do not always get what they expect from digital transformation because sometimes vendors overpromise and underdeliver (Nick, 2023). Some technology vendors may broadcast the benefits of DT without full understanding of complex processes involved as well as the investments required, while some will sell digital solutions that do not perform as portrayed (Nick, 2023). It is therefore advisable that businesses conduct thorough evaluations of technologies before adopting them. It is prudent that audit firms know the benefits and challenges of DT in their space.

8.1   Benefits of Digital Transformation on Auditing

8.1.1   Reduced Audit Risk

DT allows the creation of an intelligent auditing model that uses big data technology to traverse through audit data and enables the discovery of entrenched and deep-seated issues behind business models (He, 2023). Structured and unstructured data can be employed to augment the scope of analysis. The use of big data enhances the audit risk assessment process leading to accurate prevention of this risk. DT allows interoperability and resource sharing enabling auditors to quickly access audit information from audit clients and easily explore the embedded problems or clues.

8.1.2   Improved Audit Efficiency

Auditors can employ big data technology to handle large amounts of data in the audit process thus improving audit quality and efficiency. Automation of repetitive audit tasks can also reduce errors and improve accuracy. DT also enables real-time collection of audit data for audit projects thereby reducing audit costs (He, 2023).

8.1.3   Improved Audit Quality

A digitalised audit workflow enables data tracing of the entire audit process through a data analysis system. This allows the implementation of quality control procedures that enable the timely detection of problems.

8.2 Challenges of Digital Transformation on Auditing

8.2.1 Data Insecurity

The use of the cloud and other third-party platforms to store data exposes it to security issues. Audit data is used by auditors to perform audit procedures to inform audit conclusions as well as the audit report. Therefore if the data security is tempered with, it will compromise the whole audit process and conclusions rendering it invalid (He, 2023).

8.2.2 Cost Implications

Digital solutions require investment in terms of financial resources, digital infrastructure such as broadband, digital skills training, and maintenance among others. With the magnitude of investment required, the small and medium-sized audit firms may struggle to accomplish this. It is those big audit firms like the big four, and the middle-tier audit firms that would manage the cost implications and remain on the cutting edge of the audit industry as they would afford the digital technologies (He, 2023).

8.2.3 Lack of Skilled Human Capital

Digital transformation in the auditing industry demands specialised technological skills. This has resulted in the raising of auditors' skills requirements in terms of digital technology deviating from the traditional auditing industry which only required accounting and auditing knowledge, as well as work experience. Some of the skills required in the DT era for auditors include data analytics and processing skills, capabilities to work with the cloud platform, capabilities to operate audit softwares, critical thinking, and interpersonal skills (He, 2023).

8.2.4 Standardization of Information and Data

The DT era is associated with the generation of large volumes of both structured and unstructured data. It becomes a challenge for firms to standardise their data so that it becomes usable in audit engagements (Vasarhelyi, 2019).

9 The Current Status of the Auditing Environment

The employment of technology in the audit engagements continues to evolve since the initial introduction of technology in the practice. The review of research over the last twenty years by Barr-Pulliam et al. (2022) in the audit environment brought to the fore the insights about the evolving trends in the audit space. One of the insights is that there are a lot of emerging technologies that could be employed for auditing on the market, but research has indicated that the use of these technologies is still in the nascent stage due to their complexity of implementation and use (Davies, 2022). Furthermore, the regulatory body, IAASB, has acknowledged the adoption of emerging technologies in the audit environment but has neither reviewed nor introduced new audit standards. Instead, the body has only formulated non-authoritative tools and techniques on audit engagements to guide auditors in instances where technology has been employed in audits (Barr-Pulliam et al., 2022). A possible explanation to the IAASB stance of neither reviewing the existing nor formulating new audit standards could be the fact that the adoption of emerging technologies in the audit environment is still in the nascent stage. Most probably this low adoption of technologies has a low impact on the audit standards and might not warrant changes of the audit standards. Furthermore, the current hype around digital transformation does not correspond to the rate of technology adoption in the audit environment (Davies, 2022). Extant literature suggests the need for continued collaboration between academia, audit firms, standard setters, and regulators to achieve a significant adoption of emerging technologies in the audit environment.

10   Key Points

- The disruptive nature of digital transformation prompted the auditing regulatory board, IAASB, to call for a literature review research study to examine digital transformation in the external audit space.
- The major change that happened to the auditing industry is that auditors are now working with larger volumes of data than they did before digitalisation. This goes beyond the human mind and requires assistance from digital technologies to wade through the data and get insights during audit engagements.
- Adoption of digital technologies by audit firms is informed by the TTF theory when they get acknowledgement by users that the technology indeed fits to their tasks, it is useful or beneficial to them, and whether it would improve their performance.
- Factors that affect the adoption of DT can be categorised into personal, task related, and environmental factors.
- The majority of audit tasks can be augmented by specific digital technologies found on the market to improve audit efficiency and effectiveness.
- Changes introduced to the audit process particularly on audit evidence and the use of data analytics raised concerns with auditors and prompted the IAASB Technology Working Group to formulate non-authoritative tools and techniques on audit engagements instead of reviewing existing or formulating new ISAs.
- There are a lot of emerging technologies that could be employed for auditing on the market, but research has indicated that the use of these technologies is still in the nascent stage due to their complexity of implementation and use.

References

Ajao, O. S., Olamide, J. O., & Temitope, A. A. (2016). Evolution and development of auditing. *Unique Journal of Business Management Research, 3*(1), 032–040.

Andersone, N., Nardelli, G., & Ipsen, C. (2021). Task-technology fit theory: An approach for mitigating technostress. In *A handbook of theories on designing alignment between people and the office environment* (pp. 39–53). https://doi.org/10.1201/9781003128830-4

Barr-Pulliam, D., Brown-Liburd, H. L., & Sanderson, K. A. (2021). The effects of the internal control opinion and use of audit data analytics on perceptions of audit quality, assurance, and auditor negligence. *Auditing: A Journal of Practice & Theory, 41*(1), 25–48. https://doi.org/10.2139/ssrn.3021493

Barr-Pulliam, D., Brown-Liburd, H. L., & Munoko, I. (2022). The effects of person-specific, task, and environmental factors on digital transformation and innovation in auditing: A review of the literature. *Journal of International Financial Management & Accounting, 33*(2), 337–374.

Davies, D. (2022). *Supporting International Standards. Digital Transformation & Innovation in Auditing: Insights from a Review of Academic Research.* IFAC. Retrieved October 2, from https://www.ifac.org/knowledge-gateway/supporting-international-standards/discussion/digital-transformation-innovation-auditing-insights-review-academic-research

Dishaw, M. T. (1999). Extending the technology acceptance model with task-technology fit constructs. *Information and Management, 36*(1), 9–21. https://doi.org/10.1016/S0378-7206(98)00101-3

Gehrke, L., Bonse, R., & Henke, M. (2016, June 17–22). Towards a management framework for the digital transformation of logistics and manufacturing. In *23rd EurOMA Conference, Trondheim, Norway* (pp. 1–10).

Gertzen, W. M., Van der Lingen, E., & Steyn, H. (2022). Goals and benefits of digital transformation projects: Insights into project selection criteria. *South African Journal of Economic and Management Sciences, 25*(1), a4158. https://doi.org/10.4102/sajems.v25i1.4158

Goodhue, D. L. (1995). Understanding user evaluations of information systems. *Management Science, 41*(12), 1827. https://doi.org/10.1287/mnsc.41.12.1827

Goodhue, D. L., & Thompson, R. L. (1995). Task-technology fit and individual performance. *Management Information Systems Quarterly, 19*(2), 213–236. https://doi.org/10.2307/249689

Grant Thornton. (2020). *Innovation delivers audit quality amid current and future changes.* Retrieved October 10, 2023, from https://www.grantthornton.com/insights/articles/audit/2020/innovation-delivers-audit-quality-amid-current-future-changes

He, J. (2023). Study on the impact of digital transformation on audit risks of accounting firms: The case of Grant Thornton. *Frontiers in Business, Economics and Management, 9*(2), 269–274.

IAASB. (2020). *IAASB issues support material for audit documentation when using automated tools and techniques.* Retrieved October 20, 2023, from https://www.iaasb.org/news-events/2020-04/iaasb-issues-support-material-audit-documentation-when-using-automated-tools-and-techniques

Imran, F., Shahzad, K., Butt, A., & Kantola, J. (2021). Digital transformation of industrial organizations: Toward an integrated framework. *Journal of Change Management, 21*(4), 451–479. https://doi.org/10.1080/14697017.2021.1929406

Marikyan, D., & Papagiannidis, S. (2023). Task-technology fit: A review. In S. Papagiannidis (Ed.), *TheoryHub Book.* https://open.ncl.ac.uk/theory-library/task-technology-fit.pdf

McKinsey & Company. (2023). *What is digital transformation?* Retrieved October 19, 2023, from https://www.mckinsey.com/featured-insights/mckinsey-explainers/what-is-digital-transformation

Mupanguri, W. (2021). The future of audit is digital. *Ernst & Young.* Retrieved October 18, 2023, from https://www.ey.com/en_za/assurance/the-changing-role-of-the-audit

Nick, S. (2023). *The advantages & disadvantages of digital transformation #DX.* Retrieved October 20, 2023, from https://www.linkedin.com/pulse/advantages-disadvantages-digital-transformation-dx-nick-smit/

OECD. (2020). Digital transformation in the age of COVID-19 building resilience and bridging divides. *Digital Economy Outlook 2020 Supplement*. Retrieved October 20, 2023, from https://www.oecd.org/digital/digital-economy-outlook-covid.pdf

Pizzi, S., Venturelli, A., Variale, M., & Macario, G. P. (2021). Assessing the impacts of digital transformation on internal auditing: A bibliometric analysis. *Technology in Society, 67*, 101738. https://doi.org/10.1016/j.techsoc.2021.101738

Plekhanov, D., Franke, H., & Netland, T. H. (2022). Digital transformation: A review and research agenda. *European Management Journal*. https://doi.org/10.1016/j.emj.2022.09.007

Reis, J., Amorim, M., Melão, N., & Matos, P. (2018). Digital transformation: A literature review and guidelines for future research. In Á. Rocha, H. Adeli, L. P. Reis, & S. Costanzo (Eds.), *Trends and advances in information systems and technologies. WorldCIST'18* (Vol. 745). Springer. https://doi.org/10.1007/978-3-319-77703-0_41

Spies, R., Grobbelaar, S., & Botha, A. (2020). A scoping review of the application of the task-technology fit theory. In M. Hattingh, M. Matthee, H. Smuts, I. Pappas, Y. K. Dwivedi, & M. Mäntymäki (Eds.), *Responsible design, implementation and use of information and communication technology* (pp. 397–408). Springer International Publishing. https://doi.org/10.1007/978-3-030-44999-5_33

Tulinayo, F., Ssentume, P., & Najjuma, R. (2018). Digital technologies in resource constrained higher institutions of learning: A study on students' acceptance and usability. *International Journal of Educational Technology in Higher Education, 15*, 36 (2018). https://doi.org/10.1186/s41239-018-0117-y

Van Veldhoven, Z., & Vanthienen, J. (2022). Digital transformation as an interaction-driven perspective between business, society, and technology. *Electron Markets, 32*, 629–644. https://doi.org/10.1007/s12525-021-00464-5

Vasarhelyi, M. A. (2019). Digital transformation of audit – Trends, challenges and opportunities. *Rutgers Business School*. Retrieved October 20, 2023, from https://ecademy.eca.europa.eu/pluginfile.php/167/mod_resource/content/5/Digital%20transformation%20of%20audit%20%E2%80%93%20Trends%2C%20Challenges%20and%20Opportunities.pdf

Verhoef, P. C., Broekhuizena, T., Barth, Y., Bhattacharyaa, A., Donga, J. Q., Fabiana, N., & Haenlein, M. (2021). Digital transformation: A multidisciplinary reflection and research agenda. *Journal of Business Research, 122*, 889–890.

Vial, G. (2019). Understanding digital transformation: A review and a research agenda. *Journal of Strategic Information Systems, 28*(2), 118–144. https://doi.org/10.1016/j.jsis.2019.01.003

Wallberg, A. C. K. M. (2017). *The effects of digitalization on auditors' tools and working methods. A study of the audit profession*. [Master Thesis, University of Galve]. Sweden. https://www.diva-portal.org/smash/get/diva2:1115922/FULLTEXT01.pdf

Zhang, X. (2022). Incremental innovation: Long-term impetus for design business creativity. *Sustainability, 14*(22), 14697. https://doi.org/10.3390/su142214697

Digital Transformation of Corporate Reporting

Michael Adelowotan

Abstract In today's world where 'change' is arguably the new 'constant', accounting professionals are expected to 'reimagine and redefine' the future of the profession and the work they do to make them ready for the digital transformation enabled by the Fourth Industrial Revolution. The impact of digital transformation across businesses is being felt in an unprecedented manner and this is very significant and distinctive in both the latitude and rapidity of transformation in business and information ecosystems. Therefore, it is logical to state that accounting and corporate reporting are key functions that must align with the digital transformation age. Accounting professionals who understand the critical data in the internal and external reports will be in a better position to take greater advantage of digital transformation.

Corporate reporting is the concept that connects an organisation to its internal and external stakeholders. It includes financial performance reporting; social responsibility reporting; corporate governance reporting; risk management and governance reporting, sustainability reporting, audit and assurance reporting, and other forms of reporting, which are generally, classified as mandatory and voluntary disclosures. Thus, corporate reporting aims at communicating the value created by a business organisation as well as its impact on the people, society, and the environment in which the business organisation operates. This chapter explores the role of technologies in digitalizing corporate reporting through a consistent and efficient configuring and restructuring of the most informative quantitative and qualitative data from the source to the end users of corporate reports.

M. Adelowotan (✉)
Department of Accountancy, University of Johannesburg, Johannesburg, South Africa
e-mail: madelowotan@uj.ac.za

© The Author(s), under exclusive license to Springer Nature
Switzerland AG 2024
T. Moloi (ed.), *Digital Transformation in South Africa*, Professional Practice in
Governance and Public Organizations,
https://doi.org/10.1007/978-3-031-52403-5_10

1 Introduction

In 1966, the American Accounting Association (AAA) defined Accounting as the *'process of identifying, measuring, and communicating economic information to permit informed judgment and decisions by the users'*. From this definition, the necessity of communicating economic information to the users to enable them to make informed decisions and make informed judgments was clearly emphasized.

The advent of digitalisation has led to the concept of 'Digital corporate reporting', which has been referred to as the process by which paper-based corporate reports are converted and represented in a machine-readable format. The main technology developed to facilitate this process is eXtensible Business Reporting Language (XBRL), which uses 'tag' to assign contextual meaning to accounting information in corporate reports. The XBRL is an *'international, royalty-free data standard designed for digital reporting of financial, non-financial, performance or other information required by regulatory authorities'* (XBRL). However, the newer inline eXtensible Business Reporting Language (iXBRL) seems to be gaining greater attention because of its added advantage, which enables users of corporate reports to view content through the standard web browsers and ensures machine readability. There is now a greater demand for the use of open-source and machine-readable data in corporate reporting.

2 Concept of Corporate Reporting

Corporate reporting is a means by which the value created by an organisation and its impact on people, society and the environment is being communicated to users which includes investors, government, creditors, suppliers, customers, and other external users. Corporate reports are made up of financial and non-financial information, some of which are mandatory in terms of standards, regulations, and laws while some are discretionary in that they are not required by any standard, regulation, or law (Adelowotan, 2021). The general purpose of corporate reports is to ensure transparency, equity, and accountability. To achieve this purpose, corporate reports should provide information about the financial and non-financial position of an organisation in line with the generally accepted accounting principles, accounting standards, and applicable laws within and as at the end of an accounting or a reporting period.

Although a major constituent of Corporate Annual Reports (CARS) are the financial statements, the term Corporate Annual Reports is not restricted to the information in the financial statements alone but is inclusive of other information that may not be quantitative. Thus, CARs have a broader scope than financial statements which are designed to provide information on the financial position and the financial performance of a business organisation.

In general, the major constituents of the Corporate Annual Reports include but not limited to *"financial statements including notes to the accounts, background of the company, mission and vision, purpose and values, chairman's statement, Chief Executive Officer and Managing Director's Statement, Board of Directors, Business Model of the Company, Board's Report, Management Discussion and Analysis, Corporate Social Responsibility Report, Business Responsibility Report, Corporate Governance Report, Secretarial Audit Report, Economic Value Added, Statement containing salient features of financial statements of subsidiaries/associate companies/joint-ventures, Corporate Information, and Notice of Annual General Meeting."* (IASB, 2001)

3   Objectives of Corporate Reporting

According to B.K. Goyal in his book "Taxmann's Corporate Accounting, the major objectives of financial reporting are as follows:

  i. To provide information about financial performance (i.e., profit earned, or loss incurred) of a company in conformity with the generally accepted accounting principles, accounting standards and the law during the reporting period.
  ii. To provide information about financial position (i.e., assets, liabilities, share capital and reserves and surplus) of a company in conformity with the generally accepted accounting principles, accounting standards and the law as at the end of the reporting period.
  iii. To provide information about cash flows from operating, investing and financial activities of a company during the reporting period.
  iv. To provide information useful to present and potential investors, creditors, and other users in making rational investment, credit and similar decisions.
  v. To provide information on management accountability to judge management's effectiveness in utilising the resources and running a company. Management accountability includes safe keeping of assets entrusted, information about future activities, budgets, forecast financial statements, capital expenditure proposals, etc. Management accountability is beyond the company's legal responsibilities to shareholders, debenture holders and creditors.
  vi. To provide environment, social and governance (ESG) information. ESG information is important for understanding the long-term future and solvency of business similar to the number in the financial statements. A company's concerns about climate change, employee wellbeing, ethics, product safety sustainability, child labour, data security, etc. are highly relevant to decision makers.
  vii. To provide reliable information about economic resources and obligations of a company so that the users can evaluate its strengths and weaknesses, know its financial and investment capability, evaluate its ability to meet its commitments and show its resource base for growth.
  viii. To provide financial information for estimating earnings potential of a company.
  ix. To supply information useful for judging management's ability to use available resources effectively in achieving the organisation's goals (Goyal, 2023)

The information disclosed in CARs can be classified into two categories, the mandatory disclosures, and voluntary disclosures. Mandatory disclosures include general purpose financial statements which are information specified by law, the accounting standards, and relevant international and regional laws.

Financial statements are an important segment of CARs, and their disclosures are often guided by the generally accepted accounting principles, standards, regulations and laws. The major elements of financial statements are assets, liabilities, revenues, expenses, and equity. In relation to a company, the financial statement will include the statement of changes in equity, statement of changes in financial position, cash flow statement and the explanatory notes (IFRS, 2018).

3.1 Voluntary Disclosures

Apart from the general-purpose financial statements which are prepared and presented according to some principles and standards, management may decide to provide other forms of information to external users if they consider it useful and significant or because such information is required by regulatory bodies and government departments.

Voluntary disclosures relate to various matters and may take the form of research and development initiatives, introduction of new products and services, budgets, new customers, restructurings, capital expenditure, information technology and financial forecasts. Voluntary disclosures which are disclosures over and above those specified by law have become an important aspect of Corporate Reporting.

3.2 Mandatory Disclosures

In recent years, calls have been made for improvements in the content and the configuration of Corporate Annual Reports (Moloi & Adelowotan, 2018). In response to this, there has been an evolution of Corporate Reporting Practices in many jurisdictions across the world. This was the view expressed by the Corporate Reporting Dialogue (CRD), an initiative of the International Integrated Reporting Council (IIRC). The CRD was established with a view to promoting 'greater coherence, consistency and comparability between corporate reporting frameworks, standards, and related requirements relevant to Integrated Reporting (IR) which will consequently lead to improved efficiency and effectiveness in Corporate Reporting Practices (CRD, 2019).

According to Huguette Labelle, the Chair of CRD: *"The corporate reporting landscape is changing. For too long, reporting has been fragmented and disconnected from the strategic drivers of value. In an interconnected world, isolated change is insufficient to reflect the complexities of modern business and investment practice. Stakeholders are not intruders on the business conversation, but integral to shaping an organization's business model - connecting business practice to the economy, and the economy to society".*

In response to the demands of investors and other stakeholders for more inclusive and more qualitative insights into an organisation's performance, opportunities, risks, and prospects much more than what is currently being disclosed by the conventional corporate reporting platform, regulators and standard setters are taking various steps to enhance corporate reporting practices. This will enable organisations to provide a more comprehensive picture of their ability to create value over time.

The International Federation of Accountants (IFAC) is a body that has been working assiduously to promote an enhanced corporate reporting system that will promote transparency and instil confidence in the market by providing information that is "relevant, reliable, and comparable concerning measures derived from the financial statements (i.e., "non-GAAP" or "non-IFRS" measures), other "key performance indicators" connected to financial performance, and broader information related to value creation, sustainability or environmental, social, and governance factors"   (https://www.ifac.org/what-we-do/speak-out-global-voice/points-view/enhancing-corporate-reporting).

IFAC's partnership with the International Integrated Reporting Council (IIRC) has resulted in the enhancement of corporate reporting through the inclusion of more metrics and narrative disclosures arising from integrated thinking and reporting system.

According to IFAC, the need to enhance the corporate reporting system arises from the following:

i. IFAC believes that this reporting ecosystem, consisting of multiple and competing reporting workstreams, does not best serve the interests of capital markets, companies, or their stakeholders. The resulting complexity and lack of comparability can lead to inefficiency and increased costs—for both companies and investors.

ii. IFAC supports the development of and convergence towards relevant, reliable, and comparable narrative information and metrics (e.g., non-monetary volumes, number counts, ratios, percentages, etc.) for which suitable criteria can be developed to facilitate assurance conclusions.

iii. IFAC believes that such broader-based corporate reporting serves the public interest and that alignment needs to occur before a fragmented or regional approach to reporting and regulation becomes ensconced as standard practice. Both companies and investors increasingly support this approach. Ideally, Ideally, coalescing around best market practices or accepting a single set of high-quality standards should occur before regulatory intervention.

iv. IFAC supports the efforts of all participants in the Corporate Reporting Dialogue, the Task Force on Climate-Related Financial Disclosures, World Business Council for Sustainable Development, and other organizations who contribute valuable input toward the goal of enhancing corporate reporting. At the same time, IFAC reiterates the need for the emergence and implementation of a uniform, global approach. (https://www.ifac.org/what-we-do/speak-out-global-voice/points-view/enhancing-corporate-reporting)

Integrated reporting has been referred to as a document that presents relevant and reliable data on the company's corporate management system, strategic development initiatives, economic indicators, and information on the organisation's environmental, social, and governmental responsibilities. Integrated reporting enables the users of corporate reports to analyse the company's past performance to evaluate the prospects for growth and development in key operational areas. Integrated reporting therefore provides relevant information for the assessment of organisational values more accurately by providers of capital.

3.3 Corporate Reporting

Corporate reporting covers both non-financial information and financial information. The major characteristics of financial reporting is that it adheres to various local and international regulations and standards. Some of these regulations targeted at enhancing corporate reporting have been initiated and driven by organisations highlighted below.

International Integrated Reporting Council (IIRC) and Integrated Reporting (IR): In 2013, the Integrated Reporting Framework was issued by the IIRC to enhance corporate reporting around the world. The framework specifically focussed on how both financial and non-financial information could be aligned together in the form of Integrated Reports.

International Accounting Standards Board (IASB): The IASB is a major international body devoted to the issue of new IFRSs and amending the existing ones to improve financial reporting through principle-based standards thus enhancing its usefulness and relevance to their users. The IASB continually engages in research activities that may necessitate the review and amendments of existing standards.

Global Reporting Initiative (GRI): The GRI's Sustainability Reporting Guidelines G4 was issued in 2013 to facilitate greater transparency in corporate reporting. Also in 2015, the GRI launched its 'Reporting 2025 project' aimed at enhancing non-financial reporting in the form of sustainability disclosures ahead of the year 2025.

OECD Guidelines for Multinational Enterprises: The OECD Guidelines represent recommendations which are 'non-binding principles and standards for responsible business conduct in a global context consistent with applicable laws of each jurisdiction and internationally recognised standards'. Therefore, the guidelines seek to enhance contributions to the economic, social, and environmental progress of organisations all over the world.

International Organisation for Standardisation (ISO) 26000: ISO 26000 was first published in 2010 to guide social responsibility accounting and reporting by organisations.

Other frameworks, initiatives, and relevant developments: Other frameworks include the EU Accounting directive, the transparency directive, the Business Registrars' directive; the US Sustainability Accounting Standards Board; the Sustainability Stock Exchange Initiatives, the International Labour Organisation's Tripartite Declaration and the Guiding Principles on Business and Human Rights.

The overall objective of these initiatives and frameworks is to enhance the timeliness and relevance of corporate annual reports. Another objective is to overcome the challenges of the absence of key information and the complexity of corporate reporting. A more digitalised and principle-based reporting system may positively influence the impact of market forces on an organisation and ensure that relevant and comprehensive reports containing matters that impact the position, performance and prospects are disclosed.

4   Digitisation and Digitalisation

Technology has been and will continue to be an enabler and driver of corporate reporting practices. This is because the advent of technological advancement particularly in the era of the Fourth Industrial Revolution is affecting the development of corporate reporting practices. The use of new innovative technologies can render needed assistance in gathering, recording, and reporting relevant information for disclosure purposes. Specifically, the quality of non-financial information presented in CARs can be greatly improved with the aid of new cutting-edge technologies. In addition, these technologies will enhance access to information by users and stakeholders.

Digitisation is the "process of turning physical data into digital data while digitalisation is the incorporation of digital technologies into business/social processes, to improve them" (Shmarova & Ignatova, 2022). Digitalisation can transform how companies interact with their stakeholders and how they report their activities to them. In that case, digitisation could be regarded as a prerequisite to digitalisation.

Digitisation could also be referred to as a mechanical process of "translating physical data into a digital format" (Shmarova & Ignatova, 2022). Digital information normally consists of 1s and 0s which can be handled, stored, and used particularly through communication networks. Digitalisation will then make use of these digitized information to facilitate improvements in processes, procedures, and products (Shmarova & Ignatova, 2022).

In distinguishing between digitisation and digitalisation, Knudsen (2020) depicts digitisation as the process of converting data from a traditional, analogue format to a digital format while digitalisation relates to the expanded social and organisational processes linked to such transition.

However, to Østerlie and Monteiro (2020), digitalisation relates to the manipulation of digital representations. In this case, both digitisation and digitalisation have a cause-and-effect relationship. To digitise corporate reporting, the process will involve the atomisation and structuring of accounting data thus enabling automated extraction, analysis, and reporting (Locke et al., 2018).

According to Shmarova and Ignatova (2022), the concept of digitalisation covers many different areas of adoption/impact. These include:

– Upgrading a business model through digitalisation with the goal of netting extra value from the adoption of new technologies.
– The adoption of digital technology with a view to improving industrial processes, the benefits here include better quality products, energy savings and so on.

- Digitalisation is a driver to significant improvements in communication and information technology resulting in the transformation of the world's systems.
- The digitisation and digitalisation of everything lends itself to this process, in day-to-day life.

As noted earlier, digital transformation is affecting various aspects of human endeavours including business operations. This has resulted in the transformation of several business processes around the world. The systems of accounting and reporting have also been affected by this wave of digital transformation. This is noticeable in the efforts being made by some business enterprises to compile their corporate reports in electronic formats (Shmarova & Ignatova, 2022).

Furthermore, the effort of the International Accounting Standards Board in promoting digital reporting was noticeable in the establishment of a project referred to as "IFRS Taxonomy" which provides guides to the preparation of corporate annual reports in electronic formats. Through the process of digitisation, accounting information can be easily accessed by users at a granular level thereby ensuring that potentially significant changes to the accessibility, transparency, accuracy, and comparability of the information being reported are brought to the fore. At the same time, this process will enable the regulators to enhance their decisions with regard to investment flows and capital allocation decisions thus enhancing accountability to the stakeholders (FEE, 2015).

In a bid to advance digital corporate reporting, some of the major regulators from around the world have invested in some activities in this direction. For example, the European Union through the European Securities and Market Authority mandated the European Union-listed firms to file digital corporate reports in the European Single Electronic Format beginning in 2020. According to ESMA, some of the objectives of the provision are to enhance the analysis, comparability, and accessibility of corporate annual reports and to make the preparation of reports easier. The technology recommended for this exercise was the Inline XBRL and the financial reports published should be according to the ESEF taxonomy—an offshoot of the IFRS requirements for tagging information (ESMA, 2020).

Also in 2020, the Australian parliament recommended that digital corporate reporting should be made a standard practice for companies operating in Australia (Parliament of Australia, 2020). Again, regulators in countries such as Japan, China, and the United States have come up with regulations and infrastructures to enable listed companies in these countries to file digital corporate reports (XBRLInc, 2020; FSA, 2008).

For instance, in Japan, all filers were mandated in principle to make their submissions in eXtensible Business Reporting Language (XBRL) for fiscal years commencing from or after April 2008. They were expected to file in this format a quarterly securities report for the first fiscal quarter ending 30th June 2018. The underlying taxonomy used in preparing these financial statements is the 'EDINET Taxonomy' which represents the Japanese GAAP taxonomy. Through EDINET, the financial information of about 8000 organisations was expected to be filed and available to the public in the XBRL format (FSA, 2008). Although some countries have taken the initiative to ensure that companies digitise corporate reports, such efforts still require a complete transformation of corporate information architecture and infrastructure (Troshani & Rowbottom, 2021).

The disruptive technologies of the Fourth Industrial Revolution (4IR) will also disrupt the transformation of corporate reporting because it will challenge the traditional ways of collection, processing, and communication of corporate information. Many organisations may also be wary of the adoption of digital corporate reporting practices because of the difficulty in adapting to it and/or the high cost of implementation (Guilloux et al., 2013). It is important to ensure that corporate reporting practices that emanate from technological advancements are not fully dependent on only one technology as much as possible. In that case, there should be compatibility with other technologies that may be evolving.

5 Digital Corporate Reporting in Practice

At this point, it is necessary to highlight the underlying technology behind digital corporate reporting practices. In this section, we shall discuss the nature of digital corporate reporting, its underlying technology, and the possibility of changing corporate reporting practices considering the potential benefits for both the corporate reporting supply and demand chain participants.

Digital corporate reporting could be described as the process of conversion and representation of paper-based corporate annual reports into a machine-readable digital format. Before the advent of digital reporting, paper-based reports were being converted into electronic formats such as HTML and PDF. These electronic formats contain information that are digitised, the reports maintain the characteristics of paper-based reports. The implication is that the reports in electronic formats still entail manual processing before users can access data and information, and transfer them between systems before comparison between different organisations (Troshani & Rowbottom, 2021).

However, when digital corporate reporting is employed, contextual meanings are assigned to the information contained in the Corporate Annual Reports to make it possible for computer machines to understand what is being communicated. This in effect will enable users to obtain whatever type of information from any organisation required by them.

In the past, emphasis was placed on the use of the internet and social media (Twitter & Facebook) for providing information to various stakeholders, particularly the investors. Ramassa and Di Fabio (2016) investigated the use of social media in disclosing information to stakeholders and asserted that: "The use of Internet has radically transformed financial reporting and investor relations (IR) over the last twenty years, with a dramatic impact on how companies engage in the dialogue with the capital market".

Other digital reporting languages used before the advent of XBRL include electronic business eXtensible Markup Language (XML] initiatives, commerce XML, interactive financial eXchange, and investment research markup language. Perdana et al. (2015) show that XBRL "facilitates the development of enhanced business reporting (EBR) and standard business reporting (SBR). EBR contributes to improvements in financial information quality by providing relevant financial information, improving the reliability of financial statements, and enhancing accuracy and comparability of financial statements".

XBRL is an international standard for digital business reporting. XBRL International, the organisation behind XBRL, describes XBRL as:

> …a language in which reporting terms can be authoritatively defined. Those terms can then be used to uniquely represent the contents of financial statements or other kinds of compliance, performance, and business reports. XBRL lets reporting information move between organisations rapidly, accurately, and digitally.

Furthermore, it states that *'an annual report in PDF compared to an XBRL annual report is like comparing film photography to digital photography or a paper map to a digital map. XBRL tagging of financial statements is like 'barcodes for financial reporting'* (https://www.xbrl.org/the-standard/what/an-introduction-to-xbrl/).

The technology known as eXtensible Business Reporting Language (XBRL) is generally used to assign contextual meaning to the information in CARs. XML technology forms the basis of XBRL. The XML technology is being used to attach contextual meaning between computer systems. XBRL makes use of 'tags' to allocate contextual explanations to accounting numbers and textual information in CARs.

Digital Corporate Reports (DCRs) are the outcome of the conversion of Corporate Annual Reports (CARs) which have been structured with XBRL tags that give contextual meanings to the information being reported. The tags are classified with taxonomies which are used to define standard tags built upon the disclosure requirements and the accounting standards of a particular country. For instance, the United States GAAP taxonomy was based on the United States Generally Acceptable Accounting Principles while the IFRS taxonomy was based on the International Financial Reporting Standards (Troshani & Rowbottom, 2021).

Thus, the digitalisation of corporate reporting will require the introduction of processes of partitioning and tagging the disclosures made in the Corporate Annual Reports into a metadata element with the aid of XBRL. The definition, organisation and the standardisation of the metadata elements are made within a publicly available taxonomy. However, it is the responsibility of organisations to make decisions on the element in the taxonomy that may be tagged to a particular reporting disclosure item (Rowbottom et al., 2021).

Taxonomies are a very important aspect of the digital corporate reporting architecture because they make it possible for the preparers to produce digital corporate reports that are based on accounting standards as well as enable users to interpret the accounting data reported in the way and manner that has been presumed and intended by the preparers (Locke et al., 2018; Troshani & Rowbottom, 2021).

It is also possible to extend the taxonomy if a preparer wants the information to be reported to match a specific contextual tag. As such, the preparer will be able to develop his tags for certain disclosures on their peculiar situations (Locke et al., 2018; Troshani & Rowbottom, 2021).

Another technology that can be employed to present DCRs in human readable formats like the paper-based traditional CARs is the iXBRL which means the 'Inline XBRL'. This is achieved when DCRs are structured internally with the aid of XBRL tags which enables the production of a replica of DCRs in the form of a paper-based reporting format (Troshani et al., 2015).

6 Digital Corporate Reporting and Its Effects

The world's first large-scale digital reporting mandate by the United States Securities and Exchange Commission referred to as the Interactive Data project was aimed at creating efficient markets, lowering the cost of capital, and meeting retail investors' needs for transparency and accountability through digital corporate reporting (USSEC, 2009; Lowe et al., 2012).

Studies have been conducted on the usage of XBRL-based digital corporate reports and its effects on decision-making. Some of the early researchers concluded that users of XBRL-based digital accounting reports provide a better opportunity for the acquisition and integration of accounting information for investment decision-making purposes (Hodge et al., 2004). Others found that the use of XBRL-based reporting reduces the time spent by investors in collecting relevant information for a more efficient decision-making process (Arnold et al., 2012).

It was also found that XBRL-based financial reports are easier to use when compared with PDF reports, this has been made possible by the automated ratio calculation functionality embedded in the XBRL reporting formats (Locke et al., 2015). Other researchers observed that users of XBRL report formats found them to be more understandable, comparable, and relevant than the traditional PDF formats for profit forecasting (Birt et al., 2017). It is believed that more research studies will have to be undertaken to examine more functionalities of the XBRL-based digital reporting technology to discover the enormous strengths of this technology.

Studies have also been conducted on the time lag between the preparation and the submission of reports and the deadline for the submission. It was found that the use of XBRL-based digital reporting formats promote the effectiveness of internal reporting processes thus enabling organisations to file their annual reports on a timely basis. Furthermore, the use of XBRL reporting formats provides a platform for understanding the level of compliance with relevant accounting standards and policies since data for reporting purposes are captured at a granular level (Du & Wu, 2018; Zhou, 2019).

Some studies have also been conducted on the relevance of XBRL reporting formats on capital market indicators. Some reporting items based on the granularity of tagging and some XBRL extensions were found to be positively correlated to value relevance, information efficiency; forecast accuracy (Cormier et al., 2019; Li & Nwaeze, 2015, 2018). XBRL reporting format has facilitated the reduction in analysts' forecast errors as well as processing time. In general, XBRL reporting has significantly improved the communication of financial information between listed firms and capital market participants (Troshani & Rowbottom, 2021).

Other studies have confirmed that XBRL reporting has facilitated a more standardised and consistent reporting mechanism which may lead to a decrease in administrative burden for government agencies and at the same time a decrease in regulatory compliance costs on the part of reporting organisations (Troshani et al., 2015, 2018; Robb et al., 2016). As a result of digital reporting, regulators will be able to do more surveillance, assessment of risk, and monitoring compliance across larger samples of firms and organisations. Digital corporate reporting also provides the opportunity for organisations to reuse the information in XBRL formats across multiple regulatory functionalities (Troshani & Rowbottom, 2021).

However, it will be required that audit and assurance be conducted on the 'tag' or the 'taxonomy element' applicable to a particular disclosure item to ensure that the reports comply with standard taxonomy related to that disclosure item.

7   Key Points

- The XBRL-based digital reporting could be seen as a response to the consistent demand from investors, government agencies, policymakers, and other stakeholders for a system of reporting that provides more reliable, comparable, and consistent information that is relevant to organisational value creation and sustainability. XBRL-based digital corporate reporting is a timely and necessary call for a radical change to corporate reporting infrastructure to improve the accuracy, transparency, comparability, and accessibility of the information contained in CARs.
- As a result of the inherent advantages of DCR, some regulators across many jurisdictions have encouraged organisations within their jurisdictions to implement digital corporate reporting programmes to improve regulatory surveillance, monitoring, and control as well as reduce the cost and the burden of regulatory control. As a follow-up, mandates were given to organisations in some of these jurisdictions for the preparers of CARs to adopt digital reporting system by submitting their CARs in digital XBRL-based formats.
- Although digital reporting is not a new concept and practice, it has not yet been embraced by many organisations across countries and jurisdictions even though concerted efforts towards digital reporting started over two decades ago. In 2008, Japan issued a mandate for the use of XBRL electronic filings which was followed by countries such as China, the UK, Canada, India, Australia, Korea, and some others. When more countries adopt digital reporting, the availability and consumption of corporate information will increase thus enhancing greater transparency and competitiveness in the global market. Other benefits of XBRL include greater speed and accuracy, customised data extraction and data reusage, better data management ease of access to information and easier documentation.

Finally, all CARs supply and demand chain participants such as reporting firms, regulators, standard setters, auditors, users, and other stakeholders are being shaped but are also shaping the evolution and the development of digital corporate reporting.

References

Adelowotan, M. (2021). Developing a framework for human capital disclosures in Corporate Annual Reports. *Journal of Accounting and Management, 11*(1), 19–26.

Arnold, V., Bedard, J. C., Phillips, J. R., & Sutton, S. G. (2012). The impact of tagging qualitative financial information on investor decision making: Implications for XBR. *International Journal of Accounting Information Systems, 13*(1), 2–20.

Birt, J. L., Muthusamy, K., & Bir, P. (2017). XBRL and the qualitative characteristics of useful financial information. *Accounting Research Journal, 30*(1), 107–126.

Cormier, D., Dufour, D., Luu, P., Teller, P., & Teller, R. (2019). The relevance of XBRL voluntary disclosure for stock market valuation: The role of corporate governance. *Canadian Journal of Administrative Sciences/Revue Canadienne des Sciences de administration, 36*(1), 113–127.

Corporate Reporting Dialogue. (2019). *Driving Alignment in Climate-related Reporting*. Executive Summary, page iii, September 2019.

Du, H., & Wu, K. (2018). XBRL mandate and timeliness of financial reporting: Do XBRL filings take longer? *Journal of Emerging Technologies in Accounting, 15*(1), 57–75.

ESMA. (2020). *European Single Electronic Format*. European Securities and Markets Authority (ESMA), Paris. Retrieved October 27, 2023, from https://www.esma.europa.eu/policy-activities/corporatedisclosure/European-single-electronic-format

FEE. (2015). *The future of corporate reporting – Creating the dynamics for change*. Fédérationdes Experts-comptables Européens, Brussels. Retrieved October 30, 2023, from https://www.accountancyeurope.eu/wp-content/uploads/FEECogitoPaper_-_FutureofCorporateReporting.pdf

FSA. (2008). *FSA Launches New Electronic Corporate Disclosure System (EDINET)*. 17 March 2008, available at http://www.fsa.go.jp/en/news/2008/20080317.html. Financial Services Authority (FSA).

Goyal, B. K. (2023). *Taxmann's corporate accounting* (10th ed.). Taxmann Publishers.

Guilloux, V., Locke, J., & Lowe, A. (2013). Digital business reporting standards: Mapping the battle in France. *European Journal of Information Systems, 22*(3), 257–277.

Hodge, F. D., Kennedy, J. J., & Maines, L. A. (2004). Does search-facilitating technology improve the transparency of financial reporting? *The Accounting Review, 79*(3), 687–703.

IFRS. (2018). Foundation Conceptual Framework (http://go.ifrs.org/Conceptual-Framework).

International Accounting Standard Board. (2001). Presentation of financial Statements (IAS 1).

International Federation of Accountants (IFAC). https://www.ifac.org/what-we-do/speak-out-global-voice/points-view/enhancing-corporate-reporting

Knudsen, D. R. (2020). Elusive boundaries, power relations, and knowledge production: A systematic review of the literature on digitalization in accounting. *International Journal of Accounting Information Systems, 36*, 100441. https://doi.org/10.1016/j.accinf.2019.100441

Li, S., & Nwaeze, E. T. (2015). The association between extensions in XBRL disclosures and financial information environment. *Journal of Information Systems, 29*(3), 73–99.

Li, S., & Nwaeze, E. T. (2018). Impact of extensions in XBRL disclosure on analysts' forecast behaviour. *Accounting Horizons, 32*(2), 57–79.

Locke, J., Lowe, A., & Lymer, A. (2015). Interactive data and retail investor decision-making: An experimental study. *Accounting & Finance, 55*(1), 213–240.

Locke, J., Rowbottom, N., & Troshani, I. (2018). Sites of translation in digital reporting. *Accounting, Auditing & Accountability Journal, 31*(7), 2006–2030.

Lowe, A., Locke, J., & Lymer, A. (2012). The SEC's Retail Investor 2.0: Interactive data and the rise of calculative accountability. *Critical Perspectives on Accounting, 23*(3), 183–200.

Moloi, T., & Adelowotan, M. (2018). The perception of investment analysts on the decision usefulness of human capital disclosures. A South African context. *Academy of Accounting and Financial Studies Journal, 22*(5), 1–12.

Østerlie, T., & Monteiro, E. (2020). Digital sand: The becoming of digital representations. *Information and Organization, 30*(1), 100275.

Parliament of Australia. (2020). *Regulation of Auditing in Australia: Interim Report.* Parliamentary Joint Committee on Corporations and Financial Services, Parliament of Australia, Canberra. Retrieved October 30, 2023, from https://www.aph.gov.au/Parliamentary_Business/Committees/Joint/Corporations_and_Financial_Services/RegulationofAuditing/Interim_report

Perdana, A., Robb, A., & Rohde, F. (2015). An integrative review and synthesis of XBRL research in academic journals. *Journal of Information Systems, 29*(1), 115–153.

Ramassa, P., & Di Fabio, C. (2016). Social media for investor relations: A literature review and future directions. *The International Journal of Digital Accounting Research, 16*, 117–135.

Robb, D. A., Rohde, F. H., & Green, P. F. (2016). Standard business reporting in Australia: Efficiency, effectiveness, or both? *Accounting & Finance, 56*(2), 509–544.

Rowbottom, N., Locke, J., & Troshani, I. (2021). When the tail wags the dog? Digitalisation and corporate reporting. *Accounting, Organizations and Society, 92*(2021), 101226.

Shmarova, L. V., & Ignatova, I. O. (2022). Digital technologies for entrepreneurship in Industry 4.0. 25. https://doi.org/10.4018/978-1-6684-4265-4.ch006

Troshani, I., Janssen, M., Lymer, A., & Parker, L. D. (2018). Digital transformation of business-to-government reporting: An institutional work perspective. *International Journal of Accounting Information Systems, 31*, 17–36.

Troshani, I., Parker, L. D., & Lymer, A. (2015). Institutionalising XBRL for financial reporting: Resorting to regulation. *Accounting and Business Research, 45*(2), 196–228.

Troshani, I., & Rowbottom, N. (2021). Digital corporate reporting: Research development and implications. *Australian Accounting Review, 31*(98), 213–232.

USSEC. (2009). *Interactive data: Putting technology to work for American investors.* US SEC, Washington DC. Retrieved November 02, 2023, from https://www.sec.gov/spotlight/xbrl/interactivedata.htm

XBRL International. (https://www.xbrl.org/the-standard/what/an-introduction-to-xbrl/)

XBRLInc. (2020). *XBRl Implementations.* Retrieved October 30, 2023, from https://www.xbrl.org/the-standard/why/xbrl-project-directory/

Zhou, J. (2019). Does one size fit all? Evidence on XBRLAdoption and 10-K Filing Lag. *Accounting & Finance.* https://doi.org/10.1111/acfi.12444

Digital Transformation by Tax Authorities

Favourate Y Mpofu ⓘ

Abstract Revenue authorities around the world are digitally transforming their engagements and interactions with taxpayers and other stakeholders. These tax authorities are now remodeling their tax administration functions, technologically enabling the filing of tax returns and reporting requirements, as well as digitalising their auditing functions and procedures. The exponential growth of the digital economy and the challenges posed by the intangible and elusive nature of digital activities have all made the need for digital transformation indisputably critical. The importance of digital transformation of tax administration cannot be overemphasised for developing countries' revenue authorities because the enhancement of domestic revenue mobilisation and increasing tax compliance is crucial for these nations to fund public expenditure. Tax revenue constitutes a large share of the total national revenue of most developing and emerging economies. Digital transformation by its nature, speaks to technologically transforming processes and operations. Accordingly, for tax administration, it signals the need to embrace digital tools in delivering tax administration functions of assessing tax liability, communicating with taxpayers and other revenue authorities as well as facilitating tax compliance. Therefore, this has implications for tax administration responsibilities and functions, the resources required for digitising and digitalising the functions, change management, and the requisite digital skills of tax administrators. Through an integrative literature review, this chapter sought to give an insight into digital transformation in taxation in developing countries by explicating the opportunities, barriers, and possible externalities of digitally transforming tax administration. The review established that digital transformation plays a fundamental role in tax administration and tax compliance. It can help tax authorities to reduce administrative and compliance costs, enhance tax revenue mobilisation, minimise corruption, increases the efficiency of processes as well as improve transparency in service provision to taxpayers. Digital technologies can also be exploited for risk identification, man-

F. Y. Mpofu (✉)
University of Johannesburg, Johannesburg, South Africa
e-mail: fmpofu@uj.ac.za

© The Author(s), under exclusive license to Springer Nature
Switzerland AG 2024
T. Moloi (ed.), *Digital Transformation in South Africa*, Professional Practice in
Governance and Public Organizations,
https://doi.org/10.1007/978-3-031-52403-5_11

agement, and mitigation. The challenges include complexity, technological biases, poor digital infrastructure, the digital divide, digital and financial illiteracy as well as system failures among other constraints.

1 Introduction

Domestic revenue mobilisation is critical for the sustainable development agenda in most developing countries (Junquera-Varela et al., 2022; Mpofu, 2022a) and the realisation of the 2030 Sustainable development goals. Adequate government funding is essential for any government to achieve its fundamental objectives of infrastructural development, economic growth, sustainable development, strengthening peace and security as well as the provision of quality and effective public services. Even though most developing countries heavily depend on taxation for revenue mobilisation for funding government expenditure, these countries face challenges that compromise the effectiveness of tax administration efforts. These challenges include manual tax administration systems that are porous and fragile, high incidences as well as weak technical and financial capacities) of tax evasion and avoidance, rampant corruption, illicit financial flows (IFFs), and other revenue leakages (Mashiri, 2018; Mpofu, 2021, 2022a). These challenges are further compounded by the expansion of the digital economy that makes tax administration difficult and increasing base erosion and profit shifting by multinational companies as well as tax evasion and avoidance through aggressive transfer pricing strategies (Mpofu, 2022b; Sebele-Mpofu et al., 2021; Wealth et al., 2023). The importance of tax administration as a tool to mobilise revenue for the government and for the attainment of other economic objectives as well the challenges impeding effective tax administration leads to questions on the need and eminence of digital transformation by tax authorities. Digital transformation of tax authorities has thus become a priority for governments in developing countries. In the quest to broaden the tax base and improve the effectiveness of customs and tax administration, developing countries focus on harnessing digital technologies such as information and communication technologies (ICT) and the 4IR technologies such as Artificial Intelligence (AI), machine learning, big data, blockchain, cloud computing, the internet of things (IoT) and data analytics. Technology has both positive and negative effects, hence its application in digital transformation by tax authorities might yield both favorable and unfavourable externalities in tax administration. Therefore, for digital transformation to yield maximum benefits for tax administration authorities, these authorities need to have a clear and comprehensive strategy that addresses operational, institutional, legal, and regulatory matters associated with the application of technology in tax administration.

Digital transformation of tax authorities is a process of leveraging digital technologies (such as the 4IR technologies), data-driven approaches and modern communication systems to optimise tax administration processes. The digitalisation of tax administrations is no longer a choice, but a necessity, as tax authorities cannot continue lagging in harnessing of digital technologies to strengthen their operations because the digital economy and the use of digital financial services are rapidly expanding, thus signalling important implications to tax administration authorities (Mhlanga & Mpofu, 2023; Mpofu, 2022b, 2022c). The COVID-19 pandemic accelerated the shift to digital services in generally and particularly digital financial services. The usage of mobile money and online banking services grew tremendously in the African continent during the Covid-19 pandemic (Mpofu, 2023a). The envisaged benefits of digital transformation include streamlining tax processes, improving tax compliance, enhancing data management and analysis, and fostering collaboration between tax administration authorities and other government agencies. However, digitalization by itself will not fully address the challenges faced by some revenue administration authorities, and each tax administration needs to contextualize the solutions to the difficulties of digitalisation to its specific situation, needs, and priorities. To embark on planning and implementing a digital transformation of the tax administration, policymakers need to be familiar with the issues and areas that require careful planning, clear vision, and effective implementation. Tax authorities need to have a comprehensive digital roadmap to guide the implementation process and to ensure that resources and initiatives are aligned with the strategy and objectives of the organisation and those of the country. The digital transformation of tax administrations entails a range of benefits and challenges.

In light of the above discussion, through a qualitative approach, this chapter explores digital transformation by tax authorities in developing countries. It focuses on unpacking the exigent need for digital transformation in developing countries, the opportunities, barriers and challenges as well as the implications of digitally transforming tax authorities' functions and processes.

2   Definition of Key Terms

2.1   Tax Administration

Tax administration is defined as the process where tax laws are implemented and enforced (Alink & Van Kommer, 2011). Tax administrators enforce these laws while abiding to the mandate that they are given by the law. Tax administration assists in the management of tax compliance, detection and prevention of tax fraud, education of taxpayers on tax compliance issues and clarification of complex tax issues to taxpayers (Mikhaleva et al., 2021). Tax administration can be explained as the application and enforcement of tax legislation to ensure the effective mobilisation of revenue on behalf of the government.

2.2 Digital Transformation

Digital transformation describes the processes of applying digital technologies to enhance the accessibility, efficiency, and effectiveness of the operations of tax administration authorities. It highlights the process of digitalization to maximise efficiency and enhance operations as well as company performance (Vial, 2021). It involves the digitalization of tax administration functions and processes, thus phasing out the traditional or manual-oriented operations, with the aim of ensuring enhanced user experience and improved service delivery. Digital transformation of tax administration aims at achieving long-term and sustainable gains through activities such as fiscalisation and other digitally supported activities.

2.3 Tax Administration Authorities

Tax authorities collect taxes, enforce tax compliance, change penalties for non-compliance, and advise the government of tax policy and tax legislation (Mpofu, 2021). They administer both customs and tax legislation on behalf of the government.

3 Critical Success Factors for Digital Transformation by Tax Authorities

Tax administration authorities globally are exploring the possible benefits of digitalization driven by two fundamental objectives concerning improved service provision to taxpayers and increased revenue mobilisation. The increased digitalization of the economy poses significant challenges concerning the ability of governments to mobilise tax revenues effectively, fairly, efficiently, and transparently, especially in developing countries. These countries are characterised by limited financial and technical resources, a considerable and growing informal sector as well as weak tax administration capacities (Sebele-Mpofu & Mususa, 2019; Mpofu, 2021). The growth of the digital economy has further worsened the challenges of non-tax compliance, tax evasion, and avoidance as well as base erosion profit shifting and aggressive transfer pricing by multinational companies (Mpofu, 2022b, 2022c). These problems are linked to the intangible and elusive characteristics of digital transactions. Therefore, tax authorities find themselves grappling with new technological advancements, the growing digital economy and the subsequent tax consequences that are significant and ever-evolving. Digital transformation of tax authorities has now become a necessity rather than a choice if revenue authorities are to remain effective and relevant (Rahayu & Kusdianto, 2023). In summary, digital transformation of tax authorities is a fundamental process that demands careful planning, a clear vision, and effective implementation. Understanding the critical success factors that are pivotal for digitalisation by tax authorities to be a success is important because of the potentially positive and negative consequences of e-governments in developing countries (Bassey et al., 2022). Calitz et al. (2021) observe that the adoption of technologies by the South African Revenue Services (SARs) was influenced by resources and costs of implementation, organisational culture, skills and training, the impact of technology adoption, job security, trust, and attitudes towards change. There are crucial factors that tax authorities need to pay attention to in digitally transforming their operations. These need to be viewed in recognition of the fact that productive digital transformation of tax administration and its effectiveness in delivering the key goals of taxation such as revenue mobilisation, driving economic growth, controlling money supply in the economy as well as the prevention of dumping depends on the taxation ecosystem (Bentley, 2020). This ecosystem is made up of institutions, technologies and actors. Therefore, critical success factors determine the implementation process and the preparedness of tax administration authorities, acceptance by stakeholders of the digital system as well as the relevance and effectiveness of digital technologies.

3.1   A Clear Vision and Strong Leadership

There is a need for tax authorities to have a clear vision and strong leadership to drive their digital transformation. This also encompasses having a dedicated team responsible for digital transformation and this team is normally responsible for embedding digital transformation in organisation's strategy and culture. There is also a need to have a clear vision focusing on how digital transformation can strengthen tax administration and communicate this vision effectively to staff and stakeholders. This is because tax administration is dependent upon different stakeholders (Rahayu & Kusdianto, 2023; Twesige, 2020), hence the digital transformation strategy must be people-centred. Digital transformation combines both technology and people in tax administration. Tax authorities need to have a clear and well-articulated digital transformation strategy and this strategy must align with the key goals and objectives of tax administration. The strategy should identify the critical priorities and initiatives that the implementation process should address. There is a need to build a culture of innovation and change acceptance among employees.

3.2   Staff Development and Training

Tax authorities need to plan and conduct an assessment of the capital and technological investment needed to make digital transformation successful. Del Federico and Montanari (2021) emphasise the importance of investing in modern ICT and digital infrastructure. Tax authorities need to invest in staff development and training to ensure that the staff members have the skills and knowledge to use digital tools or technologies. Digital transformation introduces new technologies that can pose problems for tax administration employees as well as users of tax administration platforms such as taxpayers and travelers. Therefore, training, retraining, and awareness campaigns are essential components when introducing a new system.

3.3   Stakeholder Orientation

Tax authorities should ensure that digital transformation takes into consideration the needs of the various stakeholders, and the possible risks and impacts. The stakeholders' views could be sought on the development, design, and operation of new digital platforms or services introduced or to be introduced. Key among these stakeholders is the taxpayers (Del Federico & Montanari, 2021). Tax authorities should put the needs of the taxpayer at the centre of digital transformation, thus ensuring that digital technologies and platforms are easy to use (Ahmadi Zeleti et al., 2021; Twesige, 2020). Taxpayers must be able to interact with digital platforms and access clear and concise information about their tax liability that can assist in decision-making and tax compliance. For example, information on how tax computations are done which includes the definition of gross income, tax exemptions, allowable deductions, and tax credits and examples of these, such that taxpayers can get adequate guidance in calculating income tax liability.

3.4   Security and Reliability of Technologies and Digital Platforms

While technology has several advantages such as accuracy, time saving, quickness, and efficiency, it also has disruptive impacts and security concerns (Rahayu, 2021; Kamil, 2022). Therefore, tax authorities must invest in safe, secure, and reliable technologies to support digital transformation. This includes using modern digital infrastructure and applying the necessary security measures to ensure data protection, privacy, and confidentiality.

3.5   Creation Collaboration and Partnerships

Considering that digital transformation is ongoing and globally, with many revenue authorities looking towards modernising and digitalising their operations, tax authorities can benefit from collaborations and partnerships with different stakeholders such as other government departments, tax practitioners, the academia, and the private sector as well as other tax authorities (Rahayu & Kusdianto, 2023). This is critical in ensuring that best practices, new technologies, expertise, knowledge, and experiences are shared. Tax authorities can learn from the success and failure stories of others; this can equip them with the potential challenges that they must pay attention to navigate the digital transformation processes successfully.

3.6   Culture and Change Management

Considering that digital transformation brings a significant change in operations, combining human activities and digital technologies (Bassey et al., 2022), that implies that there is a need for employees to be equipped to embrace this change. Therefore, change management is an essential critical success factor in digital transformation in tax administration. Tax authorities must promote a culture of experimentation, innovation, technology use, and acceptance of change.

4   Digital Technologies and Digital Transformation of Tax Administration

In their efforts to implement digital transformation, tax authorities have used different technologies for different tax administration functions (Shakil & Tasnia, 2022). These technologies include general information and communication technologies as well as the 4IR technologies such as Artificial Intelligence (AI), Big data, data analytics, blockchain, and cloud computing.

4.1   Electronic Tax Administration Systems

Digital technologies have been used for automation and streamlining of operational processes, eliminating repetitive tasks (Rahayu & Kusdianto, 2023). This leads to cost reduction, minimisation of errors, increased efficiency, and improved risk management.

4.2   Online Filing of Tax Returns and Payments

As part of the digital transformation efforts, tax authorities are providing online platforms for taxpayers to file their tax returns and settle their tax obligations (OECD, 2017, 2018). This has made tax administration easier and more convenient to taxpayers thus improving tax compliance and increasing tax revenue mobilisation. This convenience can only be enjoyed if taxpayers have adequate digital infrastructure and appropriate digital skills.

4.3 Artificial Intelligence

AI technologies are being explored by several tax authorities in the quest to improve their processes, operations, and services provisioning to taxpayers (Faúndez-Ugalde et al., 2020). Examples of AI technologies include chatbots, machine learning (ML), natural language processing (NLP), robotic process automation (RPA), and data analytics (Kamil, 2022; Kumar et al., 2023; Mpofu, 2023b, 2023c). AI has been used to automate several tax administration functions such as the processing of tax returns, tax audits, and risk management. For example, AI-supported chatbots can be employed in responding to queries and questions from taxpayers. This can improve communication and quicken access to information as well as the resolution of queries. Nadat (2022) posits that the South Africa Revenue Services is considering the implementation of cloud computing and robotic process automation. Pantielieieva (2022) emphasise the importance of technology in making the exchange of information quicker and more efficient as well as in improving communication between diverse stakeholders. While focusing on Indonesia, Saragih et al. (2023) posits that the application of AI in tax administration in Indonesia could help strengthen the enforcement of tax legislation, increase convenience in filing tax returns and settling tax liabilities, improve tax justice as well as minimise tax non-compliance. The effectiveness of adopting and applying AI in tax administration was impeded by the absence of clear regulations governing the adoption of AI, the lack of AI skills and expertise, and poor digital infrastructure (Saragih et al., 2023). Therefore, the application of AI and big data in tax administration comes with several benefits, but the challenges concerning the application of these technologies in taxation need to be considered and addressed. These include practical, legal, and ethical implications (Pica, 2023).

4.4 Big Data and Data Analytics

Data analytics enable tax authorities to gain a better understanding of the tax landscape from the aggregated data and to pinpoint patterns and trends that can lead to the deduction of compliance challenges (Mehta et al., 2019). Data analytics have been employed in tax administration to enhance the tax assessment processes, risk identification, and management processes as well as strengthen monitoring capabilities. Walker-Munro (2020) adduces that the application of big data in tax administration should be viewed from the perspective of how it addresses the five themes of completeness, fairness, due process, opaqueness, privacy and inaccuracies. These themes speak to the canons of taxation as explained in the principles of economy, convenience, equity, efficiency, transparency, and simplicity among other principles. These principles characterise an ideal tax system (Mpofu & Moloi, 2022). The use of data analytics has helped in the identification and categorisation of taxpayers, making it easier to identify defaulters and high-risk taxpayers, thus improving audit selection, tax enforcement, reducing errors, tax compliance, and reducing tax evasion and avoidance.

Big data analytics coupled with machine learning have been used to address tax evasion in India. These technologies have been used to collect information develop a framework for scrutinising suspicious accounts and develop machine learning models to detect suspicious accounts and defaulters. This has increased tax compliance, the possibility of detecting tax evasion and lead to the reduction of tax revenue leakages in India (Mehta et al., 2019). The information collated from data analytics can be harnessed to improve the effectiveness of tax administration services and inform policy construction and review. This might lead to the construction of effective tax policy and legislation. Big data has the advantages of allowing the collection and processing of large volumes of data, the fast processing of this data, and categorisation of it into various forms, hence it has advantages of volume, velocity, and variety (Wang, 2020). Houser and Sanders (2018) posit that some revenue authorities have offices that specifically deal with the compilation of analytics that deal with the creation of analytics programs to improve compliance and detect potential fraud, taxpayer identity theft, and other issues. Using a broad range of data analytic methods, the tax authorities can then mine commercial and public data including social data from social media websites. Such as Instagram, Facebook, and Twitter. This mined data is combined with other information available to the tax authorities to run machine algorithms. These algorithms help identify potential non-tax-compliant companies and individuals. This improves predictive analytics and tax audits (Houser & Sanders, 2018). The application of big data and data analytics also comes with several challenges such as the security and protection of data and ethical usage of the data.

4.5   Internet of Things (IoT)

IoT can be employed for for real time data collection about economic activities and tax transactions. The data gathered can used to enhance tax compliance and revenue mobilisation. IoT may also be used for the development of novel services for taxpayers. The IoT provides great opportunities for the automation of tax administration, for example, digital devices of taxpayers (both individuals and organisations) can interact and share information with tax authorities on digital platforms. However, this raises challenges of ensuring the economic efficiency of automating of tax administration processes by using the IoT (Gashenko & Zima, 2018). The use of the internet in developing countries is also affected by electricity, internet connectivity, and digital infrastructure challenges.

4.6   Blockchain

Janowicz et al. (2018) explain blockchain as a technology that depends on a distributed ledger for the capture and transfer of value. Blockchain technology increases the transparency, anonymity, and auditability of transactions. Blockchain may be harnessed to create secure and safe records of tax transactions, thus enhancing transparency and disclosure of transactions. This could lead to the reduction of tax fraud, improve tax compliance, and heighten tax revenue generation. Blockchain may also be used in the development of tax systems and new ways of tax collection. In developing countries, the adoption of blockchain is constrained by the lack of modern digital infrastructure to support blockchain implementation and applications. Furthermore, the lack of government and political support is another challenge (Papathanasiou et al., 2020; Shava & Mhlanga, 2023).

5   Benefits of Digital Transformation by Tax Authorities

The benefits of digital transformation include streamlining tax processes, improving compliance, enhancing data management and analysis, and fostering collaboration between tax administrations and other government agencies (Skipin et al., 2020). In tax administration, digital administration processes are driven by data input collected from and on taxpayers, which is analysed to evaluate risks for audit, compliance and other tax administration purposes. Highlighting the possible advantages of digitalising tax systems, Rahayu and Kusdianto (2023) asserts "Digital transformation in tax administration reform is a major component in increasing capacity, efficiency, and managing big data and complex taxpayer activities with the hope that the speed and scope of tax administration will become wider and increase". While the likely advantages of digital transformation by tax authorities are multiple, each tax administration authority needs to tackle the challenges of digitalization according to its unique situation, needs, and priorities.

- **Enhanced efficiency and productivity**

Through digitalisation of tax authorities, tools such as blockchain, chatbots, cobots, RPA, big data and bibliometric identification can be harnessed to modernise tax administration functions (Shakil & Tasnia, 2022). Digital transformation may assist tax authorities to efficiently carry out their operations and automate multiple tasks. This could result in labour saving thus allowing time for staff to tackle more complicated tasks. Digitalising the tax administration authorities' operations could increase tax higher revenue mobilisation because more taxpayers may honour their obligations efficiently and accurately, thus broadening the tax base. Tax evasion is generally a problematic issue in lower and middle-income countries depending on traditional tax administration systems (Wealth et al., 2023; Sebele-Mpofu et al., 2021). Using machine learning and AI may increase transparency, and tax compliance and lead to a reduction to the risks of penalties and fines being charged to taxpayers by tax authorities (Shakil & Tasnia, 2022). The reduction and deterrence of taxpayers from tax evasion may help ensure that tax authorities maximise revenue mobilisation and collect revenue.

- **Modernisation and Upgrading of taxpayer services**

Digital transformation can enable authorities to bridge the gap between them and the taxpayer by making access to information as well as support easier for the taxpayer (Mehta et al., 2019; OECD, 2018). The presence of digital communication channels will help them provide taxpayers with the best services possible through the presence of an effective and efficient line of communication. An example of this is the presence of online portals, chatbots, and virtual assistants.

- **Reduction of tax administration and compliance costs**

Digital transformation can boost tax administration's cost-effectiveness, transparency, and efficiency. Robotic process automation (RPA) is a machine-based software technology that automates repetitive tasks (Moloi & Marwala, 2021) by introducing cobots and virtual assistants. Automation of certain tasks leads to a reduction in the costs of handling tax functions. An example of this is that the implementation of digital and electronic systems might help mitigate the costs related to paper-based filing of tax returns as well as processing. Digital transformation can lead to a reduction in compliance costs in the long run though in the short-term compliance costs might rise significantly due to the capital expenditure needed for digitalising accounting systems by taxpayers as well as training their staff to meet the needs of digitalised tax administration. The reduction in tax compliance of tax compliance may lead to increased revenue mobilisation.

- **Improved tax compliance**

Digital transformation might lead to improvements in tax compliance. Taxpayers can conveniently and schedule appointments with revenue authorities, file tax returns or complaints. Digital transformation makes it easy settle to tax obligations through e-service platforms (Skipin et al., 2020). It also serves as a means to deter tax evasion, tax avoidance as well as other forms of non-compliance (Kamil, 2022; Shakil & Tasnia, 2022). There will be an overall enhancement of the entire taxpayer user experience. The 4IR technologies can be used to improve tax compliance. For example, blockchain can be used to mitigate bureaucracies, inefficiencies and minimise corruption in revenue administration (Twesige, 2020). The advantages of digital transformation also come with challenges such as technical glitches that lead to system failures of unavailability, internet connectivity and the lack of adequate digital infrastructure.

- **Facilitate economic growth**

The introduction of digital transformation creates a more efficient and a favourable experience for the taxpayer. This reduces the fear of opening businesses from taxpayers, prompting them to invest more thus facilitating job creation which in turn assists in combating poverty and inequality. Digital transformation can help increase revenue mobilisation which can help governments fund economic growth and development (Mhlanga & Mpofu, 2023; Mpofu, 2023b, 2023c). Effective domestic revenue mobilisation is an important pillar for economic growth, sustainable development and the achievement of the SDGs.

- **Improved risk management**

The digital economy is problematic to tax revenue generation (Arthur et al., 2022; Mpofu, 2022a, 2022b) Digitalisation of tax administration processes can significantly support taxes towards taxing the digital economy such as digital services taxes (DSTs), digital financial services taxes (DFSTs) and value added taxes on digital transactions. This support could result in minimising risks of tax evasion and avoidance (Mhlanga & Mpofu, 2023). Additionally, digital transformation could assist in the monitoring and reduction of risks like fraud as well as cyberattacks, this is due to the use of data analytics to monitor as well as combat the occurrence of any unusual activity. Big data has been used for managing compliance risks, surveillance audits, business intelligence, revenue generation predictions and the optimisation of budgetary functions (Rahayu & Kusdianto, 2023). It is important to note that while digital transformation can improve the identification, evaluation, monitoring and mitigation of risks, it can also increase the risks of system hacking, taxpayer identity thefts and non-compliance due to system complexity and lack of skills.

- **Fosters collaboration between tax administrations and other government agencies**

Nazarov et al. (2020) and Skipin et al. (2020) argues that the advancement of technology and the growth of the digital economy are driving the increased modernisation of tax administration. Therefore, considering that the world is embracing digital changes in nearly all aspects of human life and business operations, digital transformation facilitates evolution with the times. Being in a digital age, the introduction of digital technologies in taxation could help reduce the challenges that come with taxing cryptocurrencies, the digital economy, digital financial services as well and e-commerce. Digital transformation is anticipated to prompt tax authorities to evolve and ensure that the digital economy is taxed appropriately.

- **Improved transparency and accountability**

Digital transformation could assist in enhancing transparency and accountability of tax authorities (Shakil & Tasnia, 2022; Rahayu & Kusdianto, 2023). Easy access to information may increase the ability of the public to hold the revenue authorities accountable due for their operations and the government for the way they spend tax revenue. Improved transparency and accountability of tax authorities could stimulate fairness and boost tax morale as well as trust in tax authorities. digital transformation will help in reducing the unfairness of the tax system to taxpayers it will help gather accurate information through data analytic tools, that will assist in the spreading out of the tax burden across all taxpayer groups, as an effort to stop one specific group from feeling the weight.

6   Challenges of Digital Transformation by Tax Authorities

- **Technical complexity**

The technology acceptance model (TAM) proposes that the acceptance of new technology is influenced by two factors which are the perceived usefulness and the perceived ease of use (Davis, 1989). If the target users of a new technology view the technology as one that increases their performance and is effortless to use they are more likely to accept and use it. One of the canons of taxation is simplicity (Mpofu & Moloi, 2022). Digital transformation poses a risk of making the tax systems more complex. The complexity of tax administration systems has been generally advanced as one of the reasons for low tax compliance levels in developing countries (Wealth et al., 2023). How digital tax administration addresses this concern is fundamental to the effectiveness of digital transformation by tax authorities. Because digital transformation is still in its infant stages in most developing countries, there are still risks surmounting. For example, these might include risks of omissions and errors, system failure, cyberattacks, and fraud. Tax authorities need to be adequately prepared to address these risks and some others that might emerge, otherwise lack of adequate preparation and response to these risks might lead to the use of digital technologies being inefficient, damage to the reputation of the revenue authority and loss of trust by taxpayers resulting in low tax morale (OECD, 2018). In short, there is a need for careful planning, clear vision, and effective implementation of digital transformation taking into cognizance the principles of taxation, the needs of various stakeholders and the ability of the digitally transformed tax administration authority to meet the needs of diverse stakeholders. To achieve the objectives of harnessing digital technologies, tax authorities need to vigorously research and plan towards the implementation because, without adequate planning and preparedness, they face a risk of failure to utilise the digital technologies or respond to the negative externalities that may arise. Each tax administration authority needs to tackle the challenges of digitalisation according to its unique contextual environment, needs, and priorities.

- **Inadequate digital infrastructure and increase in costs**

A large number of tax authorities in developing countries have old and outdated IT systems, consequently, it would be difficult to facilitate the use of newer technologies. This might result in the integration of newer technology by tax authorities being difficult. Hence, tax authorities would need to invest in modern technologies that are compatible with digitalisation, robotisation and the use of 4IR technologies (Pantielieieva, 2022). Considering that many of the tax authorities in developing countries have obsolete technologies, the implementation of new digital technologies might be expensive and require large capital investments as some of the systems might require a complete overhaul as opposed to just an upgrade. Rahayu and Kusdianto (2023) posit that taxpayers' costs in capital investment, time, and effort are some of the costs hindering the acceptance of digital tax administration authorities. Taxpayers have to equally invest in digital infrastructure, and learn to appropriately and effectively use electronic declarations. Therefore, contrary to the arguments by most researchers that look at the implementation costs from the angle of tax authorities only it is important to discuss them from the angle of the taxpayer. These costs could lead to attitudes of hostility towards the digitalised system and fuel tax evasion. Additionally, both the taxpayers and revenue authorities would need to train and support their staff in continuous professional development to gain the skills that are compatible with using digital tax administration platforms. Developing countries generally suffer from having insufficient technical and digital skills. There are vast range of skills needed to efficiently implement and operate digital technologies and tax authorities that are based in less developed countries generally have challenges in attracting and retaining these due to poor remuneration and unfavorable working environments.

- **Increase in risks**

There is a likelihood of an increase in potential risks such as privacy risks and breach of confidentiality. Because tax authorities hold extremely sensitive and critical data, they must take the necessary measures to ensure maximum protection from cyberattacks and suspicious activity. Due to the magnitude of the information that their systems hold, tax authorities must implement data privacy rules, which may be hard to implement perfectly in some countries due to digital transformation being a new experience. Risks of cyberattacks, financial losses, and tax fraud may also heighten (Lipniewicz, 2017). Accordingly, tax authorities must put in place effective risk management procedures that respond to technology use-induced risks in addition to other risks associated with tax administration.

- **Hostility to change by employees and taxpayers**

Information technology, customer service, employees, and operations are considered important in the governance of tax administration as these influence relational capabilities, decision-making, and organisational culture of the tax authorities (Ahmadi Zeleti et al., 2021). Consequently, change management is very critical for the success of a new project otherwise if there is no stakeholder buy-in and ownership of the project, an antagonistic attitude towards the proposed or implemented change may fail the project. For example, employees may be unwilling to embrace technology due to several reasons taxpayers may be unwilling to shift to the use of digital technologies due to them being a foreign concept to them, this will make it hard for tax authorities to implement these changes if the individuals that are at the core of the tax system do not want to utilise it.

- **Tax authority staff redundancy and loss of jobs**

The implementation of digital technologies poses the issue of staff not being needed for certain tasks because those would have been automated (Kumar et al., 2023). This may unfortunately lead to job loss for those whose roles have been assumed by digital technologies. These job losses have significant implications for families, poverty alleviation, unemployment, loss of income, access to health and education for dependents of affected employees, and ultimately economic growth.

- **Risk to revenue mobilisation**

Although digital transformation may increase compliance it also poses the risk of new and evolved loopholes for tax evasion (OECD, 2017, 2018). Due to everything being conducted online, it eradicates the presence of a paper trail making it more difficult for the tax authorities to effectively monitor the activities of taxpayers. The digital footprints might be difficult to follow due to the elusive nature of digital transactions (Mpofu, 2023a, 2023b). This will prompt taxpayers to find new innovative ways to evade taxes for example offshore accounts which may affect tax authority revenue collection from taxpayers.

- **Lack of cooperation**

There is a need for the transformation of revenue authorities to be considered internationally and for different countries to work together because there are taxpayers with business across continents, and this may be a challenge because some countries may refuse to cooperate. Rahayu and Kusdianto (2023) point to the variation of stakeholder interests, lack of collaboration, information asymmetry, and non-availability of clear channels of integration of information as some of the challenges associated with the digital transformation of tax administration authorities. Loebbecke (2015) and Parviainen (2017) emphasise the importance of government support and commitment for the digital transformation of revenue authorities to be a success. This support and political will to adequately resource and capacitate tax administration authorities is lacking in most developing countries.

7   Implications of Digital Transformation by Tax Authorities

Digital transformation by tax authorities in developing countries has significant and far-reaching implications (Kamil, 2022). While the positive implications of reduced administrative costs and compliance costs, increased convenience and compliance, reduced tax evasion as well and strengthened accountability and transparency are possible, arguments raising negative implications are also equally pragmatic. These negative implications include the costs, capacity limitations, possibilities of exacerbating existing inequalities, the perpetuation of the digital divide, increase in poverty driven by job losses as well as the impacts of cybersecurity risks.

- **Increased convenience and compliance**

Taxpayers can access their tax records anytime and anywhere, this reduces the stress of paper filing because they can now file online (Rahayu & Kusdianto, 2023). Taxpayers could be prompted to comply because it would be easier for them, online filing could assist in the reduction of costs that are associated with filing taxes.

- **Increased clarity and transparency**

Taxpayers are better informed of the operations of the tax system due to the clear lines of communication developed with the tax authorities (Wang, 2020). Digital platforms allow taxpayers to be more involved in the filing of their taxes and gain better knowledge of their tax accounts. Tax authorities are also able to have real-time access to the tax records of taxpayers and understand the taxpayers better.

- **Enhanced services and efficiency**

The tax authorities can enhance their processes to be more efficient and other staff can focus on the more complex tasks (Del Federico & Montanari, 2021; Rahayu & Kusdianto, 2023), thus ensuring that the authorities operate at optimum efficiency. This might also ensure improved service delivery because taxpayers have easier and better access to their information.

- **Costs, capacity and equity implications**

Digital transformation is generally anticipated to be expensive and developing countries may not be able to raise enough resources to fund the necessary technology and infrastructure (Rahayu, 2021), this might continue to leave them at the mercy of more developed countries and multinationals. They can fail to deal with tax evasion and avoidance schemes as well as aggressive transfer pricing activities. Concerning the weak capacities, these might also impede the ability of developing countries to implement and manage digitalised systems productively. Lastly, digital transformation could increase the existing inequalities concerning the digital divide and lack of internet connectivity that characterise developing countries (Mpofu, 2023a, 2023c). For example, taxpayers with access to technology and resources are better positioned to make use of digital tax administration platforms and effectively comply with tax legislation. On the contrary, those without access to digital services and internet connectivity might find it challenging to comply with tax laws.

8 Key Points

- Some of the challenges of ineffective tax administration linked to traditional systems include auditing digital companies that operate across multiple jurisdictions, taxing cross-border digital transactions and equity and fairness in taxation as well as mitigating tax evasion and avoidance risks. Investing in novel technologies such as big data, data analytics, cloud computing and block chain can help in digitally transforming tax administration and to respond to the weaknesses of traditional tax systems.
- Digital transformation of tax authorities is still in its infant stages in developing countries, but it is essential for tax authorities to speed up the process. It can help tax authorities reduce the administration and tax compliance costs borne by the taxpayers, enhance efficiency and effectiveness, and increase tax compliance and ultimately domestic revenue mobilisation.
- Digital Transformation like any other new system presents challenges concerning the implementation of new technology, thus adequate steps must be taken in order to avoid failure and unintended consequences. Each tax authority would

benefit from vigorously preparing for its implementation process and tailoring the preparations to their contextual needs.

- Strategic planning—It is imperative that tax authorities develop strategic plans for the introduction of digital technologies. This plan ought to encompass the key goals, objectives, and a clear timeframe. A survey and research into the current digital position, preparedness, and possible future demands of the tax authority should inform the digital transformation process. This also assists the authorities in preparing financially for the investment into the upgrades and replacements needed for the digital technology implementation. They must also utilise data collection to identify taxpayer behaviours as well a taxpayer needs to cater to them during the implementation process.
- Transparent lines of communication with taxpayers—Tax authorities ought to ensure that taxpayers are well informed about digital transformation. They need to be transparent about the benefits of going digital while also focusing on equipping them with the knowledge and ability to utilise digital technologies and to respond to possible risks. Transparent communication, stakeholder engagement, and information sharing are important pillars of building trust and acceptance of a new system.
- Development of online portals—Tax authorities must make sure the system is convenient and user-friendly for taxpayers and that it allows them to have online access to their records. This could aid in facilitating smooth and easy tax filing and tax account management. This reduces the stress associated with paying taxes and burdensome tax compliance costs, thus promoting an increase in tax compliance. The development of online portals would also enable users to be able to file their taxes from the comfort of their phones, which upholds the principles of economy, convenience, and simplicity that must characterize a good tax system.
- Stakeholder Collaboration—This would help in the development of innovative means of problem-solving due to the presence of input from multiple other organisations not just the tax authorities. Thus, tax authorities need to collaborate with other agencies like the government as well as the taxpayers to come up with a well-versed outlook on the different challenges as well as the means to combat them. This could also assist in decreasing of the costs of implementation if they were to collaborate with the private sector and partner towards the implementation of digital technologies.
- Training and staff development—Tax authorities should ensure that their staff is well equipped for the changes that are to come with the use of digital technologies. This can be done through adequate training for their staff, upskilling, and reskilling. This might also reduce the number of employees that become redundant. Continuous staff development is important to ensure that the is staff continuously equipped with the relevant digital skills to deal with activities that are more complex since automating manual tasks will reduce the number of workers needed for that process. It might also ensure that the staff can utilise the digital technologies efficiently and effectively and remain up to date with the ever-changing technology and its accompanying risks.

- Monitoring—It is crucial that even after implementation the tax authorities monitor the progress of the digital transformation process, and the emerging risks and always be ready to update the system in response to the advancement in technologies, emerging novel technologies, and loopholes in tax systems. Monitoring might also assist in identifying the different ways that taxpayers may try to evade and avoid paying taxes. Awareness of the tax evasion and avoidance schemes ensures that the necessary updates are made to combat the arising weaknesses in the system. Digital transformation is an ever-evolving process, which will require constant modification of the systems to cater to the needs of the current and future tax systems, thus constant innovation is crucial.
- Implementation of privacy and security measures—It is important for the tax authorities to invest in privacy and data protection measures because the implementation of digital transformation poses a risk of cyber-attacks, thus ensuring that the security measures are effective and dynamic might ensure the reduction in those risks and instill confidence in taxpayers.

References

Ahmadi Zeleti, F., Walsh, G. S., Ojo, A., & Mulligan, E. (2021, October). A case of the governance of digital technology in tax administration. In *Proceedings of the 14th International Conference on Theory and Practice of Electronic Governance* (pp. 298–307).

Alink, M., & Van Kommer, V. (2011). *Handbook on tax administration*. IBFD.

Arthur, P., Hanson, K. T., & Puplampu, K. P. (2022). Revenue mobilization, taxation and the digital economy in post-COVID-19 Africa. *Journal of African Political Economy & Development, 7*(1), 1–12.

Bassey, E., Mulligan, E., & Ojo, A. (2022). A conceptual framework for digital tax administration-A systematic review. *Government Information Quarterly, 39*(4), 101754.

Bentley, D. (2020). Digital tax administration: Transforming the workforce to deliver. *eJTR, 18*, 353.

Calitz, A. P., Cullen, M., & Ferreira, M. C. A. (2021). Software robot process automation at the South African Revenue Service (SARS). *Cell, 83*, 6049777.

Davis, F. D. (1989). Perceived usefulness, perceived ease of use, and user acceptance information technologies. *MIS Quarterly, 13*(3), 319–340.

Del Federico, L., & Montanari, F. (2021). OECD approach on digital transformation of tax administrations and new taxpayers' rights. In *OECD Approach on Digital Transformation of Tax Administrations and New Taxpayers' Rights* (pp. 7–29).

Faúndez-Ugalde, A., Mellado-Silva, R., & Aldunate-Lizana, E. (2020). Use of artificial intelligence by tax administrations: An analysis regarding taxpayers' rights in Latin American countries. *Computer Law & Security Review, 38*, 105441.

Gashenko, I., & Zima, Y. (2018). Automation of tax administration with the help of the internet of things: Pros and Cons from the positions of economic effectiveness. In *System analysis in economics-2018* (pp. 347–350).

Houser, K., & Sanders, D. (2018). The use of big data analytics by the IRS: What tax practitioners need to know. *Houser, Kimberly and Sanders, Debra, The Use of Big Data Analytics by the IRS: What Tax Practitioners Need to Know (February, 2018). Journal of Taxation, 128*(2).

Janowicz, K., Regalia, B., Hitzler, P., Mai, G., Delbecque, S., Fröhlich, M., et al. (2018). On the prospects of blockchain and distributed ledger technologies for open science and academic publishing. *Semantic web, 9*(5), 545–555.

Junquera-Varela, R. F., Lucas, C. O., Krsul, I., Calderon Yksic, V. O., & Arce Rodriguez, P. (2022). Digital transformation of tax and customs administrations.

Kamil, I. (2022). Influence artificial intelligence technology for E-filling and Digital Service Tax (DST) in tax administration on tax compliance. *International Journal of Management Studies and Social Science Research, 4*(1), 144–156.

Kumar, R., Malholtra, R. K., & Grover, C. N. (2023, January). Review on artificial intelligence role in implementation of Goods and Services Tax (GST) and future scope. In *2023 International Conference on Artificial Intelligence and Smart Communication (AISC)* (pp. 348–351). IEEE.

Lipniewicz, R. (2017). Tax administration and risk management in the digital age. *Information Systems in Management, 6.*

Loebbecke, C. P. A. (2015). Reflections on societal and business model transformation arising from digitisation and big data analytics: A research agenda. *Journal of Strategic Information Systems, 24,* 149–157.

Mashiri, E. (2018). *Regulating Multinational Enterprises (MNEs) transactions to minimise tax avoidance through transfer pricing: Case of Zimbabwe.* PhD. University of South Africa.

Mehta, P., Mathews, J., Kumar, S., Suryamukhi, K., Babu, C. S., Rao, S. K. V., Shivapujimath, V., & Bisht, D. (2019). Big data analytics for tax administration. In *Electronic Government and the Information Systems Perspective: 8th International Conference, EGOVIS 2019, Linz, Austria, August 26–29, 2019, Proceedings 8* (pp. 47–57). Springer International Publishing.

Mhlanga, D., & Mpofu, F. Y. (2023). The impact of digital financial service taxes and mobile money taxes on financial inclusion and inclusive development in Africa. In *Economic inclusion in post-independence Africa: An inclusive approach to economic development* (pp. 81–102). Springer Nature Switzerland.

Mikhaleva, O. L., Syradoev, D. V., & Terekhova, T. A. (2021). Big data technology application in the taxation sphere. In *Engineering economics: Decisions and solutions from Eurasian perspective* (pp. 431–436). Springer International Publishing.

Moloi, T., & Marwala, T. (2021). Robotic process automation in strategy and strategy implementation. In *Artificial intelligence and the changing nature of corporations: How technologies shape strategy and operations* (pp. 97–104). Springer International Publishing.

Mpofu, F. Y. (2021). A critical review of the taxation of the informal sector in Zimbabwe.

Mpofu, F. Y. (2022a). Sustainable mobilisation of tax revenues to enhance economic growth in Sub-Saharan Africa: Challenges, opportunities, and possible areas of reform. *International Journal of Research in Business and Social Science (2147-4478), 11*(9), 222–233.

Mpofu, F. Y. (2022b). Taxing the digital economy through consumption taxes (VAT) in African countries: Possibilities, constraints and implications. *International Journal of Financial Studies, 10*(3), 65.

Mpofu, F. Y. (2022c). Taxation of the digital economy and direct digital service taxes: Opportunities, challenges, and implications for African countries. *Economies, 10*(9), 219.

Mpofu, F. Y. (2023a). Mobile money services and sustainable development effect in Africa. In *The Fourth Industrial Revolution in Africa: Exploring the development implications of smart technologies in Africa* (pp. 151–173). Springer Nature Switzerland.

Mpofu, F. Y. (2023b). Fintech, the fourth industrial revolution technologies, digital financial services and the advancement of the SDGs in developing countries. *International Journal of Social Science Research and Review, 6*(1), 533–553.

Mpofu, F. Y. (2023c). Digital entrepreneurship, taxation of the digital economy, digital transformation, and sustainable development in Africa. In *The Fourth Industrial Revolution in Africa: Exploring the Development Implications of Smart Technologies in Africa* (pp. 193–219).

Mpofu, F. Y., & Moloi, T. (2022). Direct digital services taxes in Africa and the canons of taxation. *Laws, 11*(4), 57.

Nadat, U. (2022). Analysing the journey of revenue authorities in the commonwealth realm on becoming 4IR-centric: With a focus on South Africa. *African Journal of Corporate Governance Research.*

Nazarov, M. A., Mikhaleva, O. L., & Chernousova, K. S. (2020). Digital transformation of tax administration. In *Digital age: Chances, challenges and future 7* (pp. 144–149). Springer International Publishing.

OECD. (2017). *Tax challenges of digitalisation*. OECD. https://www.oecd.org/tax/beps/tax-challenges-digitalisation-part-2-comments-on-request-for-input-2017.pdf

OECD. (2018). *Tax challenges arising from digitalisation – Interim Report 2018*. OECD. https://www.oecd.org/ctp/tax-challenges-arising-from-digitalisation-interim-report-9789264293083-en.htm

Pantielieieva, N. (2022). Digital transformation of tax administration. *Path of Science, 8*(1), 3035–3051.

Papathanasiou, A., Cole, R., & Murray, P. (2020). The (non-) application of blockchain technology in the Greek shipping industry. *European Management Journal, 38*(6), 927–938.

Parviainen, P. T. M. (2017). Tackling the digitalisation challenge: How to benefit from digitalisation in practice. *International Journal of Information Systems and Project Management, 5*, 63–77.

Pica, L. (2023). The new challenges of artificial intelligence, profiling and bigdata analysis by tax administrations: Will the right to meet these new challenges be shown? *JusGov Research Paper*, (2023-04).

Rahayu, S. K. (2021). Utilization of artificial intelligence in tax audit in Indonesia. *Management and Accounting Review (MAR), 20*(3), 135–157.

Rahayu, S. K., & Kusdianto, A. (2023). Challenges of digital tax administration transformation in Indonesia.

Saragih, A. H., Reyhani, Q., Setyowati, M. S., & Hendrawan, A. (2023). The potential of an artificial intelligence (AI) application for the tax administration system's modernization: The case of Indonesia. *Artificial Intelligence and Law, 31*(3), 491–514.

Sebele-Mpofu, F. Y., Mashiri, E., & Korera, P. (2021). Transfer pricing audit challenges and dispute resolution effectiveness in developing countries with specific focus on Zimbabwe. *Accounting, Economics, and Law: A Convivium*, 000010151520210026.

Sebele-Mpofu, F. Y., & Mususa, A. (2019). How successful is presumptive tax in bringing informal operators into the tax net in Zimbabwe? A study of transport operators in Bulawayo. *International Journal of Innovative Science and Research, 4*(3), 79–89.

Shakil, M. H., & Tasnia, M. (2022). Artificial intelligence and tax administration in Asia and the Pacific. In *Taxation in the digital economy* (pp. 45–55). Routledge.

Shava, E., & Mhlanga, D. (2023). Mitigating bureaucratic inefficiencies through blockchain technology in Africa. *Frontiers in Blockchain, 6*, 1053555.

Skipin, D. L., Koltsova, T. A., Yukhtanova, Y. A., & Ruf, Y. N. (2020, August). A person in the digital transformation of tax administration: Opportunities and reality. In *Russian Conference on Digital Economy and Knowledge Management (RuDEcK 2020)* (pp. 306–310). Atlantis Press.

Twesige, D. (2020). Smart Taxation (4Taxation): Effect of Fourth Industrial Revolution (4IR) on tax compliance in Rwanda. *Journal of Business and Administrative Studies, 12*(1), 1–27.

Vial, G. (2021). Understanding digital transformation: A review and a research agenda. *Managing digital transformation*, 13–66.

Walker-Munro, B. (2020). Use of big data analytics by tax authorities. In *Legal regulations, implications, and issues surrounding digital data* (pp. 86–110). IGI Global.

Wang, L. (2020). Research on tax collection and administration based on big data analysis. In *2020 International Conference on Intelligent Transportation, Big Data & Smart City (ICITBS)* (pp. 679–682). IEEE.

Wealth, E., Smulders, S. A., & Mpofu, F. Y. (2023). Conceptualising the behaviour of MNEs, tax authorities and tax consultants in respect of transfer pricing practices–A three-layer analysis. *Accounting, Economics, and Law: A Convivium*, (0).

Digital Transformation in the Small Businesses Sector

Stella Bvuma

Abstract This research chapter investigates the impact of digital transformation on small businesses and offers insights into best practices for its implementation. Using a mixed-method approach, the study explores the current state of digital transformation adoption, its driving factors, barriers, and methods for evaluating success among small businesses. The findings aim to provide valuable guidance for small business owners and policymakers seeking to enhance their digital transformation strategies.

1 Introduction

Digital transformation is a pivotal component of contemporary business strategies, fostering innovation, operational efficiency, and competitiveness (Chanias & Hess, 2016; Verhoef et al., 2021). However, small businesses have been slower to embrace this paradigm shift, mainly due to perceived complexities and costs (OECD, 2021; Achieng & Malatji, 2022). This paper explores the implications of digital transformation on small business success and outlines best practices for implementation. It employs a mixed-method approach, with a focus on qualitative research, to analyze current trends, benefits, and challenges associated with digital transformation adoption among small businesses. The study aims to inform small business owners and policymakers on designing effective digital transformation strategies within the small business sector.

S. Bvuma (✉)
University of Johannesburg, College of Business and Economics, Johannesburg, South Africa
e-mail: stellab@uj.ac.za

T. Moloi (ed.), *Digital Transformation in South Africa*, Professional Practice in Governance and Public Organizations,
https://doi.org/10.1007/978-3-031-52403-5_12

2 Literature Review

The literature review serves as the foundation upon which this research is built, offering a comprehensive understanding of digital transformation in small businesses. In an era marked by rapid technological advancements and digital disruption, the imperative for small businesses to engage with digital transformation becomes increasingly evident. The body of knowledge surrounding this subject is rich and multifaceted, encompassing studies from various domains, such as business management, technology, and entrepreneurship. Central to this discussion is the role of digital transformation as a strategic tool for small businesses. Digital transformation refers to the integration of digital technologies into various facets of business operations, aimed at enhancing productivity, customer experiences, and competitiveness (Chanias & Hess, 2016; Verhoef et al., 2021; Chen et al., 2012). Despite its recognized benefits, the adoption of digital transformation in small businesses has been characterized as sluggish, primarily due to the perceived complexities and costs involved (OECD, 2021; Achieng & Malatji, 2022). Previous research on small and medium enterprises (SMEs) has explored the influence of digital involvement on the overall business model process from a strategic viewpoint, particularly through customer acquisition and retention (Bowman, 2018; Dholakia & Durham, 2010; Paulus-Rohmer et al., 2016; Scuotto et al., 2017). The literature further highlights the challenging nature of digital transformation in small businesses. Understanding the complexities, opportunities, and constraints surrounding this critical transformation is vital for enhancing the competitiveness and sustainability of small enterprises. Hence, this literature review seeks to provide an overview of existing research on digital transformation in small businesses, exploring its current state, drivers, barriers, and potential benefits.

The digital transformation landscape in small businesses is continually evolving. These businesses are known as the backbone of the economy in many countries (Kuan & Chau, 2001). Several studies have aimed to shed light on the current state of digital adoption in small businesses. These studies underscore the significance of understanding the extent to which small businesses engage with digital transformation (Verhoef et al., 2021; Achieng & Malatji, 2022). While digital transformation adoption rates vary across regions and sectors, the prevailing theme is one of gradual progress. Small businesses recognize the importance of digitalization, albeit at different paces (OECD, 2021; Dholakia & Durham, 2010). Small businesses are increasingly exploring digital solutions to enhance various aspects of their operations, encompassing marketing, customer service, supply chain management, and internal processes (Chen et al., 2012). This diversification in the dimensions of digital adoption underscores the versatility and adaptability of digital technologies to cater to the diverse needs of small businesses. Understanding this diversification is fundamental to grasping the intricate dynamics of digital transformation in the small business sector.

The driving forces behind digital transformation in small businesses are multifaceted and underscore the strategic implications of this adoption. Competitive pressure emerges as a central driver, with small businesses recognizing the need to remain competitive in dynamic markets (Chanias & Hess, 2016). The competitive landscape, marked by peers and larger corporations embracing digital transformation, prompts small businesses to take action (Paulus-Rohmer et al., 2016). Cost reduction serves as another compelling incentive for digital transformation. Small businesses anticipate cost savings through process automation, improved efficiency, and optimized resource allocation (Verhoef et al., 2015). The pressure to meet customer expectations acts as a significant driver, especially for businesses in service and retail sectors (Scuotto et al., 2017). The evolving digital preferences of customers necessitate businesses to provide seamless online interactions and personalized experiences (Bowman, 2018). These drivers, while diverse, collectively emphasize the strategic importance of digital transformation as a means to adapt, compete, and thrive.

Conversely, small businesses face several barriers that hinder their engagement with digital transformation. One of the most prominent barriers is financial constraints, characterized by limited budgets and resources (Achieng & Malatji, 2022). Small businesses often perceive the initial investment in digital tools, software, and expertise as a substantial challenge, particularly when operating with tight budgets (OECD, 2021). The lack of expertise in digital technologies is another notable barrier (Paulus-Rohmer et al., 2016). Small businesses often grapple with the knowledge and skills required to navigate digital complexities, such as data analytics and cybersecurity. Resistance to change is a prevailing theme in small businesses, stemming from concerns about the disruptions and challenges associated with digital transformation (Chen et al., 2012). Overcoming this resistance necessitates effective change management and communication strategies. Recognizing and addressing these barriers is paramount for small businesses and policymakers seeking to enhance digital adoption in this sector.

The measurement of success in digital transformation initiatives is a fundamental aspect of assessing the impact of digitalization (Dholakia & Durham, 2010). Small businesses adopt a variety of metrics that align with their goals and the nature of their business. Customer feedback is a prominent metric, reflecting the importance of understanding the impact on customer satisfaction (Verhoef et al., 2021). Increased website traffic is another key metric, particularly for businesses with an online presence. It signifies the effectiveness of online strategies in driving visitor engagement. Conversion rates, measuring the percentage of website visitors completing desired actions, serve as critical success metrics for businesses aiming to drive customer engagement and sales (Bowman, 2018). Some small businesses adopt a more data-driven approach, focusing on cost savings through process optimization and reduced operational expenses (Scuotto et al., 2017). The choice of metrics underscores the diversity of objectives and goals among small businesses engaging in digital transformation.

This literature review provides a holistic understanding of digital transformation in small businesses, encompassing the current state, drivers, barriers, and success metrics. Digital transformation is no longer a choice but an imperative for small businesses in today's competitive landscape. Understanding the multifaceted dynamics of digital transformation is fundamental for enhancing the competitiveness and sustainability of small enterprises. As small businesses continue to adapt and evolve, digital transformation emerges as a strategic tool that can redefine their future, positioning them for growth and success.

3 Methodology

We outline the research methodology employed to investigate the impact of digital transformation on small businesses. The study combined both qualitative and quantitative research methods to gain comprehensive insights into the adoption, drivers, barriers, and success measurement of digital transformation in the small business sector.

3.1 Qualitative Research

Qualitative data was collected through an extensive and structured approach to ensure a deep understanding of the challenges and benefits of digital transformation among small businesses. The qualitative research process included the following elements:

3.1.1 In-Depth Interviews

In-depth interviews were conducted with a diverse sample of small business owners and experts in the field. These interviews provided an opportunity to explore nuanced aspects of digital adoption, individual experiences, and the specific contexts in which digital transformation initiatives were undertaken. The qualitative interviews were semi-structured, allowing for open-ended questions to elicit rich, detailed responses.

3.1.2 Focus Group Discussions

Focus group discussions were organized to encourage group dynamics and the exchange of diverse perspectives. These discussions involved small business owners, employees, and other stakeholders, promoting an interactive environment where participants shared their experiences and viewpoints on digital transformation.

3.1.3 Thematic Analysis

Qualitative data from interviews and focus group discussions were analyzed using thematic analysis. This involved the identification of recurring themes, patterns, and key findings within the qualitative data. The analysis allowed us to extract meaningful insights from the narratives of small business owners and participants.

3.2 Quantitative Research

Quantitative data was collected through structured surveys distributed to a diverse sample of small businesses. The quantitative research process included the following elements:

3.2.1 Survey Design

The research team designed a comprehensive survey that included a range of questions related to the adoption of digital transformation, its driving factors, barriers, and methods for evaluating success. The survey was structured to provide quantitative data that could be analysed statistically.

3.2.2 Survey Distribution

The surveys were distributed to a stratified sample of small businesses, ensuring representation across various sectors, regions, and business sizes. The survey distribution was conducted both online and in person, and participants were assured of data confidentiality and anonymity.

3.2.3 Data Analysis

Quantitative data obtained from the surveys were subjected to rigorous statistical analysis. Descriptive statistics, such as means, frequencies, and percentages, were used to summarize key findings. Inferential statistics, including regression analysis and correlation, were employed to identify significant relationships and patterns within the data.

This mixed-method approach allowed for a comprehensive examination of digital transformation in small businesses. Qualitative research provided valuable qualitative insights, while quantitative research provided statistical evidence and trends. By combining these two methods, the study aimed to offer a holistic view of the state of digital transformation adoption, its drivers, barriers, and success measurement in the small business sector.

4   Ethical Considerations

Ethical considerations were paramount in conducting this research. Participants in both the qualitative and quantitative research were informed about the purpose of the study, their rights as participants, and the use of their data. Informed consent was obtained from all participants, and their identities were kept confidential. The research adhered to ethical guidelines and principles to protect the rights and privacy of the participants.

5   Findings

5.1   *Current State of Digital Transformation Adoption*

The findings of this research provide a comprehensive overview of the current state of digital transformation adoption among small businesses. Through a mixed-method approach involving both qualitative interviews and quantitative surveys, we gathered a wealth of data that collectively portrays a detailed picture of the digital landscape in small businesses.

Our quantitative survey, distributed to a diverse sample of small businesses, revealed that approximately 62% of respondents had initiated digital transformation projects in various facets of their operations. This statistic underscores the considerable interest and investment that small businesses are directing toward digital transformation. The remaining 38% of businesses, although not yet involved in formal transformation projects, expressed their intent to explore digital solutions in the near future. In our qualitative interviews and focus group discussions, we sought to gain deeper insights into the nuances of digital transformation adoption. These discussions reinforced the quantitative findings and added depth to our understanding. Small business owners and experts participating in these qualitative sessions shared valuable perspectives on their digital journey.

An emergent theme from these qualitative interviews was the diversification of digital adoption across different operational areas. Small businesses were keen to leverage digital tools and technologies to enhance various aspects of their operations. These included marketing, customer service, supply chain management, and even internal processes like human resources and accounting. One interviewee, the owner of a small e-commerce business, highlighted how digital transformation had revolutionized the way they interacted with customers and managed inventory. They implemented e-commerce platforms and automated inventory management systems, allowing them to offer a seamless online shopping experience to their customers and manage inventory more efficiently. In another instance, a small restaurant owner detailed their experience with digital transformation in the context of food delivery services. They had integrated an online ordering system and delivery management software to streamline their delivery operations and reach a broader customer base, especially during the COVID-19 pandemic. These stories of transformation exemplify the diverse ways small businesses are incorporating digital solutions into their daily operations.

5.2 Primary Drivers of Digital Transformation

The research revealed several primary drivers motivating small businesses to embrace digital transformation. These drivers play a pivotal role in shaping the decisions and strategies of these businesses.

5.2.1 Competitive Pressure

Small businesses are acutely aware of the competitive landscape they operate in. Our data indicated that the perceived competitive pressure from both peers and larger corporations acted as a significant driving force behind digital transformation initiatives. Small businesses recognized the importance of staying relevant and competitive in the market. As one interviewee put it, "We saw our competitors rapidly adopting digital tools, and we couldn't afford to be left behind."

5.2.2 Cost Reduction

The potential for cost reduction emerged as a compelling incentive for small businesses to embark on digital transformation journeys. They realized that digital solutions could enhance resource allocation, improve operational efficiency, and streamline various business processes. By automating tasks and improving process efficiency, small businesses anticipated significant cost savings. "We knew we could do things more efficiently with digital tools, and that would ultimately save us money," shared one participant.

5.2.3 Customer Demand

The voice of the customer was a clear motivator for many small businesses. Responding to customer expectations and the need for better online experiences was a primary driver, especially for businesses in the service and retail sectors. Small businesses recognized that their customers increasingly expected seamless online interactions, easy access to information, and personalized experiences. As a result, they felt the pressure to meet these expectations.

One example that encapsulated this driver was a small boutique clothing store owner. They described how they had initially hesitated to set up an online store due to concerns about the cost and complexity. However, as customer inquiries for online shopping options grew, they recognized the need to meet this demand. The boutique owner acknowledged that digital transformation was a necessity to provide the convenience their customers desired.

5.3 Barriers to Digital Transformation

While small businesses are eager to reap the benefits of digital transformation, they face several notable barriers in their journey toward digital adoption. The research illuminated these challenges, which must be addressed to facilitate successful transformation.

5.3.1 Financial Constraints

A common challenge encountered by small businesses is limited budgets and resources. Many small business owners expressed concerns about the financial implications of digital transformation. They perceived the initial investment in digital tools, software, and expertise as a significant barrier. These businesses often operated with tight budgets and were cautious about allocating funds to transformation initiatives. One survey respondent, who owns a small consulting firm, explained that while they recognized the potential of digital marketing, the costs associated with creating and implementing a robust online marketing strategy were daunting. They were concerned that the initial investment might not yield immediate returns.

5.3.2 Lack of Expertise

Small businesses often lack the necessary knowledge and skills to implement digital transformation effectively. This skills gap was identified as a critical barrier. In the survey, over 48% of respondents cited the absence of in-house expertise as a challenge in their digital transformation efforts. The complexities of digital technologies, data analytics, and cybersecurity were areas where businesses felt they lacked the requisite skills. In our interviews, small business owners shared their experiences of grappling with the learning curve associated with digital tools. Some described challenges in finding and hiring talent with digital expertise, while others had invested in employee training to bridge the knowledge gap.

5.3.3 Resistance to Change

A prevailing theme in our qualitative interviews was resistance to change. Many employees and business owners were apprehensive about the disruptions that digital transformation might bring to their existing processes. Resistance manifested in various forms, from reluctance to adopt new software to concerns about employee morale during the transition. One small manufacturing business owner recounted how the introduction of digital manufacturing tools led to resistance from some long-time employees who were accustomed to traditional manufacturing methods. To address this, the business had to invest time in change management and communication to ease the transition.

5.4 Measuring Success

Small businesses adopt a variety of metrics to measure the success of their digital transformation efforts. The research found that the choice of metrics often aligned with the specific goals of the transformation initiative and the nature of the business. Key metrics for measuring success included:

5.4.1 Customer Feedback

Many small businesses recognized the importance of gathering direct feedback from customers. They relied on customer surveys, reviews, and direct feedback to gauge the impact of digital changes on customer satisfaction. Positive customer feedback was considered a strong indicator of success. Negative feedback, on the other hand, triggered adjustments and refinements to digital strategies. More importantly, it has been the driving force behind the change of the customer care process and made it possible to incorporate insightful consumer feedback into other business domains (Galliers & Leidner, 2003).

5.4.2 Increased Website Traffic

For businesses with an online presence, measuring the increase in website traffic was a common success metric. A surge in website visitors, especially those arriving through digital marketing efforts, indicated the effectiveness of the online strategy. A small bakery owner, for example, monitored website traffic to understand the impact of online promotions and social media campaigns.

5.4.3 Conversion Rates

Conversion rates, such as the percentage of website visitors who make a purchase or complete a desired action, were considered a vital success metric. Many e-commerce businesses and service providers closely tracked their conversion rates. Improvements in conversion rates validated the effectiveness of digital initiatives in driving customer engagement and sales.

5.4.4   Cost Savings

Businesses that integrated data analytics into their operations had a more structured approach to measuring success. They monitored cost savings resulting from process efficiencies and reduced manual labor. These businesses used data-driven insights to optimize operations and reduce operational costs. One small logistics company, for example, tracked the reduction in delivery times and associated fuel costs due to digital route optimization. The research further revealed that the definition of success was not one-size-fits-all. Small businesses had diverse objectives for their digital transformation initiatives, which influenced their choice of success metrics. While some businesses prioritized revenue growth and customer acquisition, others focused on operational efficiency and cost reduction. Regardless of the specific metrics, small businesses shared the goal of achieving tangible, data-driven outcomes to validate their digital investments.

5.5   Discussion

The findings of this research have shed light on the complexities and nuances surrounding the digital transformation of small businesses. In this discussion, we will explore and analyze these findings in greater depth, examining the implications for small businesses, policymakers, and the broader business landscape.

5.5.1   Digital Transformation: A Necessity for Small Businesses

The research findings unequivocally highlight that digital transformation is not merely a trend but a necessity for small businesses. The pressures of competition, the changing demands of customers, and the allure of cost savings are driving small businesses to embrace digital solutions. Small businesses, regardless of their size or sector, are recognizing that digital transformation is a means to enhance their competitiveness and relevance in the evolving business landscape. Chanias and Hess (2016) emphasize the transformative nature of digital technologies, positioning them as essential tools for enhancing competitiveness in the business environment.

5.5.2   Competitive Pressure as a Motivator

One of the central findings is the role of competitive pressure as a driving force behind digital transformation in small businesses. In a market environment where innovation is accelerated, and consumers are offered an array of choices, small businesses find themselves compelled to adapt rapidly. They are no longer competing only with local counterparts but with online giants and businesses worldwide. This competitiveness dilemma has forced small businesses to consider digital transformation as a tool for survival and growth. Small business owners and stake-holders who participated in the research consistently highlighted the urgency of staying competitive through digital means. This competitive motivation is reflected in their stories, where they observed competitors adopting digital tools and recognized the need to keep pace. This realization led to a sense of urgency and an impetus for change. Small businesses understand that they must be agile and adaptive in their strategies to remain relevant and competitive. Dholakia and Durham (2010) discuss the impact of innovation and competition on the strategic choices of small businesses, highlighting the need for adaptability in dynamic markets.

5.6   Cost Reduction as a Motivator

The potential for cost reduction emerged as another strong driver of digital transformation. Small businesses, often constrained by tight budgets and limited resources, see digital transformation as a means to improve operational efficiency and reduce costs. The research revealed that many small businesses consider digital solutions as cost-effective alternatives to traditional manual processes. The implementation of digital tools can lead to significant savings by streamlining operations, reducing human error, and optimizing resource allocation. For instance, automating routine tasks, such as inventory management and order processing, not only minimizes errors but also reduces the time and effort required to perform these tasks manually. Small businesses recognize the financial benefits of such improvements. An interesting finding is that the potential for cost reduction is particularly appealing to small businesses in industries characterized by slim profit margins. For example, restaurants and small retailers, which often operate on thin margins, are motivated by the promise of cost savings through digital solutions. These savings can have a substantial impact on their profitability, making digital transformation an attractive proposition. Bowman (2018) notes the increasing interest of small businesses in cost-effective alternatives, aligning with the findings that emphasize the financial benefits of digital solutions.

5.7   Customer Demand as a Motivator

The influence of customer demand on digital transformation adoption is evident in the research findings. Small businesses are increasingly cognizant of the expectations of their customers, who have grown accustomed to seamless online experiences. Today's consumers expect easy access to information, personalized interactions, and the ability to make transactions online. Small businesses must respond to these customer expectations to retain and attract clients. Many of the research participants, particularly those in service-oriented and retail sectors, voiced the importance of meeting customer demands. For instance, the owner of a small boutique clothing store shared how customer inquiries about online shopping options prompted their digital transformation journey. This is a reflection of how small businesses are influenced by customer feedback and preferences. It's worth noting that in some cases, customer demand is a catalyst for digital transformation rather than a reactive response. Small businesses that proactively anticipate customer needs and align their digital strategies accordingly are positioned to gain a competitive advantage. They understand that embracing digital channels, e-commerce platforms, and digital marketing tools is a means to enhance customer experiences and build lasting relationships. Scuotto et al. (2017) discuss the impact of customer expectations on small businesses, highlighting the need for businesses to align with evolving customer preferences.

5.8 Barriers to Digital Transformation

While the research illustrates the compelling motivations for digital transformation in small businesses, it also uncovers the multifaceted barriers that these businesses face. Recognizing and addressing these barriers is essential to facilitating successful digital transformation. Paulus-Rohmer et al. (2016) emphasize the challenging nature of digital involvement for small and medium enterprises, aligning with the identified barriers.

5.9 Financial Constraints as a Barrier

Financial constraints emerged as a prominent barrier to digital transformation in small businesses. Many small businesses operate with limited budgets and financial resources, making it challenging to allocate the necessary funds for digital initiatives. The initial investment required for digital tools, software, and expertise can be intimidating, particularly for businesses with tight financial margins. Achieng and Malatji (2022) discuss the challenges small businesses face in allocating funds for digital initiatives, resonating with the identified barrier of financial constraints.

The cost of digital transformation can vary widely, depending on the scope of the project and the specific tools or technologies involved. For example, implementing a comprehensive digital marketing strategy or adopting an enterprise resource planning (ERP) system can involve substantial costs. These financial implications can deter small businesses from initiating digital transformation projects. Small businesses often walk a tightrope, balancing the desire for digital transformation with the need to manage operational costs. They must carefully assess the potential return on investment (ROI) and the long-term benefits of digital initiatives. In some cases, businesses might opt for gradual digital adoption to minimize upfront costs, while others may seek external financial support.

5.10   Lack of Expertise as a Barrier

A lack of expertise in digital technologies is another critical barrier that small businesses encounter. Many small business owners and their employees may not possess the requisite knowledge and skills to effectively implement digital solutions. The complexity of digital technologies, data analytics, and cybersecurity can be daunting, particularly for businesses that lack an IT department or digital specialists. The skills gap is exacerbated by the rapid pace of technological change. Digital tools and platforms evolve continuously, requiring businesses to remain up-to-date with the latest developments. The absence of in-house expertise can hinder the successful adoption and integration of digital solutions. Several interviewees highlighted their experiences of grappling with the learning curve associated with digital tools. While some businesses invested in employee training to address this barrier, others opted to outsource certain aspects of digital transformation to experts or service providers. This outsourcing allowed them to leverage specialized knowledge and skills without making significant internal investments. Verhoef et al. (2021) highlight the importance of digital expertise for successful digital transformation, aligning with the identified barrier of a lack of expertise.

5.11   Resistance to Change as a Barrier

Resistance to change, both among employees and business owners, was a recurrent theme in the research. Small businesses often encounter reluctance and apprehension when introducing digital transformation initiatives. The fear of disruptions, concerns about employee morale during the transition, and the inertia of sticking to familiar processes are key factors contributing to resistance. Small business owners and managers shared their experiences of managing resistance within their organizations. For instance, the introduction of digital manufacturing tools in a small production facility led to resistance from employees accustomed to traditional methods. In such cases, change management and communication strategies were essential to ease the transition and gain employee buy-in. Resistance to change can be a formidable barrier to digital transformation. It can impede the adoption of new technologies, slow down the implementation process, and hinder the realization of digital benefits. Overcoming this barrier requires a combination of leadership, communication, and a supportive organizational culture that values innovation and embraces change. Chen et al. (2012) discuss the challenges of resistance to change in the context of digital transformation, supporting the identified barrier.

5.12   Measuring Success in Digital Transformation

Small businesses employ diverse metrics to measure the success of their digital transformation efforts. The research indicates that these metrics align with the specific objectives and goals of the transformation initiative. While the choice of metrics varies, businesses universally aim to achieve tangible, data-driven outcomes that validate their digital investments. Donati emphasizes the importance of metrics in assessing the success of digital transformation initiatives, aligning with the identified metrics such as customer feedback, increased website traffic, and cost savings.

5.13   Customer Feedback as a Success Metric

Gathering customer feedback emerged as a vital success metric for many small businesses. Businesses recognize that direct customer feedback is a valuable source of insights into the effectiveness of their digital initiatives. Positive feedback, such as customer satisfaction ratings, reviews, and testimonials, is seen as a strong indicator of success. Small businesses often collect customer feedback through surveys, online reviews, and direct communication channels. This feedback helps them gauge the impact of digital changes on customer satisfaction, identify areas for improvement, and refine their digital strategies accordingly. Positive customer feedback not only validates the effectiveness of digital initiatives but also enhances a business's reputation and trustworthiness.

5.14   Increased Website Traffic as a Success Metric

For businesses with an online presence, measuring the increase in website traffic is a common success metric. An upsurge in website visitors, especially those arriving through digital marketing efforts, indicates the effectiveness of the online strategy. Small businesses closely monitor website traffic to understand the impact of online promotions and social media campaigns. Small business owners and marketers recognize that increased website traffic can lead to greater brand visibility and, subsequently, improved conversion rates. By tracking website traffic, they gain insights into the performance of digital marketing efforts, the effectiveness of content, and the resonance of their online brand presence.

5.15   Conversion Rates as a Success Metric

Conversion rates, such as the percentage of website visitors who make a purchase or complete a desired action, hold great importance for many small businesses. E-commerce businesses, service providers, and even non-profit organizations closely monitor their conversion rates. An increase in conversion rates indicates that digital initiatives are successfully engaging customers and driving desired actions. Improvements in conversion rates validate the effectiveness of digital initiatives in converting website visitors into customers or leads. Small businesses use A/B testing, analytics tools, and user journey analysis to optimize their online processes and enhance conversion rates. The data-driven approach helps them refine their digital strategies for greater impact.

5.16   Cost Savings as a Success Metric

Small businesses that integrate data analytics and process automation into their operations often use cost savings as a key success metric. By tracking the reduction in operational costs resulting from process efficiencies and reduced manual labour, these businesses assess the tangible benefits of digital transformation. The research uncovered examples of small logistics companies tracking the reduction in delivery times and associated fuel costs due to digital route optimization. In manufacturing, improved inventory management systems reduced the costs of overstocking or understocking, ultimately impacting the bottom line. Cost savings are a concrete metric that appeals to small businesses, particularly those operating with slim profit margins. Businesses are keen to measure the return on investment (ROI) associated with digital transformation initiatives and ensure that their digital investments yield tangible financial benefits.

5.17   Tailored Definitions of Success

The research illustrates that the definition of success in digital transformation is not one-size-fits-all. Small businesses have diverse objectives for their digital initiatives, which influence their choice of success metrics. While some prioritize revenue growth and customer acquisition, others focus on operational efficiency and cost reduction. Regardless of the specific metrics, small businesses share the goal of achieving tangible, data-driven outcomes that validate their digital investments. It's important to recognize that the success of digital transformation is contingent on the alignment of digital strategies with business objectives. Small businesses must define their success metrics based on their unique goals and challenges. This tailored approach allows businesses to gauge the impact of digital initiatives in a manner that directly resonates with their strategic priorities. The diverse objectives for digital initiatives align with the findings, resonating with the idea that success metrics should be aligned with unique business goals (Verhoef et al., 2015).

5.18   Recognizing the Imperative of Digital Transformation

The research reinforces the imperative for small businesses to recognize digital transformation as an essential aspect of their strategic arsenal. In a rapidly evolving business landscape, the pressures of competition and customer expectations compel small businesses to act swiftly. Understanding the role of digital transformation in staying competitive and meeting customer demands is the first step in this journey. Small businesses must be proactive in assessing their competitive positioning and understanding their customers' preferences. This proactive approach will help them identify the areas where digital transformation can have the most significant impact. Whether it involves establishing an online presence, automating manual processes, or enhancing data analytics capabilities, small businesses should strategically plan and align their digital initiatives with their overarching business objectives.

5.19   Addressing Financial Constraints

To overcome the barrier of financial constraints, small businesses should explore diverse strategies. One approach is to consider incremental digital transformation. Instead of pursuing large-scale initiatives that require substantial upfront investment, small businesses can opt for phased, manageable projects. This allows them to allocate resources gradually and observe the impact of digital changes before committing to more extensive transformations. Another avenue to explore is external funding or support. Small businesses can investigate grants, subsidies, or government programs designed to encourage digital transformation. These resources can help offset the initial costs and facilitate digital adoption. Additionally, businesses should conduct a cost-benefit analysis to assess the long-term financial benefits of digital transformation. While the initial investment may seem significant, evaluating the potential cost savings, revenue growth, and improved operational efficiency can help justify the expense. Small businesses should recognize that digital transformation is an investment in their future sustainability and growth.

5.20   Bridging the Skills Gap

To address the barrier of a lack of expertise, small businesses can take a multi-faceted approach. Employee training and upskilling are critical components of building internal digital capabilities to ensure that the small business's digital transformation is sustainable (Westerman et al., 2014). Businesses should invest in training programs, workshops, and certifications that equip their employees with the necessary digital skills. Cross-functional teams that bring together individuals with diverse skill sets can collaborate on digital initiatives. Small businesses can also explore partnerships and collaborations with external experts, digital agencies, or consultants. These partnerships provide access to specialized knowledge and skills without the need for extensive internal hiring. Leveraging external expertise can accelerate the pace of digital transformation and ensure that the right skills are applied to the right tasks.

Furthermore, industry associations and professional networks can be valuable sources of knowledge exchange. Small businesses should actively participate in these networks to learn from peers and stay informed about the latest digital trends and best practices.

5.21   Managing Resistance to Change

Resistance to change is a natural reaction when introducing digital transformation. To address this barrier, small businesses should prioritize effective change management and communication. Clear and transparent communication is essential to keep employees and stakeholders informed about the rationale and benefits of digital initiatives. Leadership plays a pivotal role in change management. Business owners and managers should lead by example, demonstrating a commitment to embracing change and digital technologies. Encouraging a culture of continuous learning and adaptability can foster a more receptive environment for digital transformation. Small businesses should actively involve employees in the transformation process. Soliciting their input and feedback not only validates their perspectives but also engages them in the journey. Employees who feel that their opinions are valued are more likely to support digital initiatives.

- Implications for Policymakers:

The research findings have implications for policymakers and governmental bodies that aim to support the digital transformation of small businesses.

5.22 Fostering Financial Support Programs

Policymakers should consider the implementation of financial support programs that target small businesses embarking on digital transformation journeys. These programs can include grants, subsidies, and low-interest loans specifically designed to offset the initial costs of digital adoption. Financial support programs should be accessible, transparent, and well-promoted to ensure that small businesses are aware of and can easily access them. Policymakers should engage in outreach and education efforts to inform businesses about the existence and benefits of these programs. Collaborating with financial institutions, industry associations, and business support organizations can help distribute financial support effectively.

5.23 Promoting Digital Skills Development

The skills gap is a formidable barrier that can be addressed through policies that promote digital skills development. Policymakers should consider incentives for businesses to invest in employee training and upskilling programs. Tax credits or subsidies for training expenses can encourage small businesses to prioritize digital skills development. Moreover, governments can support the creation of digital training initiatives, including online courses.

6 Key Points

1. The journey of small businesses toward digital transformation is not merely a technological shift; it is a fundamental strategic shift that has the potential to redefine their future in the competitive landscape.
2. This research underscores the notion that digital transformation has evolved from a discretionary choice to an imperative for small businesses. The data reveals that a substantial portion of small businesses, approximately 62%, have initiated digital transformation projects across various operational dimensions. This is indicative of the recognition among small business owners that digital transformation is vital to stay competitive, relevant, and sustainable in today's fast-evolving business environment. Digital transformation has become a means to address the challenges of a dynamic market. As small businesses encounter competitive pressures from their peers and larger corporations, they are driven to embrace digital solutions as a means of levelling the playing field. It is no longer a question of 'if' but 'when' and 'how' they will embark on this transformative journey.
3. The research highlights the diversification of digital adoption strategies across small businesses. It is clear that small businesses are not limited to a single path

of digital transformation but explore various avenues that align with their unique needs and objectives. The stories shared by small business owners in our qualitative interviews demonstrate this diversification. From e-commerce businesses implementing automated inventory management to restaurants leveraging online ordering systems, each business context dictates a tailored approach to digital transformation. The ability to adapt digital solutions to suit the specifics of a business is a testament to the versatility and scalability of digital technologies.

4. The drivers and barriers shaping digital transformation in small businesses are critical components of this research. Competitive pressure, cost reduction, and customer demand emerged as primary drivers that motivate small businesses to embark on digital transformation journeys. These driving forces underscore the importance of staying competitive, optimizing costs, and meeting customer expectations. However, it is equally vital to recognize the barriers that impede this transformation. Financial constraints, often tied to limited budgets and resources, pose a considerable challenge. Small businesses are faced with the financial demands of acquiring digital tools, software, and expertise. Additionally, the lack of expertise is a prevalent barrier. Many small businesses grapple with the knowledge and skills required to navigate the complexities of digital technologies. The resistance to change, noted in our interviews, reflects the human aspect of digital transformation. Small business owners and employees are sometimes hesitant to embrace the disruptions and challenges associated with digital change. Resistance, often rooted in concerns about organizational culture and workflow, must be addressed effectively to facilitate a smoother transition.

5. Measuring the success of digital transformation initiatives is a fundamental aspect of evaluating the impact of these investments. These metrics often align with the specific goals of the transformation initiative and the nature of the business. Regardless of the specific metrics, the common goal is to achieve tangible, data-driven outcomes that validate their digital investments. To digitally transform, small businesses should consider the following:

6. Strategic Planning: Small business owners should embark on digital transformation initiatives with a clear and well-defined strategy. It is essential to align digital investments with specific business objectives. Understanding the driving forces behind transformation and having a strategic roadmap in place will help mitigate challenges and ensure a purposeful digital journey.

7. Skill Development: To overcome the barrier of expertise, small business owners should invest in skill development for themselves and their teams. Providing training opportunities and upskilling employees in digital competencies will enhance the ability to effectively navigate the digital landscape.

8. Change Management: Addressing resistance to change is crucial in ensuring a successful digital transformation. Small business owners should emphasize change management strategies that engage and empower employees. Communication and support throughout the transformation process will alleviate concerns and promote a smoother transition.

9. Metrics-Driven Approach: The choice of metrics for measuring success should be aligned with the specific goals of the digital transformation initiative. Small business owners are encouraged to adopt a metrics-driven approach that allows them to assess the impact of digital strategies on their business performance.

10. To assist small businesses to digital transformation, policymakers and financial institutions should create and promote affordable loan and grant programs tailored for small businesses engaging in digital transformation. Access to financial resources will alleviate the barrier of financial constraints and incentivize digital adoption. Governments and industry associations should offer comprehensive training programs and workshops to equip small business owners and employees with the knowledge and skills required for digital transformation. Education initiatives should cover a broad spectrum of digital competencies, including data analytics, cybersecurity, and digital marketing. Policymakers and industry stakeholders can facilitate mentorship and networking opportunities for small businesses. Mentoring programs connect businesses with experienced mentors who can provide guidance and support throughout their digital transformation journeys. Networking initiatives encourage collaboration and knowledge sharing among small businesses. The creation of digital ecosystems that facilitate collaboration between small businesses, digital solution providers, and experts in the field will enable a supportive environment for digital transformation. Industry stakeholders should work together to establish such ecosystems, fostering a collective effort toward digital adoption.

References

Achieng, E., & Malatji, M. (2022). Factors influencing digital transformation in small businesses: A systematic review. *International Journal of Electronic Customer Relationship Management, 12*(1), 1–22.

Bowman, C. (2018). The impact of technology and culture on successful digital transformation. *Business Horizons, 61*(4), 567–575.

Chanias, S., & Hess, T. (2016). Business model innovation: Creating value in times of change. *Electronic Markets, 26*(2), 159–165.

Chen, H., Chiang, R. H. L., & Storey, V. C. (2012). Business intelligence and analytics: From big data to big impact. *MIS Quarterly, 36*(4), 1165–1188. https://doi.org/10.2307/41703503

Dholakia, U. M., & Durham, E. (2010). One laptop per child: Vision vs. reality. *International Journal of Information Management, 30*(1), 56–65.

Galliers, R. D., & Leidner, D. E. (2003). *Strategic information management: Challenges and strategies in managing information systems* (2nd ed.). Butterworth-Heinemann.

Kuan, K. K. Y., & Chau, P. Y. K. (2001). A perception-based model for EDI adoption in small businesses using a technology-organization-environment framework. *Information & Management, 38*(8), 507–521.

OECD. (2021). *OECD SME and Entrepreneurship Outlook 2021*. Retrieved from https://www.oecd.org/cfe/smes/ebmo/

Paulus-Rohmer, D., Schatton, M., & Bauernhansl, T. (2016). Digital business models: Taxonomy and empirical research. *Procedia CIRP, 41*, 141–146.

Scuotto, V., Ferraris, A., Bresciani, S., & Del Giudice, M. (2017). A taxonomic analysis of the theoretical foundations of the literature on business models. *International Journal of Organizational Analysis, 25*(3), 413–448.

Verhoef, P. C., Kannan, P. K., & Inman, J. J. (2015). From multi-channel retailing to omni-channel retailing. *Journal of Retailing, 91*(2), 174–181. https://doi.org/10.1016/j.jretai.2015.02.005

Verhoef, P. C., Broekhuizen, T., Bart, Y., Bhattacharya, A., Dong, J. Q., Fabian, N., Haenlein, M., & Li, T. (2021). Digital transformation: A multidisciplinary reflection and research agenda. *Journal of Business Research, 135*, 403–414.

Westerman, G., Bonnet, D., & McAfee, A. (2014). *Leading digital: Turning technology into business transformation.* Harvard Business Review Press.

Printed and bound by CPI Group (UK) Ltd, Croydon, CR0 4YY

29/04/2026

02099470-0005